Ross and Cromarty

Tim 'na stad air an aonaich
agus faoin ne mo dheòin-sa
on's co-ionann do m' rùn-sa
luchd an dé is a' bhòn-dé.

Is co-ionann do m' aire
na tha maireann no faondrach . . .

Time stops on the mountain
and is idle in my desire
for in my thoughts they are equal,
those of yesterday and the day before it.

Equal in my thoughts
those lasting and those gone and neglected . . .

SORLEY MACLEAN
Tim is Sgùrr Urain (Time and Sgurr Urain)
Sgurr Urain is the highest peak of the Five Sisters of Kintail.

. . . And the dead
Who lodge in us so strangely, unremembered,
Yet in their place. How can we reject
The long last look on the ever-dying face
Turned backward
from the other side of time?
And how offend the dead and shame the living
By these despairs? And how refrain from love?
This is a difficult country, and our home.

EDWIN MUIR
The Difficult Land

Ross and Cromarty

A Historical Guide

David Alston

Birlinn

First published in Great Britain, 1999
by Birlinn Limited
8 Canongate Venture
5 New Street Edinburgh EH8 8BH

Cover Picture Acknowledgments [clockwise from top]:

Dun Telve Broch, by Moses Griffiths, from
A Tour in Scotland and Voyage to the Hebrides, 1772, by Thomas Pennant.

Cromarty Court House, courtesy of Cromarty Court House.

Cromarty Court House and Cromarty Bay, from *Voyage Round Great Britain*, by William Daniell,
courtesy of the Mitchell Library, Glasgow City Libraries and Archives.

Sir John Gordon of Invergordon, courtesy of Cromarty Court House.

British Library Cataloguing-in-Publication Data
A catalogue record for this book is available from the British Library

ISBN 1 874744 48 3

Typeset by Waverley Typesetters, Galashiels
Printed and bound in Finland by Werner Södeström OY

CONTENTS

INTRODUCTION

I would like this Guide, which contains many hard and perhaps dry facts, to be not just of the head but also of the heart, and with this intention have prefaced it with two quotations from Scottish poets which convey both thoughts and feelings about landscape.

Ross and Cromarty is, like Scotland as a whole, a difficult country – particularly, a historian might add, since the deterioration of the climate around 1200 BC. It has been a continuing challenge to find the right balance between arable farming, grazing and fishing, and attempts to introduce industry and manufacturing have seldom been successful. Struggles between rival groups for control of limited resources have been bitter and the difficulties, and the rivalries, have been greatest in the Highland and western parts.

The present landscape reflects the problems, struggles, successes and failures of the past. It has been moulded to its shape by the labours of many generations – not primarily by those who can be named but by those gone and neglected who still, if we are concerned with the place and its history, make their claim on us from the other side of time.

The labours of the dead, those of yesterday and the day before it, and the labours of those living today have an equal value. The dead are, nonetheless, gone and our only way to engage with them is by making the effort to see their lives and their times as they were – in truth and without romanticism. To give sufficient attention to see things both as they are, and as they were, is an act of love, from which we should not refrain – for this, although a difficult country, is our home.

ACKNOWLEDGEMENTS

The information contained in this Guide has been gathered over some ten years and it is, as a result, impossible to thank all those who have contributed. I began knowing little about history. My first attempts at research were tentative and I gratefully acknowledge the help and encouragement I received at that early stage from Marinell Ash, Malcolm Bangor-Jones, Elizabeth Beaton, Robin Callander, Monica Clough and Jane Durham. More recently my understanding of historical method has been greatly enhanced by Prof. Christopher Whatley of the University of Dundee.

In the course of writing the book I have been helped by material made available by Jean Munro, Graham Ritchie and Audrey Henshall, by the continued oversight and help of Richard Oram, editor of the series, and by Hugh Andrew of Birlinn. Help with illustrative material has been given by Colin Dunn, Mike Taylor and Andrew Dowsett. Iain Crichton Smith kindly gave permission to quote from his translation of William Ross's *Oran Eile*.

I have been able to explore history largely because I have been employed as curator of Cromarty Courthouse Museum and would like to take this opportunity of thanking the Courthouse Trustees and both the Highland Council and its predecessor, Ross and Cromarty District Council, who have supported the museum.

I dedicate this book to my children –
CHIHIRO, AIDAN AND NAOMI

HOW TO USE THE GUIDE

The Guide covers the modern administrative area of Ross and Cromarty within Highland Region and Kintail in the south-west. Kintail has been included for two reasons. First, because it was originally part of the medieval diocese of Ross and the church has over the centuries been an important force in forging the area's identity; second, because it was from Kintail that the Mackenzie family rose in the sixteenth and seventeenth centuries to dominate both the east and the west coasts of Ross and Cromarty. The parish of Kincardine, although historically an integral part of the area, was transferred to Sutherland District in the 1970s and is dealt with in other volumes in this series. The period covered by the Guide is from the appearance of the first known human inhabitants *c.*7000 BC to *c.*AD 1850.

Throughout the book I use the term 'Ross and Cromarty', rather than Ross-shire, where this is appropriate. Ross and Cromarty was created in 1889 by the amalgamation of Ross-shire and Cromarty-shire. The shire, or sheriffdom of Cromarty originated in the thirteenth century and was the smaller but senior partner. To refer to the result of the union simply as 'Ross-shire' is equivalent to using the term 'England' when 'Great Britain' is meant.

The aim of the Guide is to provide an outline of the history of Ross and Cromarty, setting this in the wider context of Scottish history, but always trying to identify what is special to the area. The chapter headings give the periods of time covered, and a series of gazetteers and associated maps within the chapters identify sites through which this history can be explored. Some gazetteers, such as those for Neolithic chambered tombs or medieval castles, give a complete listing of sites. Other gazetteers are selective, but it has been my intention to provide, as a minimum, information on all historical and archaeological sites marked on the Ordnance Survey Landranger Map Series. For every site, the number of the OS map is given, followed by an asterisk where it is marked on the map as an '*antiquity*'. The maps for the area are numbers 15 (Loch Assynt), 19 (Gairloch & Ullapool), 20 (Beinn Dearg), 21 (Dornoch Firth), 24 (Applecross), 25 (Glen Carron), 26 (Inverness), 27 (Nairn) and 33 (Loch Alsh and Glen Shiel). Where maps 21 and 27 overlap, a reference to the former has been given. To use the Guide effectively it is important to be able to use six figure map references. Instructions are given on all OS Landranger maps and it is worth taking some time to understand the system. The inclusion of sites in the Guide does *not* imply that there is a public right of access and permission should be sought where appropriate.

The Guide is wide ranging and in many parts comprehensive – but I have also provided a personal list of sites which I consider *Essential Viewing*. These are all sites of particular importance, which are easily accessible and are likely to make a profound impression on the visitor. I have also included a chapter on the art and culture of the area, with suggestions for *Essential Reading* and *Essential Listening*, and the concluding bibliography contains what I consider to be the best sources of additional information.

Further detail on almost all sites can be had from the Sites and Monuments Record held and administered by the Archaeology Service of Highland Council (01463 702250). I would also commend the many museums in the area: Cromarty Courthouse (01381 600418), Groam House in Rosemarkie (01381 620691), Tain Museum (01862 894089), Dingwall Museum (01349 865366), The Highland Museum of Childhood in Strathpeffer (01997 421031), Tarbat Archaeological Trust (01862 871790), The Clan Munro Centre (01349 830000) at Foulis, Gairloch Museum (01445 712287) and Ullapool Museum (01854 612987).

LIST OF GAZETTEERS

LIST OF PLATES

Plates 1–4 and 15–16 are by Andrew Dowsett.

Plates 5–12 and 14 are Crown Copyright: Royal Commission on the Ancient and Historical Monuments of Scotland.

Plates 11 and 12 are by Susan Seright.

Plate 13 is reproduced with permission of Cromarty Court House.

MAPS

LIST OF ILLUSTRATIONS

All illustrations credited Audrey Henshall are taken from *The Chambered Tombs of Scotland* (Edinburgh University Press, 1984), reproduced with permission.

All illustrations credited MacGibbon & Ross i are taken from David MacGibbon and Thomas Ross, *The Castellated and Domestic Architecture of Scotland* (Mercat Press, 1991).

All illustrations credited MacGibbon & Ross ii are taken from David MacGibbon and Thomas Ross, *The Ecclesiastical Architecture of Scotland* (Mercat Press, 1991).

ESSENTIAL VIEWING IN ROSS AND CROMARTY

THE MESOLITHIC
*c.*7000 BC–*c.*4000 BC

We do not know when humans first inhabited the place we now call Ross and Cromarty. While there are traces of people in southern Britain from half a million years ago, the glaciers which covered the north of Scotland scoured the land on which any vestiges of settlement might have been found, and it is only in places such as caves that evidence may remain. At Inchnadamph in Sutherland, fragments of animal bone have been found deep in limestone caves, but it is unclear if these were gathered together by human hands or have been moved by the natural forces of underground water systems. For the time being the evidence is inconclusive and we must begin an account of the people of the north of Scotland, and of Ross and Cromarty, at a later date.

By 10,000 BC, the glaciers had retreated and Scotland had emerged from the last Ice Age. The landscape, barren at first, was gradually covered by grass plains over which herds of reindeer, giant fallow deer and elk roamed. As new soils began to form and the climate became warmer, trees reappeared. First there were birch and hazel, then, between 6500 and 6000 BC, elm and oak, and from 5500–5000 BC pine forest began to dominate the north-west. With the trees came other plant species – edible herbs, berries and roots – and a wider variety of animal species.

Into this slowly changing landscape came humans. They lived by hunting and gathering and, adapting to the changing environment, they began to produce smaller and finer stone tools than their ancestors. Bone and antler were also put to new uses. It is this change in technology – the use of new tools – which marks this as a new age: the Mesolithic or Middle Stone Age. We should not, however, allow the label of a 'new age' to mislead us into thinking that change was necessarily sudden and dramatic. The new skills in working stone, antler and bone may have developed slowly.

The people of the Mesolithic have left little behind them. These hunters and gatherers – perhaps hunters, fishers and

gatherers would be more accurate – stayed only for short
periods in one place, so while they may have returned to the
same sites year after year, we cannot talk of settlements, but
only of traces of temporary camps. We should think of these
as being located near seasonal sources of food – including
fish, shellfish, fruits, small mammals and birds. Occasionally
such sites can be identified from accumulated midden debris
and by finds of tools and weapons. We must remember that
most of the objects fashioned and used by the Mesolithic
people would have been made of perishable materials, such
as skin and bark, of which we have almost no trace. They had
no pottery and no metals. What remains are these tools of
stone, antler and bone. However, with modern archaeological
techniques it is possible to glean further information from a
range of other sources such as traces of postholes, charcoal
from hearths, and shells.

The earliest remains discovered from this period in
Scotland are on the island of Rum and date from a little before
7000 BC. Although the next oldest sites are 1000 years younger,
these are distributed across Scotland, suggesting that the
colonists had penetrated most of the country. Two such sites,
at Redpoint and Shieldaig, lie within the area of this guide
(*see* Gazetteer 1). These are lithic scatter sites – that is, sites
known only from the scattered remains of stone tools and not
from any excavated remains of a campsite.

Evidence from elsewhere shows that Mesolithic people were
highly mobile and often travelled by water, making use of
coastal camps. The river estuaries and firths of the east coast
would have been a rich source of food, and the sheltered waters
would have allowed relatively easy and safe movement in log
boats. There are a number of Mesolithic sites on the southern
shore of the Moray Firth. It is likely that there are similar
undetected sites along the east coast of Ross and Cromarty,
particularly along what were once the tree-lined and marshy
shores of the Beauly, Cromarty and Dornoch Firths.

At this point it is worth mentioning changes in sea level in
the area. There were two effects of the melting of the ice sheets
as the earth's climate changed. First, a great weight of ice was
removed from some areas and, as a result, the land itself began
to rise. Second, the water which had been trapped in the ice

was released to increase the volume of the oceans. Since both some land and the absolute level of the oceans were rising, there is no simple relationship between the end of the Ice Age and sea levels on the coast. Although we might expect the sea level to have risen after the ice melted, in fact water levels in the area, relative to the surrounding land, were lower *c.*6000 BC than today because the land had risen and there had not yet been a corresponding rise in the oceans. It is, therefore, likely that many coastal Mesolithic sites were later submerged.

We also know of one natural disaster during the Mesolithic which would have affected coastal sites, when a huge wave, known as a *tsunami*, swept across the North Sea as the result of a huge landslide on the Norwegian coast. A wall of water, several metres high, was carried up the firths. Traces of sand displaced by the wave have been found on high ground in Castle Street, Inverness.

Information gained from the sparse material remains of the Mesolithic in Scotland can be augmented by what we know of the period elsewhere in Europe, and by study of later nomadic peoples. We would expect, for example, that the basic social unit would be an extended family group of ten to twenty individuals, large enough to gather sufficient food in an area, but not too large for the available resources. There must have been contact between such groups to avoid in-breeding. This contact also allowed the spread of information from one group to another, as is shown in the development of regional styles of flint and bone working. Also from European sites comes evidence of a wider and more complex social structure. There is no reason to suppose that Mesolithic society in Scotland would have been different or less complex. In some parts of Europe, more permanent and larger settlements evolved over time, probably as bases from which groups went out on hunting and foraging expeditions.

The shared culture of many Mesolithic peoples involved elaborate burial rituals and offerings that suggest belief in an afterlife. Although we have no such evidence from Scotland, excavations in continental Europe offer us tantalising glimpses into the life of our predecessors. These can be profoundly moving – as, for example, the burial of a child resting on a swan's wing.

But these are only glimpses, and perhaps the most difficult task facing us when we contemplate this period is to accept the great void in our knowledge. It is tempting to fill this void by imagining what life might have been like, and sometimes there is a danger of projecting our own wishes onto the blank screen of the past. For example, Mesolithic society is sometimes presented as egalitarian, with little concern for territorial boundaries. Perhaps it was, but we must be careful that this conclusion is based on evidence and not on our own longings for a particular kind of society. Real understanding can only be advanced by painstaking and disciplined research.

THE NEOLITHIC
*c.*4000 BC–*c.*2500 BC

A radical, but not a sudden, change began in Scotland around 4000 BC when a new people arrived with a new way of life – the first farmers, who cleared land to grow crops and kept animals. They were, in these ways, quite different from the Mesolithic people, who lived by gathering food, hunting and fishing. Although the ways of life were different, the two peoples appear to have survived side by side for some time, though gradually the way of the farmers came to dominate.

The farmers had to clear land of trees before they could cultivate it and, for this reason, good quality axes of flint or ground-down hard stone were important. Sometimes these were locally made, but where there were sources of particularly good stone, centres of production developed and axes were then traded over wide areas. This new technology in stone gives its name to the period – the Neolithic or New Stone Age.

Traces of early cultivation sites have been widely identified in Scotland. It seems that trees were cut at about waist height, fallen timber was burned (the ash would have helped to fertilise the soil), simple seed-sticks were used to break the surface, and seed was then planted. There may also have been rudimentary hoes. As the natural fertility of the soil was exhausted, new sites would be cleared, and the consequent expansion of cleared areas created grazing for domesticated animals.

The settled lifestyle of farming made it possible to use new types of artefact, such as heavier stone tools, furniture and fragile pottery; while keeping sheep and goats led to the production of lighter, woven clothes. Houses were probably made of wood, but no traces have been discovered in this area.

Neolithic burial sites
The principal archaeological remains from the Neolithic are the tombs in which these farming people buried their dead. These large structures – chambered cairns and barrows (earth

mounds) – could only be erected by a people who were settled in permanent communities and the evidence shows that they were used over long periods of time. Bones and 'grave goods' were inserted and removed from the tombs at various stages in their histories, and from the 350 or so which survive there is evidence of a wide variety of burial practices.

Since farming communities developed where the soils were most fertile, Neolithic tombs in Ross and Cromarty are found within a few miles of the east coast and along the sides of the firths, extending into some of the smaller valleys, such as those at Boath in the valley of the River Alness. There is some evidence that the best farming ground was avoided – cairns tend to be on hillsides, at or above the present level of cultivation (mostly sited between 60 m and 180 m above sea level) and they are entirely absent from the low-lying parishes of Fearn and Tarbat. There are, however, some surprising gaps in the distribution, with no cairns in Strath Oykell or Strath Carron. There are also no cairns in Wester Ross and only one in Kintail, although some of the valleys were capable of settlement. This can be partly explained by postulating that the tomb builders entered the area via the Great Glen and spread north and east from there, while a parallel west coast expansion was concentrated on the Western Isles.

Until recently, excavations of cairns focused on what was found within the burial chambers, but while this is still important, more attention has now been given to the way in which the tombs were built. This has revealed an evolution of styles, with many cairns having undergone reconstruction and extension. There is considerable variation from one region to another in the types of tomb, and these variations suggest patterns in the movements of people, cultural contacts and communications.

In the north of Scotland, it seems that the earliest Neolithic stone tombs were small rectangular chambers over which a cairn was built, only just large enough to cover the tomb. These modest tombs may reflect a pioneering society with limited resources in the early stages of settlement. Then, from about 3000 BC, there was the introduction from the south-west of larger passage graves, with many-sided (polygonal) or rounded chambers. A fusion of these two styles – the older, small cairn with a rectangular chamber and the larger passage grave with a many-sided chamber – led to a new and subsequently widely-spread type of cairn, with many variations, known as the Orkney–Cromarty group. (Inclusion of cairns resulting from a similar spread up the west coast to the islands constitutes a wider group known as Orkney–Cromarty–Hebridean.) Tombs of this type may be round, long, square or trapezoid. They are characterised by having entrance passages and chambers built from large stones (megaliths), commonly divided into compart-ments by pairs of upright stones.

At about the same time – *c.* 3000 BC – there was an intro-duction to the east of massive elongated long cairns, which can be more than 60 m long. Colonists from the north-east of England may have introduced them to the area. Long cairns were often built over existing structures, entirely hiding earlier round cairns with burial chambers. These long cairns were the counterparts of earth-barrows, a type of burial mound common in England and also found in eastern Scotland as far north as the Moray Firth. The remains of barrow-burials have often gone undetected, and their distribution is only now becoming apparent with the use of aerial photography.

Both long cairns and cairns of the Orkney–Cromarty group may be curved or 'horned' to create partially enclosed fore-courts, sometimes with a stone façade, which had a ritual function. There are a number of cairns with such façades in Ross and Cromarty (Balnaguie, Belmaduthy, and Kilcoy South: Gazetteer 2:7, 9, 24). The entrances to cairns are generally towards the east, though often not exactly aligned in this direction. Excavations in Orkney and Caithness have pro-vided information about the ritual use of cairns, in particular the use of ritual fires, but lack of excavation leaves a gap in our knowledge of this aspect of most of the cairns in Ross and Cromarty.

The jigsaw of styles is made even more complex by the fact that cairns were altered and enlarged over time. Since early cairns were small, the passage to the central chamber was short. When such tombs were altered to make larger cairns, either the short passage remained and the burial chamber was off-centre in the larger cairn (King's Head: Gazetteer 2:25), or the passage was lengthened, something which may be apparent in the arrangement of stones (Heights of Brae: Gazetteer 2:22). Some trapezoid-shaped cairns appear to have been added to earlier structures (Boath Long, Carn Liath in the Morangie Forest, Kinrive West and Mid Brae: Gazetteer 9:11, 16, 26, 30). At Kilcoy South (Gazetteer 9:24), one of only two cairns to have been excavated in the area, there may have been three phases of development.

Out of this complex picture, we can detect some clear regional patterns. One distinct form of the Orkney–Cromarty group are cairns with passages and rectangular burial chambers, a type mostly confined to the Black Isle, where there are six examples (Gazetteer 2:7, 9, 13, 15, 32, 45), with a seventh a short distance away at Contin (Gazetteer 2:19). This is our first evidence for the emergence of a distinctive local culture.

From about 2500 BC, some tombs went out of use and their entrances were ritually blocked, as can be seen at Kilcoy South. To the south of the Beauly Firth, at the end of the Great Glen, a further type of cairn appeared – the Clava cairn. The most recent evidence shows that Clava cairns date from *c.*2000 BC and so belong to the Bronze rather than the Neolithic Age. However, they are considered here because they have until now been considered to be Neolithic. There are two forms: a round cairn with a central circular corbel-roofed chamber, entered by a passage; and a round cairn with a large unroofed central area with no access through the cairn. In both forms the cairn has a kerb of larger vertical stones and may be surrounded by an outer ring of standing stones. It is characteristic of Clava cairns that the kerb stones and standing stones are graded in height, with the highest at the north-west. There is only one firmly identified Clava cairn on the Black Isle (Carn Urnan: Gazetteer 2:17). Two cairns on the Black Isle, at Alcaig (NH 576567: OS26) and Croftcrunie (NH 610520: OS26 marked as a 'chambered cairn'), were previously thought to be of this type, but this view has now been revised.

In considering this complicated and sometimes confusing picture, it is worth reminding ourselves that the burial customs of the Neolithic farmers were not so different from our own as we might at first imagine. Many parish churches contain hundreds of graves, and the churches, like Neolithic cairns, are large stone-built structures. The graves themselves were disturbed and re-used. Regular ritual activity still takes place around them, following a variety of practices which have changed over the centuries and which present a bewildering picture to any outsider. The graves were sealed when the Reformation put an end to burial within the building, but we still make use of other burial sites, which are often deliberately close to 'our' original communal burial cairn.

Ritual sites: henges and stone circles
Contrary to common belief, a henge is not a stone circle, but a circular enclosure consisting of a central flat area, surrounded by a deep ditch, beyond which is a bank formed by the material from the ditch. In some cases, but by no means all, they are associated with later stone circles. In Scotland henges are mainly distributed in the east of the country. The largest and most impressive henge sites are those such as the Stones of Stenness and the Ring of Brodgar (both in Orkney), Balfarg in Fife, and Cairnpapple in West Lothian. However, there are also two notable concentrations of smaller henges, one in the valley of the River Don in Aberdeenshire, the other in Ross and Cromarty at the western end of the Black Isle and along Strathconon. The group in Ross and Cromarty consists of five henges (Gazetteer 3:1–5), and there is also a possible stone circle farther north at Edderton (Gazetteer 3:6). There are no henges along the Moray coast, and as with chambered cairns, the Beauly Firth seems to have been a cultural boundary.

Henges are divided into two types – Class I and Class II – according to the number of entrances over the ditch. Class I henges have a single entrance; Class II have a pair of entrances directly opposite each other. There is one clear example of each type in the Ross and Cromarty group, but the remaining three are unusual. In most henges the entrance runs across the ditch and through a break in the surrounding bank, but in these three henges the surrounding bank is unbroken (in one case this may be the result of disturbance in creating a field boundary). It is possible that they represent some intermediate stage in the development of henge building – or that the gaps have been filled at a later date, though it is strange that this should have happened on three sites. Only excavation is likely to provide answers.

Where henges have been excavated – and there have been no excavations so far in Ross and Cromarty – they have shown that both Class I and Class II henges are of similar date, beginning around 3000 BC. A number of sites have burials within the henge and some have remains of what are taken to be ritual offerings and ritual feasting. Excavation has also revealed traces of early timber structures within henges and remains of timber circles outside the enclosing bank, as at Balfarg in Fife, where there was a circle, about 25 m in diameter, of massive wooden uprights. Since excavations at several stone circles show there to have been an earlier timber phase, it seems likely that henges played an important part in the development of stone circles. It is generally agreed that henges and stone circles had a ritual function – and some, such as Balfarg, appear to lie at the centre of a complex of monuments in a ritual landscape – but precisely what that function was is unclear.

BEAKER CULTURE AND THE BRONZE AGE

*c.*2500 BC–*c.*700 BC

Around 2500 BC a new group of people from continental Europe began to appear in Scotland. From their skeletons, we know to have been taller, more robust, and with rounder skulls than the people of the Neolithic. Associated with them we find a new style of small, decorated pottery vessel – the beaker. Studies of beaker pottery suggest that there was a migration of people from what is now the Low Countries to eastern Britain, and a parallel movement from Brittany and Spain to western Britain. There is, however, debate about the scale of this migration. Some archaeologists argue that it was more a movement of culture than of people, and that it was a relatively small group who came to dominate the native culture. Others hold that the evidence is for a profound change rather than a gradual transition, suggesting a 'take over' by a relatively large incoming population.

One aspect of the change, however it took place, was in burial customs. The communal chambered tombs of the Neolithic appear to have gone out of use from around 2500 BC, and their entrances were blocked. Burials (either of bodies or cremated ashes, but with cremation gradually becoming the norm) were now of individuals, in stone-lined graves, or cists, often with grave goods, usually including a beaker. Smaller round cairns were placed over these cist burials.

A further profound change, occurring in the north around or before 2000 BC, was the introduction of metal working. The principal metals used were copper, gold and bronze (an alloy made by combining copper and tin). It had taken around 500 years for this technology to spread from southern England. The slow pace of this change may in part be due to human factors, particularly a reluctance to share or adopt new skills, but it was also because the production of bronze required tin, and this metal was found only in Cornwall. The introduction of bronze working thus involved integration into a system of trade running the length of Britain.

The principal finds of both beaker pottery and metal artefacts are from burials. Beaker pottery, which never wholly replaced older indigenous pottery, was produced from c.2500 BC to c.1500 BC and shows several changes in style. As well as the beakers themselves, many tombs contain sherds of shallower bowls known as 'food vessels' which appear to be associated with female burials. Beaker pottery is however unevenly distributed throughout the country, being rare in the western mainland and far north, with only a thin scattering of finds north of Easter Ross. This may reflect the pattern of settlement of the 'beaker people'.

Burial sites also reveal an extensive use of bronze, gold and jet. This suggests an affluent society where power and status were expressed by possession and display of material objects. Improvements in the working of bronze after 1400 BC led to the production of more sophisticated pieces. Long-bladed swords replaced daggers, and close-fitting moulds allowed the casting of socketed axe-heads. These changes distinguish the Early Bronze Age (c.2000 BC–c.1400 BC) from the Middle Bronze Age (c.1400 BC–c.900 BC).

New burial rites led to the closing and ritual sealing of Neolithic tombs, as at Kilcoy South (Gazetteer 2:24). Bronze Age cist burials were sometimes made within abandoned tombs. More commonly, cremated bone was placed loose in small cairns bounded by stone kerbs ('kerb cairns'), or in pottery urns buried in cists, often along with richly decorated vessels and personal jewellery. Small cemeteries, with cremation pyres, appeared in some places, as at Croftcrunie on the Black Isle (Gazetteer 4:1).

Some Bronze Age cemeteries and groups of kerb cairns are associated with impressive standing stones. Other standing stones do not appear to have this connection. In addition to single standing stones there are also groups of stones which appear to be aligned in some significant way, perhaps with some role in astronomical observation or with some ritual dependent on the position of the sun, moon and stars. A further ritual alignment of stones can be found in Clava-type cairns, described in the chapter on the Neolithic.

The Bronze Age Crisis

Evidence from across Scotland shows a sudden abandoning of many settlement sites shortly after 1200 BC. The precise reasons for this are debatable, but it seems to be connected with changes in climate. Population during the Bronze Age had been increasing and agriculture had expanded into marginal areas, but the climate seems to have deteriorated from about 1600 BC. Cooler and wetter weather, with stronger winds, led to tree loss and shorter growing seasons. The cool and wet climate encouraged the spread of peat, which is formed when organic material cannot fully decompose. This material then builds up as a blanket deposit of waterlogged, semi-decayed material which inhibits further growth.

A massive eruption of the Icelandic volcano, Hekla, in 1159 BC, spread clouds of volcanic dust and may have precipitated the final disaster. There was a dramatic drop in population – perhaps as high as 50 per cent – and the remaining communities came to rely more on a pastoral economy, grazing cattle and sheep on rough pasture, and on fishing from coastal sites. The fundamental problem facing the inhabitants of the Highlands in the Middle and Late Bronze Age – that of controlling limited resources and striking the right balance between limited arable farming, grazing and fishing – remained the same for the variety of peoples in the area during its subsequent history.

Part of the Late Bronze Age 'solution' to this problem was the development of a war-like society in which groups could effectively compete for the limited resources. There is evidence of increased production of weapons – and highly ornamented metalwork may reflect the growing importance of tribal chiefs or warlords, who came to dominate a more hierarchical social structure. By about 700 BC, we see the first signs of a new cultural influence from Europe with the introduction of horses and lavishly decorated metal work for horse harnesses. This was the beginning of the age of the Celts.

Settlement sites

The most common traces of settlements of the Bronze Age are hut circles. These are the remains of the stone founda-tions of timber-built circular or oval houses. They are often associated with field clearance cairns and, where excavations have been carried out, with marks of cultivation. Gazetteer 4 lists the sites of hut circles marked on the OS Landranger maps, though many others are recorded, and it is possible, especially on the west coast, to come across sites of hut circles which are as yet unlisted. Although often regarded solely as Bronze Age remains, the roundhouses which stood on hut circles continued to be built until at least AD 500 and possibly as late as AD 1000. After this date more rectangular structures began to appear.

An especially revealing Bronze Age landscape, with fifty-four hut circles, has been excavated at Lairg in Sutherland and this is now the focus of the Ferrycroft Interpretive Centre. Although outside the area of this Guide it provides a readily accessible introduction to the archaeology of the period. The Ferrycroft site shows a rapid decline in population from shortly before 1000 BC, presumably as a result of the Bronze Age crisis described above. A similar pattern is likely to be found in other places, with a drop in population and a withdrawal of the remaining people to the protection of fortified sites.

THE HEROIC AGE
*c.*700 BC–*c.*AD 500

The period from *c.*700 BC to *c.*AD 500 is referred to as the Iron Age, or more evocatively, as the Heroic Age. It is also the beginning of the Celtic period of Scottish history, characterised by the strengthening of influences from the continent, leading to the introduction of horses (with the skills of horse riding and charioteering) and iron working. As well as a cultural influence from the Continent, there was also some migration of Celtic people to Britain, although the scale of this migration is unclear. The native peoples of the late Bronze Age probably spoke a closely related language, and their society had already become similar to that of the Celts, being ruled by a warrior elite. As a result, the incoming culture and its more advanced technology, whatever the number of immigrants, was quickly adopted by the indigenous inhabitants.

From early written accounts of Celtic society elsewhere in Britain, we are able to form a reasonably detailed picture which is likely to apply to Celtic society in the north of Scotland. The society was tribal, ruled by a chief supported by warrior aristocrats, probably from the same kin group. Within these elite kin groups, some women might have had a prominent and powerful role. There was a separate class of learned and skilled men (priests, smiths, bards, musicians, healers, etc.), who might also have been closely related to the aristocracy. Below them were free members of the tribe, who paid tribute to the chief, and finally a class of servile labourers who worked the land. Cattle were an important source of wealth, and cattle raiding among rival tribes was probably part of the way of life.

This was an ordered, hierarchical society, and we naturally know more of those who were higher in the social order. The wealth of tribal leaders and their families was flaunted in richly ornamented weapons and personal jewellery, of which some examples from the area can be seen either locally in Inverness Museum or in the Museum of Scotland in Edinburgh. The style of this ornamentation, with its later developments, is now widespread in modern 'Celtic art'. In addition to this artistic heritage, we also have a literary route into the nature of Celtic society through early Irish epic poems which portray a society of boastful, feuding warriors given to drinking and feasting, but who also valued poetry and the refinements of art.

The first map to include Scotland was made by the Roman geographer Ptolemy in the second century AD, using information gathered by Roman commanders during the previous century. He showed ten principal tribes inhabiting Scotland north of the Forth, of which the Decantae held the Black Isle and Easter Ross, the Carnonacae held Wester Ross and the Creones held Kintail. It is difficult to be sure how accurate Ptolemy's information was, especially about an area so far beyond the boundary of Roman occupation. However, his map confirms what the evidence of the Neolithic and Bronze Ages suggests (and which we would expect from the geography) – that the Beauly and Dornoch Firths had emerged as boundaries between local cultures in the east, and that different groupings and traditions had emerged on the west coast.

Hill and promontory forts

The most prominent archaeological remains from this period are forts (on hills and promontories), brochs, duns and crannogs. The largest of these, in terms of the area enclosed, are the hill forts – but they are also the least well understood. The hill fort at Ord Hill (Gazetteer 5:1), overlooking the Beauly Firth, is large enough to have contained a sizeable community, and there is another example on Knockfarril (Gazetteer 5:2) above Dingwall. There are four other smaller forts on the east coast: at Easter Rarichie near Nigg, Eathie on the Black Isle, Castlehaven in Easter Ross and in Strath Conon (Gazetteer 5:3–6). At Cnoc an Duin (Gazetteer 5:7) above Evanton, also on the east coast, there is a large unfinished fort. A number of such unfinished forts are found in north-east Scotland. It is likely that they were begun in response to the threat of Roman invasion and were abandoned after the Roman legions withdrew.

Hill forts are also found in the west, such as those at Creagan Fhamhair (Gazetteer 5:10) near Gairloch, and on both sides of Lochbroom, at Dun Lagaigh and Dun Canna (Gazetteer

5:8, 9). Dating of material from Dun Lagaigh shows that it is of a similar period to the east coast forts.

The ramparts of hill forts were built either with stone interlaced with timber, earth-faced with stone, or rubble and turf. When those which were timber-laced caught fire, either accidentally or as a result of attack, the structure pulled air through it and the heat generated by the wood burning in this furnace was enough to fuse the individual stones. This created what are called vitrified forts; not in fact a style of building but the result of a disaster. The relatively high numbers of forts throughout Scotland which show signs of vitrification may be an indication of the war-like nature of the tribal society. In this area only Creagan Fhamhair, Dun Canna and the unfinished Cnoc an Duin are unvitrified.

Brochs

The brochs of the Highlands and Islands of Scotland, massive towers of which there are over 500 examples, have been described as 'man's greatest achievement in dry-stone building'. They are concentrated in Orkney, Shetland, Skye and Caithness, though the remains to be seen in Ross and Cromarty are nevertheless impressive, and the broch at Dun Telve (Gazetteer 5:13) in Glenelg is the best preserved on the Scottish mainland.

Brochs are circular buildings, 9 m–12 m in diameter, with walls up to 4.5 m thick at the base. The inward slope of the external wall surface creates a distinctive 'cooling tower' shape and the tallest surviving example, at Mousa in Shetland, rises to a height of 13.3 m. Dun Telve, now just over 10 m high, was almost as well preserved as Mousa when it was first sketched in 1720. The distinctive features of broch architecture are detailed in the description of Dun Telve.

Most brochs were built in a comparatively short period of little more than 300 years, from sometime before 200 BC to AD 100, and probably continued in use only until around AD 200, when they were replaced by more modest circular stone houses. No buildings of a similar size appear in the area for another 1000 years (that is until the castles of the medieval period) and they were built with mortared stone. Debate continues as to why the brochs were constructed, and how their development relates both to earlier structures in the area and to building traditions in Ireland and the rest of Britain. One outcome of this debate has been the realisation that brochs may not, in fact, be primarily defensive structures, but deliberately impressive domestic buildings. This conclusion is suggested by the facts that brochs did not always occupy strong defensive positions, provided only limited space to protect people and cattle, and, with their narrow entrances, could easily have been besieged and their timber roofs set on fire. If they were domestic buildings, then it is likely that the living quarters were on a raised timber floor, with the space below used for animals. When seen as farmhouses rather than castles, brochs are more easily placed in a long tradition of round houses which is found both before and after the period of broch building.

Despite the short period over which they were built, there were some important developments in technique. An essential structural feature of brochs is that the walls are partly hollow, with two thickness of dry-stone wall linked and bonded by cross-slabs which are placed at regular intervals to create internal galleries. Some of these galleries may have been used for storage, but their structural function was to reduce the weight of the massive defensive walls. However, the largest brochs, which probably show the tradition at its most developed, have a solid base with galleried walls rising above. Such solid-based brochs are concentrated in the north, but there are at least four examples on the west coast of the Scottish mainland. Two of these are the closely neighbouring brochs of Dun Telve and Dun Troddan (Gazetteer 5:14). The southernmost of the solid-based brochs in the east was Dun Alascaig in Easter Ross (Gazetteer 5:17), though this was destroyed in 1818.

It has been argued that there was a third type of broch, a D-shaped or semi-broch built on promontories or cliff edges, which were a stage in the development of free-standing circular brochs. Alleged examples of these can be seen at Rhiroy (Gazetteer 5:16) on the south shore of Loch Broom and at Dun Grugaig (Gazetteer 5:15) in Glenelg. However, the balance of opinion is that these are structures where one wall has simply fallen away. The visitor can at least see some of the evidence at first hand.

Duns

The term 'dun' is applied to a very wide range of circular or oval stone-walled buildings, most common in Argyll but scattered throughout other areas of Scotland. They are smaller than forts and less substantial than brochs – but larger than the humbler roundhouses of which only the foundations remain as 'hut circles'. The variety means that in some cases we may be talking of a fortified house for a single family, in others, of a larger stronghold. Duns were built over a much longer period than brochs and were occupied for longer – some until the Middle Ages.

Crannogs

The third type of small defended sites are crannogs – circular timber huts, 12 m–20 m in diameter, built on artificial, or partly artificial, islands. The islands were created with timber stakes, boulders and earth, and were sometimes linked to the land by a causeway. Most crannogs date from between 500 BC and AD 100, although they continued to be a viable form of defence until the Scottish government of the sixteenth century banned further building. Many crannogs are now submerged, and views on their distribution are changing as new examples are discovered.

Recent excavation at the crannog at Redcastle (Gazetteer 5:46) on the north side of the Beauly Firth suggests a different type of structure in the inter-tidal area. There is no causeway, and changes in sea level mean that this may have had a different function, perhaps as a quay for log boats. There are also traces of Iron Age leather working and wicker work from this site.

Field systems and settlements

Many hut settlements and field systems of the Bronze Age were abandoned as the climate deteriorated and society became more warlike. However, it is not clear to what extent early Celtic society had abandoned arable farming and was dependent on a pastoral economy. Certainly cattle were important, but the evidence seems on balance to be for a mixed farming system, with the cultivation of cereals continuing on more fertile lower land. Continuing investigations at Tarbat

(Gazetteer 6:21) may tell us more about society in this latter part of the Iron Age. The abandoning of brochs and the construction of fewer crannogs after AD 200 all seem to point to a slightly more settled society, perhaps the result of the emergence of larger tribal units and a reduction in raiding between small neighbouring groups.

The impact of the Romans

In AD 83, the Roman commander Agricola led a force north in an attempt to complete the conquest of the island of Britain. He may have reached Aberdeen in that year, and in the campaign season of the following year, he pushed on west, preceded by the Roman fleet which sailed north to attack the fertile east coast plain. Agricola defeated the native tribes at an unidentified site named Mons Graupius, and it is probable that he then pursued his campaign into the inner Moray Firth. Shortly afterwards he was recalled to Rome as political crisis developed at the centre of the empire.

Aerial photography has revealed what appear to be four sites west of the Spey with features typical of ditched Roman military camps. The most northerly of these is at Tarradale on the Black Isle. Unfortunately, the sandy soil of the site has been subject to severe erosion. If this was indeed a Roman camp, it can only have been occupied for at most three years, since troops were being withdrawn from Britain by AD 86.

It had been suggested above that Iron Age society was gradually forming itself into larger and more settled tribal units. Some historians argue that the Roman threat led to a further consolidation of native tribes into larger confederations which were capable of a co-ordinated response to invasion. This may explain why some large hill forts, such as Cnoc an Duin, are unfinished. They might have been hurried attempts to consolidate the defence of the area, abandoned once the Romans withdrew.

Perceptions of the Celts

History is not only concerned with what happened in the past and why, but with changing perceptions of the past and the ways in which these perceptions influence later people. The Celtic peoples are significant because many modern Scots identify with what they take to be early Celtic culture. This has been the case for some time, and the identification with the Celtic past has led both to a valuing of Celtic heritage and to much myth-making and distortion.

There is, of course, a genuine tradition. We have artefacts from the Celtic period and there is, or at least was, an oral tradition which kept alive a body of tales of Celtic heroes such as Finn, Diarmid and the bard Ossian. A considerable number of Gaelic place-names have associations with such figures.

In the late eighteenth century, however, something remarkable happened. James Macpherson, a native of Fort William, produced poems which he claimed were translations of ancient Celtic epics written by the bard Ossian himself, and passed on over the centuries as part of an oral tradition. There is still dispute as to exactly how much original material Macpherson gathered, but he certainly added to it – and some of his critics considered the work to be entirely a forgery. These epics portrayed the ancient, native Highlanders as a noble and heroic race, a complete contrast with what had, until then, been the accepted view – that the inhabitants of the Highlands were barbaric and uncivilised. The popularity of the work throughout Europe was astonishing. Napoleon is said to have carried a copy with him on all of his campaigns, and Mendelsohn's visit to Scotland, and his composition inspired by Fingal's Cave on the island of Staffa, are indicative of the resonance which the tales had for many people. As a result, Macpherson's *Ossian* transformed perceptions of the Highlands, the value placed on Highland culture and, ultimately, the Highlanders' view of themselves and their past.

Debate as to whether or not the work was genuine gripped all levels of Scottish society in the early nineteenth century. The Cromarty writer, Hugh Miller, gives a vivid account of a visit in the 1810s to his relations at Gruids, near Lairg in Sutherland, and of the way in which the argument raged. This can be found in his autobiography, *My Schools and School-masters*. In time the accepted conclusion was that, while using some genuine source material, *Ossian* was largely a hoax. It had, nevertheless, irrevocably changed the way in which people thought about the Highlands and the value placed on their Celtic past.

A similar fascination with Celtic art and society, particularly its Pictish variant, has come to the fore in the last quarter-century. Much of this is to be welcomed since it has encouraged an increased understanding of this culture and a greater appreciation of the remarkable achievements of its artists and craft-workers. Nevertheless, there are dangers in some of the exaggerated claims of insight into Celtic society and spirituality.

PICTISH AND EARLY MEDIEVAL
*c.*AD 500–*c.*AD 1100

The Picts

The term Picts (*Picti* = painted people) was first used by a Roman writer in AD 297 to refer to the tribes of northern Britain. These were not a new people, but the indigenous Iron Age inhabitants whose culture was, by this time, largely Celtic. Other Roman sources suggest that the *Picti* could be divided into two main groups – those who lived close to the Antonine Wall and those who lived farther to the north – and it is possible that this coming together or grouping of tribes was in response to the Roman invasion itself. As in other parts of Britain, these tribal confederations developed into independent kingdoms, which we now refer to as the northern and southern Pictish kingdoms. By the sixth century, the heartland and stronghold of the northern Pictish kingdom was around the inner Moray Firth, with the great fortified site at Burghead on the Moray coast as its most visible centre of power. An independent or semi-independent Pictish kingdom continued until the ninth century when it began to be progressively absorbed into the new kingdom of Scotland – except for those parts which, at about the same date, became part of the Norse earldom of Orkney. For much of the period before AD 850, there was political stability and a slowly improving climate which is likely to have improved living conditions and provided greater wealth for the leaders of the tribal society. These were conditions favourable to the development of art. No Pictish documents have survived (unless, as is possible, the great illuminated Gospel, the *Book of Kells*, was begun in eastern Pictland), but there is a rich heritage of stone carving and some metalwork. The earliest carvings are symbol stones – that is, unworked slabs or boulders incised with one or more of a wide variety of symbols, including real and imaginary animals and the designs now referred to as 'double-disc and Z-rod' and 'crescent and V-rod'. These are known as Class I stones, which sometimes have their symbols carved on older standing stones, as at Edderton (Gazetteers 4:24 and 6:3). The function of the Class

I symbol stones in Pictish society is not clear and, for some reason, they are more common in what was the territory of the northern Pictish kingdom. Class II stones combine this symbolism with Christian images, while Class III have only Christian symbols.

Picts, Scots and the Christian mission

At some time before AD 500, another people, Scots from modern-day Antrim in northern Ireland, began to settle in south-west Argyll, in what was to become the kingdom of Dalriada. They belonged to three principal tribes – the Cenél nGábrain, the Cenél nOengusa and the Cenél Loairn. Their influence began to extend from their western base, partly through the work of Christian missionaries. The first recorded historical event of this period in the north is a visit by the Scots missionary Columba to the court of Bridei, king of the northern Picts, in AD 565, three years after he first arrived in Scotland. This is likely to have taken place either at Craig Phadrig in Inverness or at Urquhart on Loch Ness. Columba founded the monastery of Iona, probably around AD 570, but there is no evidence that he had converted Bridei or made any great impact on his kingdom.

A figure with a greater influence in the evangelising of Ross was Columba's younger contemporary, Donnan, who founded a community on the island of Eigg. Donnan and over fifty of his followers were reputedly massacred in AD 617, probably by pagan Picts. The community recovered, or was re-established, and the influence of Donnan (or of his reputation) can be seen in dedications and place-names along the west coast at Little Lochbroom (Kildonan), Kishorn (Seipeil Dhonnáin) and Loch Alsh (Eilean Donan).

The successor to Donnan's mission was that of Maelrubha, who founded the monastery of Applecross in Wester Ross in AD 673 and was abbot until his death in AD 722. In addition to this monastery, there are dedications to Maelrubha at Lochcarron (Clachan Ma-Ribhe) and at Lochmaree (Loch Ma-ruibhe with its island, Eilean Ma-Ruibhe). A further dedication at Contin, and a tradition associating Maelrubha with the parish of Urquhart on the Black Isle, suggest that his influence extended farther east. The facts that dedications

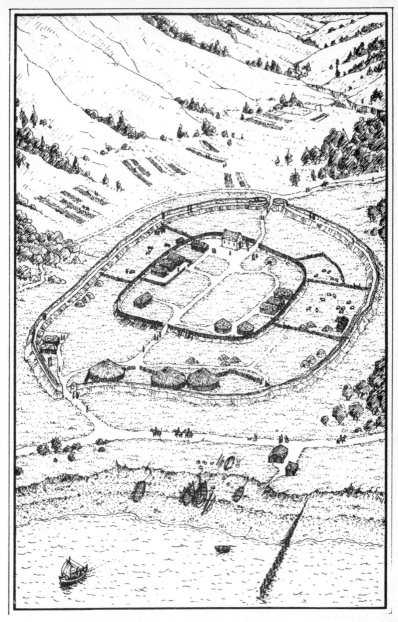

FIGURE 1.
Applecross monastic settlement – an impression of the site c.AD 700

to Columba and to Donnan/Maelrubha occur in different
areas, and that Donnan is not mentioned by Columba's
principal biographer, Adomnan, who wrote in the 680s,
suggest that there may have been some rivalry between the
two or, at least, between their followers. This may reflect
tribal or family differences within the Scots of Dalriada. In
any event, Donnan's mission among the northern Picts was
decidedly more risky, to the extent that some later followers
of Columba regarded Donnan as having deliberately sought
martyrdom.

During the eighth century the influence of Columban
Christianity increased, and from shortly after AD 750, Pictish
stones carved with Christian symbols begin to appear. Outstanding among these are four slabs carved with crosses and
other symbols at Rosemarkie, Nigg, Shandwick and Hilton of
Cadboll (Gazetteer 6:10–13). The Cadboll stone is now in
the Museum of Scotland, Edinburgh. Although the majority
of Pictish cross slabs are found in Tayside, the group from
Easter Ross are particularly important, and it has been argued
that the school of carving which emerged here influenced work
both on Iona and in the southern kingdom.

It is likely that the monasteries on Eigg and at Applecross
were abandoned c.AD 800 after a series of Viking raids, but
Christian communities in the east survived. It is not clear
if there was a single pre-eminent centre or a number of
different communities, perhaps flourishing at different times.
Rosemarkie was clearly of importance and later emerged as
the centre of the diocese of Ross. Recent and continuing
excavations at Tarbat have revealed an extensive settlement,
bounded by a bank and ditch, and dated by radiocarbon
analysis to the second to sixth century. On the evidence of
later carved stones, it is clear that this became a Christian
community. One of these stones, a fragment of an eighth- or
ninth-century carved cross shaft, is notable for having part
of a Latin inscription commemorating someone named
Reodatius (Gazetteer 6:21). There are at least two further
sites which may have been important. Duthac, associated
with nearby Tain, may have been an early Christian saint, and
his shrine may pre-date the eleventh century. Finally, the
monastery established in the thirteenth century at Old Fearn,

near Edderton, may have been a development of some earlier community.

Other early Christian sites can be identified from the evidence of place-names. The place-name element *annaid* indicates an early site, and there are seven places so named within the area covered by this book, together with an eighth in the parish of Kincardine (Gazetteer 6:24–30). It is possible that *annaid* may refer to the mother church of a local community, having precedence over other churches and holding the relics of the patron or founder. *Annaid* sites are likely to date from between AD 800 and AD 1100, and the local groupings of churches, with the *annaid* as the hub, may be the precursors of the medieval parish system. Alternatively, the name may refer to church sites abandoned at an early date. Some derived place-names refer to land owned by or associated with the church rather than the church site itself.

Early Christian sites are also indicated by the place-name element *neimhidh*, which is taken to indicate an early ritual site, perhaps supplanting a pre-Christian sacred grove. In Easter Ross there is a cluster of place-names with this derivation in the old parish of Newnakle (Dalnavie, Cnocnavie and Inchnavie), and also on the Black Isle, at Navity (Gazetteer 6:31–34).

In considering the early Christian sites and early Christian history of the area, it is important to avoid two errors which were once common. The first is to think of early Christian missionaries travelling the country and establishing churches which were then dedicated to them – leaving place-names in their wake, like a trail of breadcrumbs for later historians to follow. This mistake led to the view that the journeys of these saints could be traced, and it also confused dedications from different periods. The truth is that these charismatic men made a great impact on their followers, and it was their reputation for sanctity among their followers that led to the first dedications in their name. In consequence, place-names may indicate a sphere of influence of the followers of an early church leader, but we must remember that some saints enjoyed later periods of popularity which led to further scatterings of dedications.

A second error is the notion of a distinct 'Celtic Church', independent of and owing little to the traditions of the Roman

Catholic Church. This is little more than an invention of early Scottish historians who wished to claim the spiritual descent of the presbyterian Church of Scotland from an early, pure form of Christianity, 'uncontaminated' by contact with Rome and the papacy. This notion has no value: the church of Columba, Donnan and Maelrubha had its distinct traditions, but these Celtic saints undoubtedly saw themselves as part of a wider church centred on Rome.

Scottish control and Norse settlers
By the middle of the ninth century, Kenneth MacAlpin, King of the Scots of Dalriada, had established control over the southern Pictish kingdom. At about the same time, the northern kingdom began to come into the hands of the tribe of the rival Cenél Loairn. Rivalry between the two continued for almost 200 years, but the superior resources of the southern dynasty and a long running feud within the Moray-based northern dynasty gradually allowed the southern line to dominate.

While the Scots were consolidating their hold on Pictland, the west and north were coming under the influence of Scandinavians, who arrived first as raiding Vikings. An Irish monk recorded the first attacks in the Hebrides in AD 794, after which Iona was pillaged a number of times, and the community withdrew to Kells in Ireland in AD 807. At about the same time the monastery of Applecross was raided and was probably abandoned not long after.

Raiding was followed by settlement, and during the ninth century, the Norse earldom of Orkney was established under the powerful dynasty of Møre from western Norway. The earls of Orkney had considerable influence over Caithness and Sutherland, and the Norse sagas suggest two main periods of expansion into Ross and Cromarty: first in the late ninth century by Earl Sigurd I (the Mighty) and Thorstein the Red, a Hebridean-based Viking; and second in the early eleventh century under Earl Thorfinn. It is the second of these which is the more significant.

In AD 1029–30, Earl Thorfinn pursued a campaign against the Scots *mormaer* (steward) of Moray, winning a battle at Torfness (Tarbatness in Easter Ross). In the *Orkneyinga*

Saga, the *mormaer* is called Karl Hundason. This, which can be read as 'churl son-of-a-dog', is almost certainly an uncomplimentary by-name for Macbeth. Macbeth was in a powerful position, since by his marriage to Gruoch, he had united the rival branches of the Moray dynasty. Moreover, because both he and Gruoch were descended from tenth-century Scots kings, he presented a serious threat to the reigning monarch, Duncan I. Duncan marched north to Moray where he was defeated and killed by Macbeth. With no other adult claimant to the throne, Macbeth became King of Scotland. He ruled from AD 1040 until his defeat by Duncan's son, Malcolm III (Canmore), in AD 1054.

Various places now 'claim' the notorious Macbeth as their own. However, the alleged connection with Cawdor, near Inverness, comes only from Shakespeare's play. The earliest version of the 'story of Macbeth' is from a poem by Andrew of Wyntoun (*c.*1355–1422), in which he is described as 'thane of Cromarty'. A thane was an official who exercised authority on behalf of the king. Dingwall, on the basis that it was an early northern thanage, also alleges an association with Macbeth. None of these claims can be firmly established, and what really matters is the historical fact that Macbeth's initial power base was in the north, where it confronted that of Thorfinn.

Once Macbeth became king, however, he ruled from the southern kingdom, and it is likely that this weakened his northern boundary and allowed an expansion of Norse settlement into Ross and Cromarty. Place-names suggest that there were considerable parts of both Easter and Wester Ross in which Norse settlement was significant and perhaps even dominant. Norse farmers appear to have cultivated fertile land along the coasts, as is shown in names derived from *bólstadr*, meaning 'farmstead' (*see* note after Gazetteer 6). The name 'Dingwall' itself is probably derived from *thingvollr* ('assembly place'), and the significance of this settlement may have been that it controlled the river valleys of the Conon and its tributaries, an area from which valuable timber could be extracted. The importance of timber supply should be seen in the context of the shortage of wood in Caithness and Orkney itself. What may have been the Norse assembly site at Greenhill in Dingwall was unfortunately destroyed in the nineteenth century.

Despite the clear importance of Norse settlement in Ross, almost no archaeological remains have been discovered. North of the Oykell, in Sutherland and Caithness, there have been finds of 'grave goods' from pagan Norse burials, but no such burials have come to light south of the Oykell and Dornoch Firth. It may be that a stronger Christian influence in the area led to burial without pagan rites and so without 'grave goods' being placed alongside the body.

The other material remains of Norse culture are a hoard of silver found in the kirkyard wall at Tarbat and a discovery, in the 1880s, of what was said to be 'Viking gold' near Nigg. Unfortunately this was re-used in contemporary jewellery.

THE MIDDLE AGES

c.AD 1100–*c*.AD 1600

The geographical setting

We have seen how the natural boundaries of the area, with the Beauly Firth to the south and the River Oykell and Dornoch Firth to the north, tended to create a specifically local culture in Easter Ross and the Black Isle. The Beauly Firth marked a division between different traditions of tomb building in the Neolithic period; the Decantae tribe held this area in the Iron Age; this was a stronghold of early Christianity; and later, the Oykell marked a southern boundary of the Norse earldom of Orkney during much of its history.

As the power of the Scottish crown increased during the Middle Ages, considerable effort was expended in bringing this and other northern areas under control. It was important to push royal authority farther north than Inverness, for although Inverness was a point where routes from all directions met, it was not an easily defended border. There were more defensible lines in Easter Ross, either along the Cromarty Firth, or along the River Oykell and Dornoch Firth. There are early references to the 'stockfords of Ross' – crossings at the head of both the Beauly and Dornoch Firths, probably with wooden stakes to mark the ford and assist crossings – and control of these seems to have been sought. Ferry crossing on the firths were also important.

In the west, the geography encouraged power struggles to control the Minch – the vital seaway between the mainland and the Hebrides. In Coigach in Wester Ross, the MacNicols held sway from the tenth to the thirteenth century, when they were replaced by the MacLeods, whose power was augmented by the fact that they also held lands in Lewis on the other side of the Minch.

The advance of royal control

Macbeth's power in southern Scotland was broken in 1054, when he was defeated by Duncan's son, Malcolm Canmore (Malcolm III). Three years later, Malcolm extended his control into the north, defeating and killing Macbeth in battle at Lumphanan, Aberdeenshire. Macbeth's step-son, Lulach, was defeated the following year. This consolidation of control by the southern-based dynasty marked a turning point in the history of the north, but it was followed by almost 200 years of power struggles between the descendants of Malcolm and the remnants of the northern royal line in Moray and Ross.

The two principal rebel families associated with Ross were the MacHeths and the MacWilliams. In 1130, Malcolm Mac-Heth supported a revolt against David I, led by Earl Angus of Moray (a grandson of Lulach). Angus's defeat was followed by a march north by the royal army, possibly extending into Ross. Malcolm MacHeth had also allied himself with Somerled of Argyll, and persisted in rebellion until his capture in 1134. He was, however, not executed, and on his release in 1157 was created Earl of Ross. This was probably an attempt by the new king, Malcolm IV, to win the support of the Mac-Heths and was the first of a number of occasions when the earldom would be used by the crown to win support or reward loyalty.

A more serious threat was posed in the 1170s and 1180s by rebellions launched from a power base in the northern Highlands by Donald MacWilliam, whose father was a bastard son of Duncan II. The danger was sufficiently serious for the king, William I, to lead an army north in 1179 and establish two royal castles north of Inverness – at Eddirdowyr (Tarradale) on the north shore of the Beauly Firth and Dunskaith on the north side of the entrance to the Cromarty Firth. In 1187, MacWilliam was defeated on the moor of Mam Garvia, probably north-west of Dingwall, and his severed head was presented to the king. It was, however, another ten years before the frontier of royal authority was pushed back again into Ross.

There was a further revolt involving both the MacWilliams and MacHeths in 1211, but a turning point came when the royal house gained the support of a native northern family in the person of Farquhar Mactaggart. Mactaggart, whose name means 'son of the priest', was probably associated either with the hereditary abbots of Applecross in the west or with the sanctuary of St Duthac at Tain in the east. He was knighted in 1215 and granted lands in Easter Ross, gaining the title Earl of Ross, probably *c.*1230, after the MacWilliams were finally crushed. Mactaggart's support for the Scottish crown was of vital importance in the history of the area, and his influence seems to have allowed an expansion of feudal settlements in the north after 1215.

Feudal settlement

Royal power was exercised in the north through a combination of native noblemen such as Mactaggart and descendants of Anglo-Norman, Flemish and French families from the south of Scotland. These families, who had been part of the earlier feudal settlement of the south, now established themselves, or minor branches of their families, in the new 'border territory' north of Inverness. Royal authority was further extended in 1266, when Scandinavian territory in the west and western isles, already subdued by the Earl of Ross, was ceded to the Scottish crown by the Treaty of Perth.

The feudal system was based on the premise that all land was ultimately the property of the crown, and in return for grants of land, these families undertook to uphold the authority of the crown within their territories. Thus we find a de Monte Alto (Mowat) as sheriff of Cromarty in the 1260s and a de Moravia (Moray) castle at Ormond Hill, Avoch. The de Moravias had earlier been granted Skelbo in Sutherland, and rose to be one of the most powerful families in the area.

In some cases settlement took a form already common in the south – the establishing of a burgh on crown land, next to a royal castle held by a sheriff, situated at some strategic point. Thus the castle and burgh of Dingwall were established by 1226 on an existing site at the head of the Cromarty Firth, and Cromarty, controlling the ferry crossing at the entrance to the Firth, appears to be of a similar date. There is no trace of either of these early castles, but a moated homestead of this period survives at David's Fort near Conon Bridge, together with a simple motte near Muir of Ord (Gazetteer 7:5, 6). In the west, the fortification at Dun Lagaigh (Gazetteer 4:9) was re-worked in the twelfth or

FIGURE 2.
*Ormond Castle, Avoch, as it may have appeared c.AD 1300,
from the north-east*

thirteenth century with lime-mortared masonry to create a small motte and bailey castle, and the vitrified fort on Eilean Donan (Gazetteer 7:7) was replaced by a similar structure. It is possible that there was a re-occupation of other old fortified sites.

This was also a time with a favourable climate; a warm period which lasted from *c.*970 to *c.*1300. The area of ground under cultivation in Scotland may have reached a peak around 1280 before the beginning of a colder period, which shortened the growing season by about three weeks – a significant change in northern latitudes. The subsequent 'little ice age' lasted until *c.*1700, and later inhabitants of the area may well have looked back at what must have seemed something of a golden age. Increased productivity on the land, the extension of royal authority to the north and the formation of royal burghs encouraged trade. Coin finds from what appears to have been the fair site of medieval Cromarty (on display in Cromarty Courthouse Museum) confirm that there was an active monetary economy.

Stability and a growing southern influence also led to new religious foundations, whose clergy may have brought new farming techniques and encouraged production of wool. A community of Premonstratensian canons was brought to Old Fearn in the 1220s by Farquhar Mactaggart, and a house of the Valliscaulian order was founded in the 1230s at Beauly. Both these orders took their names from the sites of their mother houses in France, at Prémontré and Val des Choux ('Cabbage Valley'). Another Valliscaulian house at Pluscarden in Moray, founded at the same time, may have been a thanks-offering by the king for the final defeat of the MacWilliams. In 1238, the Premonstratensian house at Old Fearn was moved to a better site between Tarbat and Nigg, and in 1240, the building of a new and larger cathedral was begun at Fortrose.

While the thirteenth century was a time of prosperity and growth, the very fact that Ross had become an integral part of the Scottish kingdom involved it in the chaos of the wars with England. These began with the disputed succession to the Scottish throne in 1290 and continued intermittently for well over a century.

The Wars of Independence and after

In September 1290, the seven-year-old Queen Margaret ('the Maid of Norway'), heir to the Scottish throne, died on her arrival in Orkney. In the following year, Edward I of England was accepted by Scots leaders as arbitrator in the disputed succession. John, chosen by Edward as King of Scots, abdicated in 1296. This was followed by an English invasion and the seizure of strategic strongholds. There were six royal castles clustered around the Moray Firth – Elgin, Forres, Nairn, Inverness, Dingwall and Cromarty – all of which were taken.

Scottish resistance was successfully led by the charismatic William Wallace until his defeat at Falkirk in 1298. In the north, Andrew de Moravia was a figure of similar importance. From his stronghold at Ormond Castle, near Avoch, he led a group of noblemen in rebellion in the winter of 1296–97 and drove the English garrisons out of most of the key royal castles. This success was followed by victory for the Scots army at Stirling Bridge, where Andrew de Moravia led the northern forces but died from wounds received in the battle. Wallace remained active until his capture and grisly execution in 1305. Later traditions link Wallace with various sites in Ross and Cromarty, but the evidence for this is unreliable and tends to under-play the significance of de Moravia's leadership in the struggle. After Wallace's death, Scots' resistance to Edward was largely led by the Comyns from their power bases in Badenoch and Buchan.

In 1306, Robert Bruce, Earl of Carrick, murdered his rival John Comyn and was inaugurated King of Scots, but a civil war ensued, with Edward II of England providing support for the Comyns. William, 3rd Earl of Ross, had been a supporter of a rival claim to the throne by John Balliol. He sided with the Comyns, and in 1306, handed over Bruce's wife, daughter and sister to the English after they had sought sanctuary within the girth of St Duthac's shrine at Tain. Ross finally submitted to Bruce in 1309.

The battle of Bannockburn in 1314 was a crucial victory for Bruce, bringing a period of stalemate in the war. In 1312, Bruce, recognising the importance of the north, had made his nephew, Thomas Randolph, Earl of Moray, and in Ross he

favoured William's son, Hugh, the 4th Earl. Hugh married
Bruce's sister Maud, held the sheriffdoms and burghs of
Cromarty and Dingwall, the burgh of Nairn, estates in the Black
Isle and Easter Ross, baronies and thanages in north eastern
Scotland and the Isle of Skye. He endowed six chaplainries at
the church of St Duthac in Tain in 1320. Some of the masonry
in the roofless building in the kirkyard may date from this
period. At his death in 1333 at the battle of Halidon Hill he
was wearing the shirt of St Duthac – a relic returned to Tain
by the English. Since the shirt was meant to make the wearer
invulnerable, this act of unexpected generosity has an air of
irony.

After Bruce's death in 1329 there was a weakening of
the Scottish crown and, later in the century, a general collapse
of feudalism as a force of unity in the north. The power of
the state in the Moray Firth depended on three families –
the Randolphs, the Ross earls and the Morays (de Moravias)
– but all of these families died out in the senior male line
in the latter part of the century. In the Hebrides, the
MacDonald Lordship of the Isles emerged, bringing 150 years
of stability and a flowering of Gaelic culture in the west,
though this was perceived as a threat to the power of the
Scottish crown. The combination of this breakdown of order
in the Moray Firth and the power of the MacDonalds in the
west appears to have led to a new perception in the lowlands
of Highlanders as savage and dangerous: 'wyld wykked
helendmen.'

The Earls of Ross and the Lords of the Isles
The title Earl of Ross was granted to Farquhar Mactaggart
*c.*1230 and continued in direct male succession until the
death of William, the 5th Earl, in 1371. Nothing now remains
of the Ross castles of Dingwall, Balconie and Delny, but the
results of the patronage of this native line of earls can be
seen in Fortrose Cathedral, in the creation of the first
collegiate foundation at Tain and in the abbey of Fearn.
Fearn was a daughter house of Whithorn, and this link may
account for the introduction into the area of families from
south-west Scotland, such as the Vasses of Lochslin and the
MacCullochs of Plaids. The 5th Earl had no surviving son.

Euphemia, his daughter, became a woman of considerable importance, and her status is reflected in the magnificent surviving south aisle of Fortrose Cathedral, where she is probably buried.

Euphemia's first marriage, in 1366, was the result of the forceful policies of the king, David II, who insisted that the Earl of Ross marry off his heiress, then aged about thirteen, to Sir Walter Leslie, one of the king's closest associates. The king further insisted that Ross surrender some of his lands to Leslie and circumvented attempts to pass the earldom to another branch of the Ross family – the line of Balnagowan, which stemmed from a half-brother of the 5th Earl. This line, granted the lands of Balnagowan in 1350, eventually assumed the chiefship of the clan but the earldom passed out of Ross hands.

The Earl of Ross's protests over David II's actions led to his title being confiscated in 1371, and he died in that or the following year. Leslie became Earl of Ross and the title passed to the couple's son, Alexander. Euphemia's second marriage, in 1382, was to Alexander, Earl of Buchan, commonly known as the 'Wolf of Badenoch'. She died in 1394.

The disputes which followed were, like all disputes over inheritance, complicated, but they are essential to understanding the struggles for power within Ross and Cromarty. Euphemia's son, Alexander Leslie, Earl of Ross, died in 1402, leaving only a daughter as his heir. From this point the control of the earldom was disputed between Donald, Lord of the Isles (who had married Euphemia's daughter) and the powerful Robert Stewart, Duke of Albany and Regent of Scotland (whose daughter had married Alexander). In 1411 a force of Highlandmen marched into north-east Scotland and engaged the royal army at Harlaw. The battle was indecisive, but it effectively ended MacDonald attempts to assert power in Ross in the face of Stewart opposition. However, a change in royal policy gave the earldom to Donald's son, Alexander, in 1436, and the title was held by the Lords of the Isles until forfeited to the crown in 1475. The earldom lay dormant until James III resurrected it, raised it to a dukedom and bestowed it on his second son in 1480.

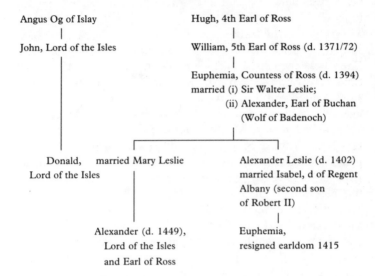

FIGURE 3.
Earls of Ross and Lords of the Isles – key relationships

There followed a period during which the MacDonalds attempted to regain control and, to this end, encouraged unrest in Ross. In 1491, Alexander MacDonald of Loch Alsh led a raid into Easter Ross and, along with Farquhar, son of the Macintosh chief, seized the castle of Inverness before being defeated at Blar na Pairc, possibly near Dingwall. The MacDonalds were finally deprived of the title Lords of the Isles in 1493.

The breaking of the power of the MacDonalds was followed by a period in which the king took a greater interest in the north. James IV travelled in most years of his reign to the shrine of St Duthac at Tain, primarily as an act of pilgrimage, but also as a mark that royal authority ran throughout the realm. His last visit was shortly before the disastrous defeat of the Scots army at Flodden in 1513 and his own death in the battle.

Royal authority in the area had been strengthened in other ways. The baronies of Eddirdour (Redcastle) and Avoch (around Ormond Castle) were held by the Douglas family, which was at first closely associated with the royal house of

Stuart. In 1455, after the Douglas faction fell from favour, these were forfeited to the crown and the land around Ormond castle became a royal hunting forest.

The rise of the Mackenzies

The Mackenzies, although originating in the area of the Beauly Firth, held the Castle of Eilean Donan, in Kintail, under the earls of Ross in the thirteenth and early fourteenth centuries. They feuded with the earls and lost control of Eilean Donan when the castle was successfully besieged in 1331. Mackenzie allies (Maclennans, MacIvers and Macleays) continued the struggle, but were finally defeated by the earls of Ross and their supporters (Munros and Dingwalls) in 1369 at the battle of Bealach nam Bròg ('the Pass of the Shoes' – so called because the men hung their shoes round their necks to provide some protection in place of shields).

Within a few years, however, the line of the earls of Ross had come to an end. The Mackenzies assisted the crown in subduing the Lords of the Isles and were rewarded in 1463 with a grant of lands near Garve. They returned to the east and established strongholds on the crannog at Achilty and soon afterwards on another crannog at Kinellan, near Strathpeffer. Many more properties were to follow.

The eastward expansion of the clan was matched in the west. They acquired Eilean Donan and lands in Kintail in 1509, and an extended feud with the MacDonalds of Glengarry finally brought them the lands of Lochbroom, Lochcarron and Loch Alsh by the 1570s. This was followed by the usurping of the lands of the MacLeods of Lewis. Feuding between various branches of the MacLeods led to them being identified by the crown as incorrigibly dangerous, and a sustained royal policy culminated in their eviction from Lewis in 1611. The Gairloch Macleods had been defeated by Mackenzies at Lochan an Fheidh in the previous year. By 1623, Mackenzie of Kintail securely held their lands and had acquired the title Earl of Seaforth.

The expanding power of the Mackenzies can be traced in the building of castles in both the east and west (*see* Gazetteer 7). The Seaforth line rebuilt Eilean Donan and made Brahan, in the east, their principal seat. A second line, who were to become the Mackenzies of Tarbat, built Castle Leod (1585) and acquired properties from the Munros (Ballone on the Tarbat peninsula and Milton on the north shore of the Cromarty Firth) and from the Vasses (Lochslin). Other branches of the clan built or expanded towers at Fairburn (*c.*1542), Redcastle (*c.*1589), Kinkell Clarsach (*c.*1590) and Kilcoy (1618).

The Brahan Seer

Coinneach Odhar, or the Brahan Seer, is a figure encountered in many collections of folklore of Ross and Cromarty and is closely associated with the Mackenzie family. Like Robin Hood, he is elusive as a historical character. Hugh Miller, writing in the 1830s, described him as having lived in the seventeenth century, working as a labourer somewhere near Brahan. Miller noted a number of his prophecies and, with some scepticism, observed that while the minor prophecies had all been fulfilled, it 'would be easier to prove that the events had taken place than that they had been foretold'. He is, among other things, said to have foretold the fall from power of the Seaforth Mackenzies. The reputed burning of Coinneach Odhar at Chanonry Point is commemorated by a plaque, but, while witches were certainly burnt here, the connection with the Brahan Seer is unproven. It is, on the other hand, as well established as any fact about his life. Rather than considering him as a doubtful historical figure, it is better to regard him as a genuine part of the folklore of the area, his name 'a magnet, drawing a host of prophetic utterances to itself'.

Other landed families

The tiny sheriffdom of Cromarty, established in the thirteenth century at the tip of the Black Isle, was at first in the hands of the de Monte Altos (Mowats), but in the early fourteenth century passed to the family of Urquhart, who held it until the 1670s. Small sheriffdoms such as Cromarty were not uncommon, though Cromarty was the only one to survive into the late Middle Ages and after.

The Munros were established at Foulis from the thirteenth or early fourteenth century and, as with the Mackenzies, branches of the family came to hold numerous properties including Milton, Culcairn, Newmore, Teaninich, Lemlair and Novar. The main line of the family ran into financial problems in the early seventeenth century, but their fortunes were restored by two generations of soldiering as mercenaries in European wars and by their adherence to the presbyterian cause at home.

After the forfeiture of the Lords of the Isles, the Bains became constables of Dingwall Castle. Their position was secured in 1542 when James V granted them land in their own right and Tulloch Castle was then built.

There has already been reference to the fate of the Macleods. They held Coigach, Gairloch and Glenelg from the fourteenth century, but rivalry and feuding between branches of the clan was endemic and they were dispossessed in the early seventeenth century. Eilean Grudidh Castle on Loch Maree may have been one of their strongholds.

Agriculture and land use in the Middle Ages
The wealth of the many landed families of Ross and Cromarty throughout the Middle Ages rested ultimately on the produce of the land. During the stable and relatively prosperous thirteenth century there was a consolidation and probably an expansion of agriculture. The most common unit of land, particularly in the fertile east-coast strip, was the 'davoch'. This was not a precise area but an amount of land paying a fixed rent. Each davoch had its own farm settlement – the fermtoun – held by one or more principal tenants, known as tacksmen (tack = lease). The tacksmen were often related to the principal landowner, and they in turn sub-let to others. At the bottom of the social pyramid were cottars, who were allowed small pieces of land in return for labour on the larger farms. A similar system of tacks, sub-letting and cottars was found in the west, but it is less clear at what period it developed. In both east and west the tacksmen played an important role as middlemen in the society. It is important to realise, when looking at the landscape, especially in the west, that the system of tenants holding individual smallholdings (crofts) was only introduced after the old social and agricultural system was swept away in the eighteenth and nineteenth centuries.

Little archaeological investigation has been carried out to reveal the medieval farming landscape of Ross and Cromarty. Some indications of the pattern of change can be gleaned from place-names. As fermtouns grew, they were often divided into two or three parts, often named Easter, Wester and Middle. In some cases the original centre of the fermtoun can still be identified by the existence of a parish church or chapel.

Many farms practised systems of transhumance, that is, the movement of animals to higher grazing ground during the summer months. The sites of mountain shielings, which were used in the summer, are considered later (Gazetteer 16:18–20), but it should be noted here that some may have been used from medieval times.

Trade in the Middle Ages
Trade in the Middle Ages was restricted to officially licensed trading towns known as royal burghs, and the creation of such towns was an important element in the feudal settlement of the north. Many of the inhabitants of such towns were incomers from the south of Scotland or farther afield, and it was the formation of these burghs that established pockets of Scots speakers in the midst of the Gaelic-speaking Highlands.

Each burgh held weekly markets at its 'mercat cross', the most visible symbol of its status. The inhabitants of the burgh traded freely, but those from outwith its bounds paid a tax – a toll – at the burgh's tolbooth. Over time, tolbooths were enlarged to contain a meeting room and a prison. Each burgh was also permitted one or more annual fairs, which would have lasted several days, all adding to the burgh income and enabling them to pay tax to the crown.

Royal burghs were at first almost democratic. Every burgess – that is every owner of property in the burgh, had an equal status and took part in the election of the burgh council and its officials, the provost and bailies. These officials, in their capacity as burgh magistrates, dispensed justice and regulated the burgh affairs. Fairly quickly, however, the system became corrupted as each burgh council simply appointed rather than elected its successor. Then, with this concentration of authority in a few hands, the more powerful burgesses began to acquire substantial parts of the common property of the town as personal possessions. However, some common property usually remained and formed the burgh's 'common good', which often still exists and is sometimes a substantial accumulated fund.

The early royal burghs of Ross and Cromarty were Dingwall and Cromarty, both established in the thirteenth century. In these places it is still possible to detect the original plan of the town – a castle and a single high street along which the citizens of the burgh held their properties. Since each burgess in the town wished to have property fronting the principal thoroughfare, the standard layout of a burgh was to have long, narrow strips of land running off the high street. As a result, houses were generally built gable end to the street, with narrow lanes running between them to give access to the land at the rear. Even now it is possible to detect this arrangement, despite the fact that the original buildings have long since disappeared.

Tain, in virtue of its status as a religious centre, claimed rights and privileges similar to those of a royal burgh, and these were finally confirmed in the sixteenth century. Fortrose traded under the authority of the Bishop of Ross and received its status as a royal burgh in 1455. The layout of both these towns, which were focused on large ecclesiastical precincts, is different from that outlined above.

THE CHURCH IN
ROSS AND CROMARTY

I. The medieval church
in the diocese of Ross

The diocese of Ross may have existed in some form in the eleventh century but, in common with much of Scotland, it was only from the time of David I (1124–53) that there was a regular succession of bishops and a clear parish structure. From then until the present century, the parish was a central point of reference in the lives of most people. In addition to the obvious religious significance of the church, the parish was a key unit of administration in civil affairs, such as the running of schools and the provision of poor relief. Because of this continuity in the importance of the parish, which transcends any division between medieval and post-medieval history, most churches and chapels in the area are described in a single gazetteer – Gazetteer 12 – which lists all buildings up to 1800. Gazetteers 9–11 list the principal medieval foundations, holy wells and medieval carved gravestones.

In medieval times, bishops were royal nominees. Because the diocese of Ross lay within the area controlled by the Scottish crown, its early history was a relatively settled affair. This was in stark contrast to Caithness, still influenced by the Norse earldom of Orkney, and more likely to oppose royal appointments. Of the diocese of Ross's thirty-seven parishes, the majority were small, clustered along the fertile east coast, with six large sprawling parishes in the west. Within each parish, in addition to the parish church, there might also be earlier Christian sites, such as chapels and holy wells. Places of worship and prayer might also be established by wealthy individuals and families, often with endowments to allow masses to be celebrated for the souls of the founders. Where the endowment was large enough to fund a group, or 'college' of clergy, a collegiate church was created, as happened at Tain, for example.

However, the focal point of religious life for most people was the parish church itself, since it was here that baptisms and burials took place. Many burials, including those of the most prominent members of the parish congregation, were made within the church building itself, under the floor of the nave. Most pre-Reformation parish churches, many of which are still in use, have several hundred burials within their walls. As noted earlier, they are in this respect more like the chambered tombs of the Neolithic than is normally recognised: both types of monument were ceremonial centres for their community and, as repositories for the remains of the dead, linked the community with the past. Both were used over many centuries. Unlike Neolithic monuments, however, we are in a position to understand the symbolism of these buildings, and a visit to even the simplest medieval church site is enhanced by a basic knowledge of its structure and meaning.

Medieval churches were built along an east–west line so that the congregation and the priest, who faced the altar to celebrate mass, looked towards the place where the sun rose – a symbol of the resurrection of Christ. At, or near the entrance to the church, was the baptismal font, placed there because baptism was regarded as the entrance to the life of faith. Running across the church and dividing the laity from the chancel, where the altar stood, was the rood screen. This was a partition surmounted by a figure of Christ on the cross ('rood' being another word for 'cross'), and the message was that progression in the Christian life was by way of suffering. Beyond, in the most holy part of the building, was the altar on which, according to the belief of the church, the risen Christ made himself present. The altar itself contained a relic of a saint. The congregation were reminded that they were members of a wider community which transcended time and space by statues of other saints and, if the church was rich enough, by wall paintings and stained glass windows. On the wall beside the altar was a water stoup (piscina), where the priest ceremonially washed his hands, a secure cupboard (aumbry) for the chalice and plate, and a 'sacrament house', where consecrated bread from the mass was reserved so that Christ remained present in the building at all times. Although much of this symbolism was swept away with the Reformation, there are sometimes remains of fonts, aumbries, piscinas and, surprisingly, sacrament houses.

David I introduced a system of 'teinds' (the Scots equivalent of tithes), whereby a tenth of the crop went to the support of the local church and its resident priest. This made possible the building of more substantial parish churches, though over time, much of this income was diverted from the parishes to support clergy in the cathedrals, who then appointed poorly paid and often badly educated deputies (variously known as vicars, curates and chaplains) to fulfil their parish duties. The magnificence of the cathedrals was achieved only at the expense of the parish ministry.

The principal medieval religious foundations in the diocese of Ross were established in the thirteenth century. During the next two hundred years, their buildings were modified and enlarged (see Gazetteer 9). The first cathedral church of Ross was at Rosemarkie, but c.1240 it was moved to a new and larger site in Fortrose. Twenty years earlier, Earl Farquhar Mactaggart had brought monks and relics of St Ninian from Whithorn in the south of Scotland to establish a religious house at Mid Fearn. This was transferred c.1238 to a better site at New Fearn in the parish of Tarbat. The Valliscaulian priory at Beauly (now in Inverness-shire, though originally in the diocese of Ross) was founded in the 1230s, and a fourth important ecclesiastical centre emerged at Tain, where a collegiate church grew from an earlier church and sanctuary. Its medieval buildings are the best preserved of all the foundations.

The skills of stone masonry which flourished as cathedrals and monasteries were enlarged and rebuilt during the fourteenth and early fifteenth centuries is also reflected in a rich collection of more than twenty-six ornamented grave slabs on the Black Isle and in Easter Ross (see Gazetteer 11). Most of these have decorated crosses, sometimes on stepped bases and sometimes flanked by long swords or other symbols.

As well as developments in architectural style, there were also changes in religious practice towards the end of the fifteenth century, with a greater emphasis on the humanity and sufferings of Christ and more attention placed on personal devotions. One unusual local trace of this is a carving, on a grave slab at Cullicudden, of a pierced hand – one of Christ's wounds. Such symbols, especially those in public places, were commonly destroyed after the Reformation.

The greater humanism of religious life was an aspect of the European Renaissance, which reached its flowering in Scotland in the reign of James IV. James has a particular importance for the area because of his annual pilgrimages to the shrine of St Duthac at Tain. His visits were partly a self-imposed penance for his part in the murder of his father and partly a way of making the point that the authority of the crown extended to the north. James also combined at least some pilgrimages with visits to his mistress at Darnaway in Moray. His route to Tain took him sometimes through Dingwall (where we know that he lost money at cards), and sometimes over the Black Isle, using the ferry between Cromarty and Nigg. Although he occasionally travelled in a small group, he was more often accompanied by members of the court and a retinue that would have included musicians, hawkers, counsellors and even the court jester.

James encouraged the work of poets such as William Dunbar, and through his work we can enter into something of the spirit of the royal parties who came to Tain in a combination of apparently sincere religious devotion and celebration of earthly, and of earthy, life. Dunbar's verse includes the *Lament for the Makaris* (poets), a moving personal meditation on death with the sonorous Latin refrain '*Timor mortis conturbat me*' ('the fear of death disturbs me'), a triumphant Easter hymn ('Done is a battlel on the dragon blak') and a wide range of comic, bawdy and satirical poems.

In 1507, also during the reign of James IV, Scotland's first printing press was established in Edinburgh, and three years later, the *Aberdeen Breviary* was published. This was a specifically Scottish service book for the Roman Catholic Church providing prayers, hymns and readings for the whole year, including the celebration of the feast days of eighty-one Scottish saints, often introduced into the liturgy for the first time. The *Breviary* was the work of Bishop Elphinstone who, with the king's encouragement, had collated manuscript sources and gathered legends and traditions from throughout the country.

Among the material gathered were stories of St Duthac, which would otherwise have been lost. It is, perhaps, not too fanciful to consider Elphinstone's *Breviary* to be, as well as a religious work, one of the first collections of the folktales of Scotland.

The Circle of Bread

In a time of dearth, a landowner in Ross sent a loaf of bread to Duthac, the leader of the local church. It was made from dough rich in butter and sweetened with honey. These were precious ingredients and Duthac could not eat such food surrounded by poverty. He sent the loaf to another.

So it continued through the day. Each one who received the bread thought of another more deserving and by nightfall it had passed to the seventh, a poor man of the parish, who brought it once more as a gift to Duthac.

Duthac retraced the circle of bread from house to house, inviting each family to join him at the chapel. There he blessed the bread and each broke a piece from the loaf as it was passed round. There was hardly a mouthful each and yet all were satisfied. One man carried away a few crumbs from the chapel and it was said that many sick people, whom no medicine could cure, were freed from their infirmities in the name of Christ, the Bread of Life, the moment they tasted, or even smelled, the smallest fragment.

Loosely based on the legends of
St Duthac in the *Aberdeen Breviary*.

In many medieval churches an ordinary loaf of bread, called the 'kirk-lafe', was blessed, broken and distributed by the priest. It was eaten by all, including those who felt themselves excluded from communion. The practice continues in the Orthodox Churches. This legend appears to link local traditions of Duthac with the sharing of the 'kirk-lafe'.

Elphinstone and a number of other churchmen in Scotland were also engaged in attempts to raise the standards of religious life and correct abuses, but the first half of the sixteenth century saw growing pressure for more radical change in the face of continuing shortcomings. From 1540, support for the Lutheran reform movement grew, and in 1560, the reformers seized the political initiative and had an act of parliament passed which abolished the authority of the Roman Catholic church.

A nineteenth-century stained glass window in the restored collegiate church at Tain shows Nicholas Ross, provost of Tain, and Robert Munro of Foulis, at the parliament in the presence of John Knox, the leading Scottish reformer. Also in the church is a substantial memorial to Patrick Hamilton, commendator of Fearn Abbey. The window and the memorial are worth some consideration because they illustrate an over-simplified view of the Scottish Reformation as a sudden transformation of Scottish church life – a view which is still encountered. In their subject-matter, however, they draw attention to some of the real complexities of the event. Nicolas Ross was head (provost) of the clergy of the collegiate church and, in virtue of this office, was also the secular head of the town of Tain. He added to his power by succeeding Hamilton as commendator of Fearn Abbey – a commendator being someone who received the income of the abbot but did not fill the office. For Ross, the Reformation offered the chance to advance his own family by acquiring church property and placing his sons in key positions in the new church. Munro of Foulis, although he also benefited, appears to have had a more genuine interest in the principles of the reform. However, the leading figure among the three was Patrick Hamilton. He was a kinsman of James V and was allocated the income of the Abbey of Fearn to fund his education in Paris, where he came under the influence of Lutheran ideas. Later, he visited Wittenburg in Germany, where he met Martin Luther in person. On his return he preached the new doctrines and was condemned as a heretic. He was burnt at the stake in St Andrews in 1528, the first protestant martyr in Scotland. Hamilton had no real connection with either Tain or Fearn, and his receipt of the income of Fearn Abbey was typical of the abuses that he came to oppose. There is, however, a strange appropriateness in the siting of a memorial here, since his execution was deliberately carried out when his kinsman James V was on pilgrimage to the shrine of St Duthac, and unable to intervene. The memorial is unfortunately graceless and misleadingly suggests that Tain was strongly affected by Hamilton's protestant ideals. The reality was that change at a parish level came only slowly.

II. The Post-Reformation Church

Much of the property of the medieval Church was by now in private hands, and arrangements were only gradually made to appoint and pay reformed parish ministers. It was not until the end of the seventeenth century that the character of the Scottish protestant church was finally established. The adaptation of earlier church buildings took place over the same long period.

From 1690, the Church of Scotland was firmly presbyterian (that is, governed by elected elders), although disputes as to who had the right to appoint ministers would continue for more than 150 years. Worship centred on preaching, and this necessitated a rearrangement within the church building. Pre-Reformation churches were built along an east–west line, with the altar at the east. Since the same church buildings continued in use, the simplest solution when the pulpit became the focus of the church was usually to locate it in the middle of the south wall, and to make new large windows in this central section of the church, often on both sides of the pulpit. As congregations increased in size, galleries, known as lofts, were built, often by the principal landowners (who owned the floor space of the church). These lofts were usually entered by external stairs. A rare survival in St Duthac's, Tain, is the front of the loft built for the Incorporated Trades of Tain, decorated with the symbols of their craft.

In small churches, significantly more accommodation could only be provided by erecting a new wing, often to the north opposite the pulpit, creating the T-shaped church. Later, new churches were built to this shape. In some cases, as in Cromarty and Nigg, these new aisles were built with money accumulated in the Poor Fund. In all churches, only the better off had pews, which they either owned or rented. Poorer people sat on stools in whatever open space remained.

During the seventeenth century, the celebration of communion (The Lord's Supper) became less frequent, but when celebrated, was an important and solemn occasion. Long communion tables were set up in front of the pulpit. Later these were replaced by long communion pews, which can still be seen in some places (Lochbroom, Lochcarron). Large crowds often travelled from neighbouring parishes, and in some places outdoor services were held, particularly where it was necessary to have services in both Gaelic and English. In the parish of Edderton there is a wooden preaching booth which was used on such occasions.

All churches issued tokens to those permitted to take communion. Early tokens were lead or pewter, marked with the name of the parish, and these can be seen on display in a number of places. Some churches also display communion plate, usually pewter. Other surviving church furniture includes collection ladles and alm stools.

It was, in general, only in the eighteenth century that larger churches were constructed on new sites and the adapted medieval buildings abandoned. Such new churches can be seen at Resolis, Urray and Urquhart, with an early nineteenth-century example at Tain.

In 1581, the reformed Church of Scotland forbade burial inside churches. Sometimes this was circumvented by the conversion of redundant parts of the church to burial vaults, but in general it led wealthier families to create their own burial chambers within kirkyards. An alternative was to use all or part of a disused church, as at Kirkmichael, Gilchrist and Fortrose. From the middle of the seventeenth century, it became more common for gravestones to be erected. Many of which are finely carved and well preserved. In looking at these, it is useful to be able to recognise the traditional symbols of mortality (skull, bones, hour-glass, coffin, death-bell and grave-digger's tools) and immortality (winged souls and resurrection scenes).

During the seventeenth century disputes within the church and between the church and the state centred on church government. The church was episcopalian from 1584–1638 and 1663–1689, with the presbyterian system finally established from 1690. The evidence suggests that church disputes in the north in the seventeenth century were perhaps less bitter than in the south of Scotland. Nevertheless, two ministers – Thomas Hog of Kiltearn and John McKillican of Alness – were imprisoned on the Bass Rock after holding conventicles (illegal religious services) under the protection of the Foulis family. They are commemorated by a memorial cairn at

Figure 4. *Outdoor preaching, Tain* c. *AD 1800*

Alness, and on Thomas Hog's gravestone, placed at the entrance to Kiltearn Church, are the words 'This stone shall bear witness against the parishioners of Kiltearn, if they bring ane ungodly minister in here'. Hog is also commemorated by a nineteenth-century plaque in the collegiate church in Tain.

Hog, who was appointed to the parish of Kiltearn in 1654, is a particularly important figure. He set about the spiritual regeneration of the parish, and it can be argued that his work influenced the nature of the church in the Highlands for centuries afterwards. Like all strict Calvinists, he emphasised personal conversion and continuous striving for assurance of salvation, but his innovation was to encourage the emergence of what came to be known as *Na Daoine* or The Men, a lay spiritual elite who later played a central role in the religious life of many congregations. They led weekly prayer meetings and, being closer to the ordinary people than the minister, had a profound influence over them.

The Men came to the fore in the evangelical revival which began in Nigg in 1739 and which spread to the west and north during the next sixty years, remaining important during the first half of the nineteenth century (and possibly for longer). There were similarities to, and links with, other revivals in the south of Scotland, but as a movement it had its own characteristics – chiefly the prominence of The Men and the fact that both evangelical ministers and The Men were often credited with prophetic powers and supernatural gifts. The revival encouraged resistance to landlord-appointed ministers and in this and other ways The Men were social leaders, an increasingly important role as traditional Highland society disintegrated.

The history of the church in eighteenth-century Scotland is much taken up with the division between Evangelicals, described above, and the Moderates, who opposed a religion dominated by emotional response and who accepted the role of landowners in the government of the church. Affairs in the Church of Scotland reached a crisis in The Disruption of 1843, when almost one-third of ministers in the Church of Scotland broke away to form the Free Church. Easter Ross and the Black Isle were, not surprisingly, among the strongest Free Church areas. *Memorabilia Domestica*, written by Donald

Sage, the minister of Resolis, is a useful account of parish life at this time. Sage joined the Free Church, and the small house he built as a manse in Jemimaville survives. The parish of Resolis is also notable for the riot which took place when the authorities appointed a new minister to the Church of Scotland. The riot was followed by a jail-breaking at Cromarty Courthouse.

A leading figure in the period leading up to the Disruption was the Rev. Dr John MacDonald, minister of Urquhart parish on the Black Isle from 1813 until his death in 1849 (from 1843 as Free Church minister). He was the best-known Gaelic preacher of his day, swaying thousands at great open-air services at a preaching site in a natural amphitheatre in the oak wood at Ferintosh.

A more widely known figure is Hugh Miller, a largely self-taught Cromarty stonemason, who became editor of the Evangelicals' Edinburgh-based newspaper, the *Witness*, in 1839. He continued in this role until his suicide in 1856, exerting a powerful influence over policies within the church and over Scottish public opinion as a whole. His birthplace in Cromarty is cared for by the National Trust for Scotland.

An account of further divisions and gradual re-unification of the Church in Scotland is beyond the scope of this guide. For those interested, a chart is provided below (FIGURE 5), and visitors should be aware that in most parishes the established Church of Scotland will own, or have owned until recently, two buildings – the original parish church and the original free church, built usually in the 1840s or 1850s. There may also be a Free Church (a minority of the original Free Church of 1843 who did not participate in later reunions, hence the by-name the 'Wee Frees') and, in some places, a Free Presbyterian church (a break-away in 1892 from the then Free Church).

Divisions in the church in Scotland
Those unacquainted with Scottish church history may find it difficult to believe that this is a simplified diagram. There is a grain of truth in the saying: wherever you find a Highlander you will find a presbyterian church – and wherever you find six Highlanders, six presbyterian churches.

FIGURE 5.

Divisions and re-unification of the Church of Scotland

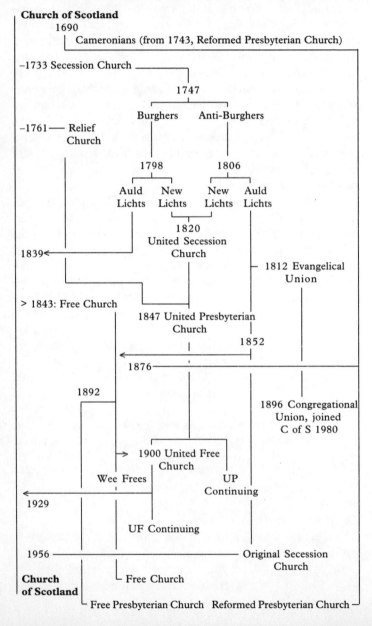

Church of Scotland
1690
     Cameronians (from 1743, Reformed Presbyterian Church)

−1733 Secession Church

1747

Burghers   Anti-Burghers

−1761 — Relief
         Church

1798   1806

Auld New   New Auld
Lichts Lichts Lichts Lichts

1820
United Secession
Church

1839◄

                     — 1812 Evangelical
                         Union

> 1843: Free Church

1847 United Presbyterian
Church

                     1852

1876

1892

                       1896 Congregational
                       Union, joined
                       C of S 1980

    → 1900 United Free
        Church
                   UP
Wee Frees   Continuing

1929

UF Continuing

1956 ——————————————— Original Secession
                        Church

Church
of Scotland └ Free Church

  └ Free Presbyterian Church Reformed Presbyterian Church ┘

A note on burials of landed families and patronage of churches

After the Reformation, many churches continued to reflect the wealth of the principal landowners of the parish who, in addition to maintaining the church, created burial places for their families, sometimes in disused chapels or other church buildings. The Mackenzies of Seaforth and of Coul are commemorated in Fortrose Cathedral; Mackenzies of Fairburn in St Clements, Dingwall; the earls of Cromartie in Kilmuir Easter; and Mackenzies of Kilcoy at Killearnan. Munro families are associated with Alness (Novar Munros), Kiltearn (Foulis Munros), Rosskeen (Munros of Newmore and Culrain) and Kirkmichael (Munros of Poyntzfield). Urquharts are interred at St Regulus in Cromarty, Cullicudden (Urquharts of Kinbeachie) and Kirkmichael (Urquharts of Braelangwell).

Carved effigies are found on tombs in Fortrose Cathedral, possibly including Euphemia, Countess of Ross. The association of the cathedral with the burial of the Seaforth Mackenzies is recorded in a poem by Duncan MacRyrie written *c.*1630. This laments the death of four Mackenzies, among them the 1st Earl of Seaforth. One was buried at Beauly Priory and the others in the cathedral of the Chanonry of Ross at Fortrose:

> *Tà fear am Manchainn nan Lios*
> *Nach léigeadh mise as mu nì:*
> *Do bhì an Cananaich nan Clag*
> *Triùir a dh'fhàg gu lag mì.*
>
> In the garden of Beauly one lies
> who will not allow me to rest:
> where the towers of Chanonry rise
> three leave my sad spirit oppressed.

There are also effigies at Fearn Abbey, including Abbot Finlay McFaed who died in 1485, at Killearnan and in the collegiate church of Tain. An obelisk near St Clements, Dingwall commemorates George Mackenzie, 1st Earl of Cromartie.

AFTER 1600

I. Land and property

In the early decades of the seventeenth century, a large part of the area covered by this guide was owned and controlled by families who can rightly be regarded as Highland clans, since their chiefs not only owned land but could call on the armed support of their people. The largest were the Mackenzies under the Earl of Seaforth, with almost the whole of Wester Ross and considerable land in the east. They were followed by the Rosses and Munros, both based in the eastern highlands of Ross. Glenelg was held by Macraes and Coigach by Macleods. In Easter Ross and the Black Isle there were lowland families, such as the Urquharts of Cromarty and the many lowland branches of the greater Mackenzie, Ross and Munro clans.

The medieval history of the area covered by this guide centres on struggles for power – the struggle of the Scottish crown to assert its authority in the north, the rise and fall of the Earls of Ross and the Lords of the Isles, and feuds between rival clans and families. By the seventeenth century, this was changing. National power struggles continued and local landowners, and consequently their tenants and followers, were involved in the wars of the seventeenth century and in the abortive Jacobite risings of 1715, 1719 and 1745. Victories and defeats advanced some families and ruined others – the Munros were rewarded for their covenanting zeal, while the royalist Sir Thomas Urquhart of Cromarty died in exile in the Netherlands. An account of the wars of the seventeenth century and of the various Jacobite risings, with a gazetteer of sites, is provided in a later section. These events, which drew the Highland clans and lowland families of Ross and Cromarty into the mainstream of Scottish and British politics, had an immediate effect on the area. But of greater importance is the fact that as society in the north became more settled towards the end of the century, and landowners became more involved in society and politics in the south, they turned their attention from defence of property to improving and increasing the income from their estates.

Service in European wars

A number of chiefs were prepared to make use of their traditional military resources by leading soldiers abroad, both for financial gain and in support of their ideals. For example, 2,000 men sailed from Cromarty in 1626 to serve as mercenaries in the protestant army of Christian IV of Denmark during the Thirty Years' War. They were men of Mackay's regiment, raised in Sutherland, but among them was the penniless Robert Munro, the Laird of Foulis, and his cousin, Robert Munro of Obsdale, who wrote a valuable account of *Monro His Expedition with the Worthie Scots Regiment (Called Mac-Keyes Regiment)*, published in 1637. Munro of Foulis sailed as a volunteer without rank, but rose to become commander of the regiment, making enough money to restore his fortunes at home. In 1631, a further regiment, under Robert Munro of Obsdale, sailed from Cromarty.

Religious disputes, civil war and military rule

Charles I came to the throne in 1625. His failure to recognise the aspirations of the Church of Scotland led, in 1638, to the drawing up of the National Covenant, a presbyterian manifesto whose signatories and supporters became known as covenanters. The royalist Thomas Urquhart of Cromarty took part in the first engagement between royalists and covenanters, the 'Trot of Turiff', in 1639. This minor battle was followed by years of intermittent war, with the covenanting cause strengthened by veterans returning from the Thirty Years' War in Europe, all culminating in the execution of Charles I in 1649. Royalist forces were finally defeated in 1651 and this was followed by the Cromwellian Union, during which Scotland was for most of the time under military rule enforced by an English army of occupation.

Throughout these affairs the Mackenzies, under the 2nd Earl of Seaforth, vacillated, constantly choosing the losing side, and were followed in these moves by the weaker Macleods and Macraes. However, the clan was not active after 1648 and held back from the abortive invasion of England in 1651. The

Munros were staunch covenanters, while the Rosses, like the Mackenzies, changed sides a number of times, finally marching with the royalist army defeated at Worcester in 1651.

One of the final royalist campaigns of the war was led by James Graham, Marquis of Montrose, who returned to the north in 1650 after a period in exile and led an army south from Orkney and Caithness. He was defeated at the battle of Carbisdale (now in Sutherland) in 1751, captured shortly afterwards, taken south (through Tain and Brahan, travelling on a pony with his feet tied underneath) and executed in Edinburgh. Montrose had expected the support of 400 Ross-shire men raised by Munro of Lemlair and Ross of Balnagowan, but these were withheld at the last moment.

There was considerable disruption in the Black Isle and central Ross during both the civil war and the Cromwellian occupation. The war was marked by pillaging by different armies and billeting of troops on impoverished tenants. During the Cromwellian union, stone from the ruined cathedral of Fortrose was taken to build a new citadel ('Oliver's Fort') in Inverness, English soldiers were garrisoned at Brahan, Chanonry and Cromarty castles, and prisoners were deported in large numbers as indentured labourers to Virginia and the West Indies. The west did not escape, for covenanting forces were stationed at Eilean Donan, and an abortive royalist rising in 1654 was followed by a systematic pillaging and burning of estates, including those in Wester Ross, by the Cromwellian army.

Restoration and Revolution
Charles II returned as king in 1660, and in the period which followed, Scotland was in effect ruled as a colony of England. The Highlands had troops quartered on the people to enforce law and order, and government involvement in Highland affairs led to troops taking part, on the losing side, in the last Scottish clan battle on the Braes of Lochaber in Inverness-shire in 1688. The commander of the government troops, Captain Kenneth Mackenzie of Suddie on the Black Isle, was killed in the fighting. Highland chiefs, seeing that their future lay in cultivating the goodwill of central government, raised rents and increased cattle droving in order to repay debts and finance their engagement with southern society.

Growing dissatisfaction with the Stewart dynasty led to the 'Glorious Revolution' of 1688, in which the protestant Queen Mary and her husband, William of Orange, were declared joint monarchs. The Mackenzies and Munros remained neutral, with the Rosses supporting William and Mary. At the end of the seventeenth century, the Mackenzies were firmly established as the most powerful family in the area, and indeed one of the most powerful in Scotland, but they were no longer a single political unit. The wily George Mackenzie of Tarbat flourished as a lawyer and statesman, deftly surviving changes in the monarchy, and was given the title Earl of Cromartie. He took his title from the town and sheriffdom of Cromarty (the difference in spelling between the two is a later convention), which he had recently acquired. Using his political influence, he had an Act of Parliament passed annexing all of his other possessions to the sheriffdom of Cromarty, thus giving him greater authority in his own lands and removing them from the sheriffdom of Ross. This enlarged jigsaw of a sheriffdom consisted of the old shire and fourteen parcels of land scattered from the east to the west coasts. It was finally merged with the shire of Ross in the 1880s to form Ross and Cromarty. The name remains as a potent source of confusion, aggravated by the fact that Mackenzie quickly disposed of the town of Cromarty itself, which then formed no part of the Cromartie estates.

Jacobite Risings
William Mackenzie, the catholic 5th Earl of Seaforth, led his followers out for the Stewarts in the Jacobite rising of 1715. After their defeat, his estate was forfeit to the crown until it was restored in 1722. Seaforth was also involved in an abortive rising in 1719, supported by 300 Spanish troops provided as a diversion from a planned large-scale Spanish invasion of England. They landed in Mackenzie territory at Glenshiel, along with some Scots who had gone into exile after 1715. Both Eilean Donan Castle and the parish church of Kintail were shelled and destroyed by government frigates, and the Spanish contingent was defeated with their Scots allies at the Battle of Glenshiel (Gazetteer 14:1).

Part of the government response to the rising of 1715 was to replace independent Highland companies of part-time soldiers with regular troops, and to augment the existing forts at Inverness and Inverlochy (later renamed Fort William) with four more forts commanding the key routes in the Highlands, all linked with a new network of military roads. As part of this policy Bernera Barracks was built in Glenelg, controlling the route to and from Skye (Gazetteer 14:2). The ruined barracks still stand as an impressive reminder of the 'pacification' of the north.

The 3rd Earl of Cromartie, George Mackenzie, supported the Jacobite Rising of 1745, while the other principal families of the area were by now either staunch supporters of the government or remained diplomatically uncommitted. During the course of the Rising and afterwards, the Cromarty Firth was patrolled by naval vessels, a foretaste of its later role as a naval base, but the only significant military action was a retreat north by Hanoverian forces under Lord Loudoun. They crossed the Cromarty–Nigg ferry, destroyed boats to prevent pursuit, and continued into Sutherland. After Culloden, the Earl of Cromartie's estates were forfeited and he was condemned to death, but the sentence was later rescinded.

More important, however, than the fate of individual aristocrats was the effect of defeat on the area. Perceptions of the '45 have been so coloured by later romanticism that it can be difficult to realise that this was not a Scottish uprising but a bitter civil war with a bitter aftermath. In the east of Ross and Cromarty, where traditional clan-based society had largely broken down, there was little popular support for the Jacobite cause. The Cromarty writer, Hugh Miller, was able to speak in the 1810s with people who remembered Culloden, having watched the smoke of the battle from the top of Cromarty Hill, and his accounts of local feelings are a useful antidote to the shortbread-tin image of Bonnie Prince Charlie. In the west, whatever the level of popular support for the Jacobites – and it is difficult to judge – the consequences of being perceived as potential rebels were serious.

After the '45

In the aftermath of the rout of the Jacobite army and the flight of Prince Charles Edward Stewart, there was a concerted government-led assault on traditional society in the Highlands by military, legislative and economic means. The army and navy began a systematic pillage of the west coast, even of the lands of clans who had supported the Government cause. In 1746, Hanoverian ships anchored in Lochbroom, ransacked Langwell House, fired the Forest of Coigach, seized cattle, sheep and other goods and generally laid waste to the area. A great military citadel was built on the east coast at Fort George and the network of military roads was extended. Hereditary jurisdictions which had allowed landowners to act as judges within their own territories were abolished and replaced by a system of government appointed sheriffs. The lands of the principal rebels, including the vast Cromartie estates, were forfeited to the crown and managed by government appointed agents until 1784; and a series of quasi-governmental bodies set about 'civilising' the Highlands and integrating them with the economy of the rest of the kingdom. Many of the government's economic measures were failures, described by Lord Kames as 'no better than water spilt on the ground', and where they were effective they benefited the east coast rather than the west. Cromarty, for example, flourished as the centre for government-subsidised flax spinning in the north of Scotland between 1749 and the 1770s.

A Jacobite 'Psalm'

By the sad Seine we sat and wept
When Scotland we thought on;
Reft of her brave and true, and all
Her ancient spins gone.

Remember England's children, Lord,
Who on Drumossie day,
Deaf to the voice of kindred love,
'Raze, raze it quite,' did say

And thou, proud Gallia! faithless friend,
Whose ruin is not far,
Just Heaven on thy devoted head
Pour all the woes of war!

When thou thy slaughter'd little ones
And ravish'd dames shalt see,
Such help, such pity mayst thou have
As Scotland had from thee.

This poem, based on the 137th psalm, was found in the early nineteenth century by the Cromarty writer, Hugh Miller. He believed it had been written in Paris shortly after Culloden. The verses describe the defeat of the Jacobites in national terms, a tragedy for Scotland – and blaming England for brutality and France (Gallia) for lack of support.

Although the '45 and its aftermath can be seen as a watershed in Highland history, changes continued which had been under-way from an earlier date. Struggles for power in the medieval period, and indeed before, had created a common interest between landowners and those within their control. Clan chiefs and heads of families needed the wholehearted support of their people; and the people needed the protection of their chief. As society became more settled and the Scottish aristocracy were absorbed into a more southern-based culture, this common interest declined. In consequence, the marks left on the landscape by history after the mid-seventeenth century are predominantly the results of ostentation by the landowning class in the building of new mansions and of sustained attempts to extract more wealth from their estates. They attempted to develop agriculture, fishing, forestry and manufacturing. They also expanded commerce in burghs of barony, thus allowing trade to take place outwith the old royal burghs.

Gazetteer 15, with the earlier gazetteer of castles, includes the residences of all the principal landowners. These build-ings, by their size and appearance, chart the fortunes of the landed families. There is, however, another aspect to the prosperity of a number of families, whose rise was the result of growing British military power and the expansion in trade which followed. It is important to see the wealth of such landowners in the context of wider, global history. The conspicuous improvements which shaped the land-scape around Tulloch Castle above Dingwall and around Novar, to take two examples, were financed respectively by the West Indian sugar trade with its labour force of slaves, and by the conquest and exploitation of the Indian sub-continent.

II. People and the economy

Agriculture

In the west, the principal wealth was in small black cattle, which were driven in herds across a network of drove roads to markets in the south (*see* Gazetteer 16:16–17). In the summer, cattle were grazed in upland shielings. Trade in black cattle grew especially after 1707, and this remained Scotland's chief export until the middle of the eighteenth century. Although trade then declined it was still of importance, and a more co-ordinated system of fairs and trysts was introduced from 1811. The largest cattle tryst in the north was originally held at Beauly (Inverness-shire), but was moved slightly to the north after 1811 to a site on the present Muir of Ord golf course. From there cattle were driven south to the great cattle trysts at Crieff and Falkirk, where they were sold on to merchants who took them south to England.

Alasdair Scolair

Cattle stealing was endemic in the middle ages and before. A late cattle reiver, and poet, was Alasdair Scolair who had a remote base at *Coire mhàileagan* (Gazetteer 16:17). He is said, after raiding a shieling, to have tied one of the women to a tree, in some accounts by her hair, when she refused to tell him where the cheeses were stored. He intended to return later in the day to release her. For some reason, he was unable to do so, and when he eventually came back weeks afterwards, there were only bones. This was, he claimed, the only one of his crimes he regretted.

After being captured and condemned to death, he asked to be allowed to walk free for 'three lengths of his gun'. His request was granted and he used this opportunity to leap over the heads of his guards and escape. He was, however, recaptured and was reputedly hung in Tain in October 1742.

In the east the fertile coastal strip yielded good crops of grain, chiefly oats and bere (a form of barley). During the seventeenth century, the advantages of shipping this to Aberdeen and Edinburgh increased with relatively higher prices in the south and greater availability of vessels, and by the end of the century, despite famine years in the 1690s, there was a well-established trade. Tenants paid their rent in kind, mostly in bere-barley, for which landowners built large grain stores or girnals, usually close to the shore. Many of these late seventeenth- and eighteenth-century girnals remain some of the most substantial buildings of their day and are still impressive (Gazetteer 16:1–9).

In both east and west, larger farms had their own barns, early examples of which survive at Flowerdale (Gazetteer 15:3) and Balnagowan (Gazetteer 9:11). In Loch Alsh, Kintail, Glenelg and Applecross, where rainfall is especially high, there were ventilated cruck-frame barns, known as creel barns, primarily for drying and storing hay and aligned to take advantage of prevailing wind (Gazetteer 16:10–14). These continued to be built until the end of the nineteenth century.

Although a number of landowners were enthusiastic agricultural improvers in the early eighteenth century, it was not until the last decades of the century that larger new farms with regular enclosed fields began to appear in any numbers. Good examples of farm buildings from this period can be seen at Tulloch, Brahan and Mains of Coul (see Gazetteer 16:31–33, with later farm buildings 34–35). High grain prices during the Napoleonic Wars (1792–1815) encouraged an influx of farmers from the south of Scotland, but a fall in prices after 1815 held back further change, and it was not until the middle of the nineteenth century that the present landscape of large farms and well-drained fields was created. Old farm settlements, with their turf-built houses and barns, usually disappeared with improvement and their remains were ploughed into the new fields. An unusual survival is the remains of a pre-improvement fermtoun at Lower Eathie, near Cromarty (Gazetteer 16:15).

A central factor in all these changes was the removal of small tenants and cottars. The many small tenants on some farms were described, disapprovingly, by one commentator in 1808 as 'a small republic', reaching communal decisions on details of farm management. On new large farms they were replaced, particularly after the 1820s, by seasonally-employed farm labourers accommodated, often in brutalising conditions, in farm bothies. Removals – clearances – were also, of course, a feature of the Highland areas (*see* Gazetteer 16:21–30).

1792 saw the first attempt to introduce sheep farming on any scale, when the Munros of Novar turned over land to sheep at Kildermorie in Strathrusdale, displacing cattle rearing tenants. This led to a riot among the displaced people, who marched south, driving the sheep before them, but who dispersed when faced by government troops. With such earlier clearances, either of Highland tenants or lowland cottars, it was common for landowners to regard the people as an economic resource, which they wished to keep on the land, though in some other location – often on pitifully small coastal patches of land where they might augment farming by fishing and be available as a source of labour. In this period emigration was discouraged, and only the slightly better off could afford to leave. The emigration of this 'middle class', who were educated and had some capital, was a profound loss to the area.

By the 1830s, labour-intensive schemes which might have brought income to Highland landowners, such as kelp manufacture, had failed, and fishing was also in decline. From this point clearances were aimed more at the removal of population; emigration was encouraged and, in some cases, assisted passages provided. Even when communities were not cleared, the loss of hill pasture, taken to create sporting estates or to expand sheep farms, pushed crofters into abject poverty. With smaller and smaller units to cultivate, the people became increasingly dependent on the potato crop, and when this failed in a series of years of blight from 1846, many were forced to leave.

The history of emigration from the area is complex. After 1808, government regulations encouraged emigration to the colonies, particularly Canada. At the same time the Napoleonic wars had brought the need to import timber from Canada, since the traditional source in the Baltic was closed. Ships sailing to Canada for timber found it economic to take an outward 'cargo' of emigrants. For ships from east-coast ports such as Aberdeen and Leith, Cromarty was the most effective point at which to make a brief stop to pick up passengers from the northern Highlands. As a result, Cromarty became a major gathering place for emigrants and remained so until larger steam ships took over the trade in the 1860s. In the late 1830s a few ships also sailed directly from Cromarty for Australia.

The most draconian of the clearances were at this time, at Glencalvie in 1845 and Greenyards in 1853 (see the guide to Sutherland in this series). However, when there were attempts to clear Coigach in 1853, resistance from the people, especially the women, led to the withdrawal of eviction notices. Public opinion expressed in the national press was beginning to have a restraining influence, and after 1855, there were no large-scale removals. Nevertheless the process of piecemeal clearance continued with the creation of sporting estates – large tracts of land given over to grouse and deer – in the latter part of the century.

The traditional Highland *baile* or township, like the lowland fermtoun, consisted of a number of tenant farmers, sub-tenants and cottars, cultivating arable ground and sharing hill pasture. This was universal throughout the Highlands in the mid-eighteenth century, but by the 1840s it had been all but eliminated and the system of holding land in small crofts had been created. In some cases the *baile* was simply cleared and let to sheep farmers. In other cases the *baile*, or a part of it, was divided into lots to create crofts; or new crofts were created on marginal ground on the coast where the tenants were expected to survive by crofting and fishing. Sub-divisions of crofts and loss of hill pasture created mounting pressure on these new communities. Gazetteer 16:21–30 is not comprehensive but provides examples of these different situations and identifies some of the main clearances.

In these changes what was wrong, above all, was the reduction of people to mere objects – pieces in an economic game-plan, moved from place to place irrespective of their needs and their roots. There were, however, exceptions to the generally callous actions of landowners and their factors. Hugh Rose, who was factor on the Cromarty estate until 1786, and was responsible for many early improvements there, became factor to the Earl of Sutherland, and argued forcefully against large-scale sheep farming. At the same time George Dempster of Skibo was articulating his 'Constitution of Creich', which would have guaranteed security of tenure and encourage new smallholdings. Rose's views did not survive his death in 1790, and Dempster's successor appears to have carried out a large number of evictions. In the west, the Mackenzies of Gairloch planned and created a system of crofts in the 1840s with the positive aim of improving agriculture and housing, basing their plans on models from England and Europe.

The expansion of land under cultivation led to pressure to enclose the commonties – that is, the lands which had been held in common by neighbouring estates and used in common by their tenants for grazing and fuel. Legislation to permit the division of commonties had existed from an earlier date, but it was principally in the late eighteenth and early nineteenth centuries that it was utilised. The commonties of Nigg Hill and Bogallan were divided in the eighteenth century, and the Mulbuie commonty, which stretched the length of the Black Isle, was divided in 1829 (Gazetteer 16:42–45). Divided land was enclosed with turf dykes and, in some cases, smallholders were settled on the land. Good examples of such turf dyke systems can be seen at various points on the Mulbuie.

Since stone dykes are so much a part of the Highland landscape, some comment may be useful. The earliest dykes were built from turf, sometimes as temporary enclosures and sometimes as more permanent boundaries. Stone dykes appear as early as the mid-eighteenth century and can still be seen in some places, such as Drynie and Resolis. These are broad based, with sloping sides, and were designed to keep livestock out of plantations. The greatest period of dyke building was, however, from the 1860s to the 1880s, and is associated with the creation of large farms, including sheep farms, and deer forests. Dykes from this period are skilfully built, tall and narrow. In the 1870s wire fencing was introduced and the properties of Portland cement were discovered, both greatly reducing the use of dry-stone building techniques. Areas which specialised in grain production and had few cattle or sheep, required few dykes.

Forestry (*see* Gazetteer 17)
The forests of oak and pine which had covered the north of Scotland from *c.*5000 BC were depleted by the climatic changes

which culminated in the Bronze Age crisis of *c.*1200 BC. The gradual reduction in temperature lowered the tree line from 600m to about 350m, but much of the remaining depletion was the result of human action. However, trees remained an important resource, and it seems likely that Norse moves to control both the Dornoch and Cromarty Firths between the ninth and eleventh centuries were partly motivated by the need to ensure supplies of timber from Strath Oykell and the group of river valleys converging on Dingwall. Oak woods were also an important source of charcoal and, as detailed below, this was exploited for iron working from the Middle Ages, though with increased production in the seventeenth century.

Even by the 1640s good timber was scarce. The Urquharts of Cromarty, for example, had to import Baltic pine to extend their castle. By the end of the century, landowners were using their authority to protect the few remaining woods, and some were beginning to plant new trees. By the 1720s there were a few identifiable plantations and some remaining natural woodland, together with ornamental plantings around castles and mansions. The most notable of the ornamental woods was at Castle Leod, where sweet chestnuts planted in the sixteenth century still flourish. Planting became more common from the mid-eighteenth century onwards, often combining the practical cultivation of trees with ornamental landscaping – both Cromarty Hill and ground above Invergordon Castle were planted in the 1750s so as to create viewpoints, with avenues between the trees radiating from the summit of the hills. Planting on the west was less extensive and by 1800 pine was three times more expensive there than in the east.

Fishing
Salmon (*see* Gazetteer 18)
Salmon fishing in the Cromarty, Dornoch and Beauly Firths is well documented from the sixteenth century. In the 1640s Gordon of Straloch noted that 'on both shores [of the Cromarty Firth] at the low edges there are numerous wooden enclosures of great use, for when the tide ebbs and the sands are dry, fish are caught with the hand'. These traps, with coble (small boat) fishing and some box traps (cruives) on rivers, are likely to have been the source of the salmon caught, salted and exported

Figure 6. *Salmon fishing at a yair in the eighteenth century*

as far as the Mediterranean. These early traps were known as yairs: 'long ranges of stakes, with wattling, somewhat resembling a hedge, carried from the land into the sea to low water mark, in the form of a crescent – with a croe, or cruive, in the centre and a curve or horn at the extremity'. Yairs were particularly destructive of herring and salmon fry, and in the early nineteenth century, fry were sold by the bushel from a yair at Tarradale. Nine cartloads were removed from one yair in the Cromarty Firth in one tide, and at Kincardine, on the Dornoch Firth, fry were commonly fed to pigs.

The early trade in salmon was in salted fish. A key advance was made by George Dempster of Skibo, who 'discovered the exporting of fish in ice to London' in 1786. Dempster, an MP, met with an Alexander Dalrymple of the East India Company in London and learned that Chinese 'coolies' used crushed ice to preserve perishable goods in transit. In 1787 Dempster persuaded the Tay fish merchant Richardson to experiment with this method. Until this point, the export of fresh salmon to London, wrapped in straw, had stopped with warmer weather in April or May. The use of ice extended the season considerably and increased demand, once fresh salmon could be provided. It also led to improved design and increased use of stake nets.

A stake net consisted of a row of poles driven into the sea bed, carrying a leader net which directed fish into a pound at the seaward end. They might be up to one mile in length. These appeared first on the Tay shortly after 1800, around Montrose in 1807, and were also in use on the Solway from an early date. Stake nets required more active management than yairs: it was, in a sense, the tide which did the fishing in a yair, leaving fish trapped on the sand at low water. The cost of the additional labour required by stake nets could only be borne with higher prices.

The expansion of stake netting had an immediate impact on river fisheries. The concern was not now the destruction of salmon fry but the number of fish, especially breeding fish, caught. The Conon, which recorded a catch of 7,656 fish before stake netting, had only 633 afterwards, while the stake nets in the lower waters of the Cromarty Firth trapped 6,500. Protests and legal action by proprietors of river fishings led to

the Tay stake nets being declared illegal in 1819, a judgement
based on an early Scots statute which banned 'fixed engines'
in rivers. The difficulty in interpretation lay in determining
what constituted a river and what a part of the sea.

Further actions were brought and decided case by case.
These 'fixed engines' became illegal in the Cromarty Firth in
the 1840s, following a Court of Session decision, and by the
1860s salmon netting was more closely regulated by statute.
From this date, bag netting outside the firths, at a series of
netting stations along the coast, became more important.

Herring and white fish

Sixteenth-century herring fishing in the North Sea was dominated by the Dutch, and the expansion of their fishery
in the northern isles continued until the mid-seventeenth
century, when cooling of Arctic waters led to a decline. From
the 1670s, a substantial herring and cod fishery developed
on the east coast, centred on Cromarty, possibly as the result
of a southward movement of shoals. Some of the substantial
merchant houses in the town date from this period of prosperity. In 1698 and again in 1712, Lord Tarbat was involved
in the promotion of herring and cod fisheries on the west coast
at Lochbroom.

In the later eighteenth and early nineteenth centuries fishing
in the Moray Firth was focused on the revived Caithness
herring fishery. This development was initiated in the 1770s
by incoming merchants from the Firth of Forth. By the mid-
1790s the reputation of Caithness-cured herring was high and
there were around 200 boats fishing. Similar developments
had taken place in the west with the establishment of a fishing
station by a Liverpool merchant on Isle Martin in Lochbroom
in 1775, followed in 1784 by a similar venture on Tanera,
established by a Stornoway man.

A crucial change came in 1785 with the introduction of a
government bounty on herring caught and cured. Earlier
bounties had encouraged the building of large vessels which
could operate as herring busses, but the new system, which
operated with various changes until 1829, increased the income
of herring fishers themselves and 'pump primed' improvements
in fishing boats and gear. This led in turn to increased catches

and allowed fishers to re-invest in yet larger boats and more nets, a process which was possible because fishers now owned their boats rather than holding them from local landowners.

The appearance of success on the west led the British Fisheries Society, founded in 1786, to plan and build a new fishing settlement at Ullapool, but it ran into difficulties as early as the 1790s. There was longer-term success in the east and the Caithness fishery drew in fishers from communities along the Moray Firth, including the Black Isle and Easter Ross. When the bounty on the catch was doubled in 1809, the number of boats engaged in the Caithness fishery increased dramatically, and both boats and curers began to look for additional bases to the south, often in small and difficult harbours.

From around 1815 the expansion in herring fishing reached Easter Ross. There followed a run of successful seasons and a company formed in 1819 established stations around the Moray Firth employing almost all the boats. In Cromarty in September 1826 there were 'no fewer than 200 women engaged in cleaning and salting the fish ... while twenty-nine masted vessels lay in the firth waiting to convey the barrels, on being made up, to various ports', and the port had become the eighth largest herring curing station in Britain, curing 20,000 barrels annually.

The policy that government should be involved in the control and development of fishing was replaced during the late 1820s by an emphasis on free trade and *laissez faire* economics, resulting in the withdrawal of bounties and the abolishing of salt duty by 1829. Herring fishing survived these changes, but there was a general decline with the loss of the West Indian market after the abolition of slavery in 1833 and the decline of the Irish market with the famine of the 1840s. Recovery came with the development of the Eastern European and Baltic markets, in which quality was of greater importance. The Caithness fishery grew further, but the prosperity of the Cromarty fishery district did not survive the decline of the 1830s and 1840s, and these factors were further setbacks to the attempts to develop the west coast fishery. A small harbour was built at Hilton in 1830 but fell into disrepair, and Balintore's harbour, planned in the 1820s, was not built until 1896.

New ports with larger harbours on the Aberdeenshire coast at Fraserburgh (1820s) and Peterhead (1830s) benefited from the expanding Baltic trade and drew on an increasingly mobile labour force of gutters, packers and fishers from the north. Many fishing communities disappeared or relied on line fishing for white fish. The closure of the Moray Firth to trawling (in 1887, with extensions in 1890 and 1892) provided protection for line fishermen whose numbers then remained substantial.

The history of fishing in Avoch is significantly different. Here the firm Falls of Dunbar provided capital and engaged fishing crews until their bankruptcy in 1788, when the Northumberland Fishing Company took their place, and by the 1790s the 'bold fishermen' of Avoch were reckoned to be more adventurous than other communities. Investment in larger boats enabled them to make longer journeys in search of fish and the community survived the decline of the 1830s.

Fishing settlements (*see* Gazetteer 19)
The nature and history of fishing and fishing settlements differs on the east and west coasts of Ross and Cromarty. In the west fishing traditionally augmented small-scale farming, and fishing settlements only appeared with planned expansion of the herring fishery in the late eighteenth century, most notably in the creation of Ullapool by the British Fisheries Society. Clearances from inland areas in the nineteenth century also created communities of crofter-fishers along the coast.

In the east there were two patterns of fishing settlement. In Easter Ross each of the small estates seems to have established its own fish boat, crewed by four to six fishers. Some of these fish boats are recorded in the sixteenth century, though they may have existed before this date. A boat and its crew not only supplied fish but also gave the estate access to sea transport, which was particularly useful in the eastern firths. Moreover, the fishing community was a useful source of labour at harvest time, and some were engaged in other work, such as digging shell lime from Nigg Bay for use as a manure.

There was a different pattern on the Black Isle, where fishing focused on the two larger fisher communities of Cromarty and Avoch. The dialect of these places, now almost extinct, retains particularly old forms of Scots, and it is likely that both were medieval fisher communities – Cromarty's in the royal burgh and Avoch established under the protection of Ormond Castle.

Some of the early fisher communities held 'fisher land' in common, as, for example, at Balintore, which was the fisher-town of Fearn Abbey. During the late seventeenth and early eighteenth centuries there was a growth of some settlements and often a loosening of ties with the land. This continued in the greater herring booms of the nineteenth century, creating the distinct fishing communities which survived into modern times.

Manufacturing and industry

Metal working (*see* Gazetteer 20)

From 1610 until 1670 one of the earliest blast furnaces in Scotland was in operation at the Red Smiddy on the east bank of the River Ewe, near Poolewe, where the bellows were driven by a waterwheel. Only earthworks can be seen, but further information is provided in Gairloch Museum. There were other ironworks around Loch Maree at Furnace, Fasadh, Talladale, Slatadale and in Glen Docherty, with a burial ground (Claod nan Sasganach) near the east end of the loch where English-speaking ironworkers buried their dead. During much of the eighteenth century local production of iron goods depended on the use of imported bars of Russian and Swedish iron. These were worked in two nail and spade manufactories in Cromarty in the late eighteenth century, and the mercat cross in front of the courthouse is repaired with iron bands from one of them.

A mine had been long established at Brora in Sutherland, exploiting deposits of Jurassic coal, and there were several attempts to find coal along the east coast of Ross and Cromarty. The water of the Coalheugh Well to the east of Cromarty is said to flow from a trial shaft sunk as early as the 1690s and there are later, nineteenth-century workings on the shore at Eathie. There was also a short-lived attempt to mine lead on the Newhall estate on the Black Isle in the 1770s, and copper for a short time after 1775 at Lochcarron, where traces of the workings can still be seen.

Many communities depended on itinerant *ceardannan* (tinsmiths) who were also horse dealers and hawkers. These travellers were not gypsies, but indigenous Gaelic speakers whose traditions are a distinctive and important, though sadly neglected, part of local culture.

Quarrying (*see* Gazetteer 20)
Large quantities of stone were required to build Fort George on the Moray coast between 1747 and 1769. Most was quarried in Munlochy Bay and moved across the firth by boat. All established communities had their own quarries, but as techniques improved in the nineteenth century, and it became possible to cut larger and more regular blocks of stone, a large quarry at Tarradale flourished, producing a distinctive sandstone used in many local buildings. Smaller quarries can be found close to many of the main settlements which grew during the century.

Some seventeenth-century buildings were roofed with heavy flagstone slate imported from Caithness and Dunrobin. In the early eighteenth century there were attempts to produce local slate from quarries at Findon and Scotsburn, but the quality was poor. The Findon quarry continued to produce stone, and structures on the shore, to the east of the Cromarty Firth bridge, may be the remains of a dock. With the opening of the Caledonian Canal in 1822 it became easier to ship slate from the west coast.

Shell deposits were an important source of lime and were exploited from the 1720s, particularly in Nigg Bay on the east and at Applecross on the west.

Textiles (*see* Gazetteer 21)
Following the defeat of the Jacobite army at Culloden in 1746 there was, in addition to repression, a sustained attempt to introduce manufactures into the Highlands as a means of integrating the Highland economy with that of the rest of the country. Three organisations – the British Linen Company, the Board of Trustees for Manufactures and Fisheries, and the Commissioners of the Annexed Estates – combined to encourage the spinning of linen yarn. The raw material (flax) was imported from the Netherlands and the Baltic, mostly to

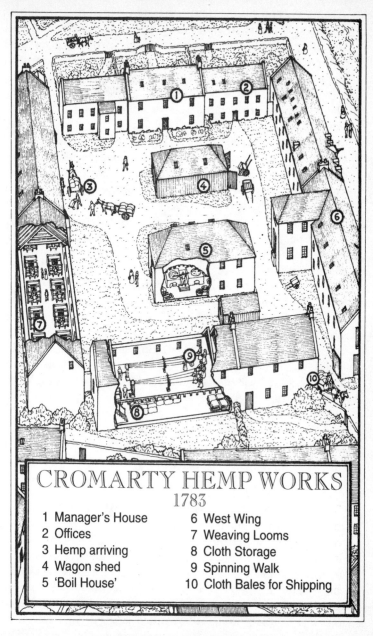

CROMARTY HEMP WORKS
1783

1 Manager's House
2 Offices
3 Hemp arriving
4 Wagon shed
5 'Boil House'
6 West Wing
7 Weaving Looms
8 Cloth Storage
9 Spinning Walk
10 Cloth Bales for Shipping

FIGURE 7. *Cromarty Hemp Works, 1783*

Cromarty, and distributed to agents there and in Dornoch, Tain and Dingwall, who organised spinning by home workers. Spinning schools were set up, including two in Wester Ross (Inverlael farm house and New Kelso, Lochcarron). Most of the spun yarn was then shipped back to Edinburgh for weaving, although some was worked locally, and small bleach fields, used to whiten the cloth, were established at Culcairn and Cromarty.

Government subsidy for this venture was withdrawn in the 1770s, but by this time, hemp working had been established in handloom factories in both Inverness and Cromarty, still using many home workers for spinning. Hemp was a coarser material used to produce sacks and bags. The Cromarty factory, which survives converted to housing, employed 200 to 250 people within the building and over 600 outworkers. Around 1800 a branch of the Cromarty factory was established in Invergordon. Hemp working continued until the 1840s, when it was superseded by jute mills in Dundee.

The introduction of sheep farming led some landowners to develop wool processing. In the 1790s a carding and spinning mill was built at Gordonsmills on the Black Isle, on the model of similar mills in the north of England, but although the building remains the venture was not successful. Other wool mills were established in the nineteenth century at High Mills, near Tain, and at Avoch.

Considerable home-based employment was provided in the late eighteenth century by thread manufacture, with 8,000 to 10,000 women in the Highlands spinning for a company based in Inverness, but this was short-lived and has left no trace.

Brewing and distilling (*see* Gazetteer 22)

In 1689 Jacobites ravaged the lands of Forbes of Culloden and burnt down his distillery at Ferintosh, on the Black Isle. In the following year Forbes was rewarded for his loyalty to the government with a grant of the right to distil whisky, duty free, on the Ferintosh estate. When demand for malt whisky grew from the middle of the eighteenth century, this became an increasingly valuable privilege, and from 1760, Ferintosh was producing more legally distilled whisky than the rest of Scotland put together. This was mostly in small stills. The population of the parish rose to around 4,000, around 1,000 of whom were engaged in distilling. When a larger distillery was built in 1782, the protests from other parts of the country led to legislation, in 1786, which ended the 'Ferintosh privilege'. The poet (and exciseman) Robert Burns lamented the loss in the verse:

> *Thee Ferintosh! O sadly lost!*
> *Scotland lament frae coast to coast!*
> *Now colic grips, and barken hoast*
> *May kill us a'*
> *For loyal Forbes' chartered boast*
> *Is taen awa'.*

Increasing demand for whisky and the outlawing of small still production led to almost forty years of illicit production, making a significant contribution to the economy of Ross and Cromarty and other northern counties. Many communities in the Highlands can identify sites associated with such stills in this (or, in some cases, more recent) times, but new legislation in the 1820s, introducing heavier fines, effectively brought to an end the period of widespread illicit distilling. Changes in excise duty in the 1820s also allowed larger distilleries to improve their product, and the principal distilleries in Ross and Cromarty were either established then or expanded from much smaller earlier enterprises. There were, it should be noted, a surprising number of licit whisky distilleries in the Black Isle and Easter Ross before the 1820s, two of which survive: one at Balblair near Edderton and the other Teaninich near Alness.

Traditionally, ale and wine had been the more popular drinks in Scotland. Growing demand in the 1760s and 1770s for imported porter (strong, dark stout) led some public-spirited landowners, such as George Ross of Cromarty, to establish their own breweries. The buildings of the Cromarty Brewery (*c.*1772) survive but it has not produced beer since the 1840s.

Other industries

Small-scale shipbuilding in the early nineteenth century is recorded at Avoch, Dingwall, Fortrose, Foulis, Invergordon,

Kessock, Munlochy, Rosemarkie, Cromarty and Jemimaville. Of these, Cromarty was the largest: at least fourteen ships were built there in the century after 1780. However, this was all on a very small scale when compared with shipbuilding on the south side of the Moray Firth, where supplies of timber were floated down the Spey to supply the industry.

In the late eighteenth century, many estates in the west, and some in the east, turned to the production of a chemical salt from the ashes of the seaweed known as kelp. The salt was sold and used in glass and soap manufacture. Kelp working was profitable but labour intensive – and it was one of the reasons why emigration was at first discouraged and land-owners preferred to relocate tenants to coastal areas rather than see them emigrate. The industry collapsed *c.* 1820, when alternative sources of the salt became available. Kelp was burnt in kilns on the shore, but no sites have been identified.

Finally, in the 1840s and 1850s, there was a brick and tile works at Phippsfield (Gazetteer 20:10), beside Glastullich, producing field drains, widely used after the Drainage Act of 1846 which provided government funds for drainage schemes.

SETTLEMENTS AND
COMMUNICATIONS

Established towns and farming communities
Until the seventeenth century the pattern of settlement remained largely unchanged. There were four burghs – Cromarty and Dingwall sited near their castles, and Fortrose and Tain around their churches (Gazetteer 23:1–4). Dingwall appears on Mathew Paris' early thirteenth-century map of Scotland, and both Dingwall and Cromarty can be found on sixteenth-century maps painted on the wall of the Doge's Palace in Venice.

On each estate there was a castle or fortified house, with a principal farm known as the Mains (from the French *demesne*). Most people lived outside the burghs in the many fermtouns, each of which was a community in its own right. In the 1650s, Sir Thomas Urquhart of Cromarty, with characteristic exuberance, described the people's attachment to their homes:

> *Each hamlet . . . having its peculiar Clan, as we call it, or name of a kindred, none whereof will from that position of land bouge with his will to any other, upon never so great advantages offered unto him, the interflitting from one parish to another, though conterminal, being of such a mutual displeasingness, that all and each of them esteem of it as of an extrusive proscription to the Barbadoes, or depulsory exile to Malagask.*

To leave one fermtoun for another was like being exiled to the West Indies or Africa – typical Urquhart hyberbole, but based on a truth which later landowners would have done well to recognise.

New settlements: burghs of barony
During the seventeenth century, the monopoly of trade held by the royal burghs was largely broken by the creation of new centres for local commerce, known as burghs of barony. By 1707 the four old trading centres of Tain, Dingwall, Cromarty and Fortrose had been augmented by a further fourteen

which held both markets and fairs, and four which held fairs
only. The creation of these new centres was an important
stage in the evolution of the modern pattern of settlement
in the area – although some were unsuccessful and simply
disappeared.

In the west there was a market at Gairloch and fairs at
Gruinard and Applecross. In the east the markets in Easter
Ross included Portmahomack, Nigg, Milton of New Tarbat
and Drummond, now part of Evanton (Gazetteer 23:5–8); on
the Black Isle, Muir of Ord, Redcastle, Balblair and Findon;
and, in the hinterland of Dingwall, Strathpeffer, Contin and
Garve.

Estate villages

Towards the end of the eighteenth century, as landowners
adopted more commercial approaches to the management of
their estates, they began to transform the traditional patterns
of rural settlement in both the highlands and the lowlands of
Ross and Cromarty. Part of this change was the creation of
villages, laid out in plots of land, usually along a single main
street (Gazetteer 23:9–23).

Villages were intended as a base for established tradesmen
– such as smiths, tailors and weavers – who, until then, had
lived on the fermtouns. But they were also regarded as a way
of establishing new forms of manufacture, which it was hoped
could be introduced to the area. Some villages succeeded, while
others simply faded away.

Two larger planned settlements were Ullapool, established
by the British Fisheries Society in 1788, and Strathpeffer, a
Victorian spa-town (Gazetteer 23:24, 25).

Building traditions

The castles and houses of the landowners have been listed
elsewhere. The dwellings of the majority of the inhabitants of
Ross and Cromarty were quite different. Until the nineteenth
century, most people lived in turf-built houses, with thatched
roofs supported on a wooden cruck-frame. The turf walls,
which were not load-bearing, were replaced every three or four
years. Thatch was generally of heather in the west and straw
in the east.

The relatively dry climate of Easter Ross makes it an area in which it is possible to build in clay. Clay was used as a mortar and many substantial, stone-built houses of the eighteenth century used no lime to bind the rubble of the walls. Clay was also used to build internal walls, daubed on to a frame of upright timbers woven with straw. More substantial walls, including external walls, were built by shuttering clay and building it up in layers. The trade of 'mud mason' survived until the nineteenth century. Clay was also used to build up straw thatch.

An unusual design of early nineteenth-century cottage can be seen in many parts of Easter Ross, including Fearn, Inver, Shandwick and Balintore. These long, low cottages are clay built and, in addition to the usual chimneys on the gables, have an off-centre chimney stack along the roof ridge. Many had central passages linking front and back entrances.

Communications

Until the latter part of the eighteenth century, overland communications in the area were very poor. Roads from east to west, other than drovers' tracks, were almost non-existent; rivers were difficult to cross; and ferries were often dangerous. Some significant progress was made in the Highlands, as a whole, with the building of military roads after the Jacobite Risings of 1715, 1719 and 1745. Most of this was in the central Highlands, but Bernera Barracks in Glenelg, completed in 1723, was linked by a road through Glenshiel to Fort Augustus on Loch Ness. The commissioners who administered the estates confiscated from the principal Jacobite landowners after 1746 carried out a number of improvements. The prominent engineer James Smeaton, who coined the term 'civil engineer', visited the area in the 1770s and produced plans for a number of public works. Only two were built and both survive (Gazetteer 24:4, 22): the bridge over the Aultgraad at Evanton (1777) and Cromarty Harbour (1782–86). Works planned but not executed were a pier at Portleich (Barbaraville) and a bridge over the Conon at Brahan.

Some simple eighteenth-century bridges, built for local landowners, can be seen at Inverlael and Dundonnel (Gazetteer

24:11, 12). At Aultbea (Gazetteer 24:13) on the east shore of Loch Ewe is a seven-span clapper bridge, that is a bridge constructed with rubble stone piers spanned by single flat slabs. This may date from the eighteenth century.

In 1792–97, a road from Contin to Ullapool was built for the British Fisheries Society, but abandoned within twelve years, and there was no satisfactory road west of Garve until 1847. The highest point of the road is An Diridh Mòr (The Great Ascent), still a lonely stretch of road. Hospitality in such places was valued, as recorded in a song of the travelling people:

> One murky night, with wind and rain
> My steps were getting weary
> A shepherd's house stood on the plain
> On the lonely strath of Dirrie.
>
> When I came knocking at his door
> His light was shining clearly
> He bade me sleep upon the floor
> Deep in the hay of Dirrie.
>
> I left my blessings on his ewes
> And on his croft sae eerie –
> 'My sorrows never on your brow
> Nor them that dwell in Dirrie.'

Roads and bridges were the responsibility of local landowners, acting in their capacity as Commissioners of Supply. Acts of Parliament enabled the commissioners to require all tenants to give six days labour on the roads, in October, after the harvest was gathered in. Statute labour in Ross-shire was converted to a cash payment in 1807. Wheeled carriages had only begun to appear in the area about 1770, but as early as 1778, a young girl was killed by the coach of Munro of Poyntzfield on the Cromarty links – one of the few places where a coach could be driven at speed.

In 1803 the government established a Highland Roads and Bridges Commission, to which landowners might apply for half the cost of new roads and bridges. This led to the building of an important bridge over the Conon in 1809 (Gazetteer 24:5) and to an expansion of the road network, allowing a mail coach to run from Inverness to Thurso from 1819. In 1807, additional funds for road building were raised by making some roads on the east coast into turnpikes, with toll houses every six miles (Gazetteer 24:1–3). Government funds were also provided for a number of harbours and ferry piers (Gazetteer 24:14–16). Safety on ferries had been a concern for some time, particularly after 1809, when the overloaded Meikle Ferry boat was swamped and sank with the loss of ninety-nine lives. One of the principal engineers in these state-funded schemes was Thomas Telford (1757–1834), who planned and built roads, bridges, harbours and piers.

Social organisation

The mid-nineteenth century was a period in which new social structures emerged and in which government accepted new responsibilities for society. The extension of voting rights in 1832 was preceded by a growth in friendly societies and political clubs. In the north, the most potent expression of popular feeling came a decade later in the creation of the Free Church. The first Free Church buildings, detailed in Gazetteer 13, are not only of religious significance, but also reflect the power of communal action. There were also many other organisations for working men which provided mutual benefits and which also gave an opportunity for ceremony and symbolism denied within the presbyterian church. Of these, the Freemasons are the best known, but there were also the Free Gardeners and the Society of Wrights and Hammermen. All built lodges, both as meeting places and as a way of investing their funds, but only the Freemasons have continued, and most of their active lodges are in later buildings. In Cromarty, however, there is both an early nineteenth-century Freemason's lodge (Bank Street, next to the post office) with an arched entrance and external stairs at the rear to an upper hall, and the Gardeners lodge of 1829, now the Cromarty Arms (Church Street), with large first floor windows which lit the meeting room.

National and local government expenditure on social problems is shown in the construction of prisons (as at Cromarty and Dingwall) and, from the 1860s, the building of 'combination' poorhouses to serve a number of parishes. All were much larger than was needed. The Easter Ross poorhouse at Arthurville, outside Tain (NH 773811: OS26) was designed to accommodate 200 people, and the Black Isle poorhouse on Ness Road, Fortrose (now Ness House) was of a similar size.

LITERATURE, MUSIC AND
OTHER ART

Poetry, literature, music, sculpture and other art produced in, or associated with, the area are an important part of our heritage. These should primarily be appreciated for their value as works of art, though sometimes these sources also add to our knowledge of historical events.

Literature

History in poetry
Bards played an important part in early society, and their poetry can provide us with a contemporary, though partial, view of events. Thus Arnor the Earl's Poet composed verses for his patron Thorfinn the Mighty after the victory over the Scots at Tarbat Ness in 1029:

> *Well the red weapons*
> *fed wolves at Tarbat,*
> *young the commander who*
> *made that Monday-combat.*
>
> *Slim blades sang there*
> *south on Oykell's bank;*
> *fresh from the fray he*
> *outfaced the Scots king.*

From a greater distance in time, the major Scots writers of the fourteenth and fifteenth centuries recounted events in the north as part of their wider histories, written with the intention of consolidating the sense of identity of the Scottish nation after the Wars of Independence. John Barbour (*c.*1320–95) and Andrew of Wyntoun (*c.*1355–1422) did so in verse, and John of Fordun (d. *c.*1384) and Walter Bower (d. 1449) in prose. Wyntoun recorded, among other things, the history of Macbeth – the Scots king 'outfaced' by Thorfinn. His *Chronicle* also includes the earliest version of the story of Macbeth and the witches, later made famous by Shakespeare.

Such accounts are more reliable when they deal with what were then events of the recent past, especially the Scottish Wars of Independence. We can read, for example, of the flight of the wife and daughter of Robert Bruce to sanctuary in Tain, where they were betrayed by the Earl of Ross:

> *The quene, and als dam Marjory*
> *Hir dochter than syn worthely*
> *Was coupillit into Goddis band*
> *With Walter Steward of Scotland,*
> *That wald on na wis langar ly*
> *In castell of Kildrumy*
> *To bid ane sege, ar riden rath*
> *With knichtis and squyaris bath*
> *Throu Ros richt to the girth of Tane:*
>
> *Bot that travale tha mad in vane,*
> *For tha of Ros that wald nocht ber*
> *For tham na blam na yhet danger*
> *Out of the girth them all has tane,*
> *And syn has sent tham everilkane*
> *Richt intil Ingland to the king,*
> *That gert draw all the men and hing,*
> *And put the ladyis in presoun,*
> *Sum into castell, sum in dongeoun.*

The fifteenth-century poetry of William Dunbar, with its insights into religious and court life during the Scottish renaissance, has already been mentioned in the context of James IV's pilgrimages to Tain.

Innovators of the seventeenth century

The area produced two notable writers in the seventeenth century. In 1660, George Mackenzie of Rosehaugh on the Black Isle published the first Scottish novel, a work named *Aretina*. It was prefaced by a dedicatory poem 'To all the Ladies of this Nation'. With only three copies surviving, it is one of the rarest of Scottish books. The tale is of two pairs of lovers and of the various misfortunes which delay their unions – indefinitely as it turns out, for the promised sequel never appeared.

1660 is also the year in which Sir Thomas Urquhart of Cromarty, an ardent royalist, is reputed to have died in exile in the Netherlands, expiring during a fit of laughter brought on by hearing news of the restoration of Charles II to the throne. Sir Thomas was an extravagant and eccentric man who, although plagued by financial problems, devised schemes to transform the economy of his estate and establish what would in effect have been a university of Cromarty. None of these were realised. He published a bizarre treatise on trigonometry, a collection of dull epigrams, musings on a universal language and a volume tracing his ancestry, generation by generation, back to Adam and Eve. Some of these are best forgotten, but he is rightly celebrated as the author of one of the greatest translations of any work of literature – his edition of the first three books of the French writer Rabelais' *Gargantua and Pantagruel*.

Rabelais' work is an earthy, rumbustious, larger-than-life story of two giants, which celebrates pleasure and satirises vanity and pedantry. Urquhart's translation is longer, bawdier and more exuberant than the original, more Rabelaisian than Rabelais himself. The twentieth-century critic Bernard Levin has said that translations, like women, are either *belle* or *fidèle* – either beautiful or faithful – but rarely both. Levin considered Urquhart's translation to be supremely *belle*, and his comments, if politically incorrect, would surely have pleased Sir Thomas, who delighted in the spirit of Rabelais rather than in accuracy. The intention of the work is conveyed is Urquhart's preface in verse:

> *Good friends, my Readers, who peruse this Book,*
> *Be not offended, whil'st on it you look:*
> *Denude yourselves of all deprav'd affection,*
> *For it containes no badnesse nor infection:*
> *'Tis true that it brings forth to you no birth*
> *Of any value, but in point of mirth;*
> *Thinking therefore how sorrow might your minde*
> *Consume, I could no apter subject finde;*
> > *One inch of joy surmounts of grief a span;*
> > *Because to laugh is proper to the man.*

Many examples could be given of Urquhart's delight in piling word on word and phrase on phrase. However, since much of this guide has been concerned with changes in land use it is fitting to use his description, from another work, of his hopes to improve agriculture on his own estate by:

> ... *teaching the most profitable way, both for the manner and the season, of tilling, digging, ditching, hedging, dunging, sowing, harrowing, grubbing, reaping, threshing, killing, milling, baking, brewing, batling of pasture ground, mowing, feeding of herds, flocks, horse and cattel; making good use of the execresence of all of these: improving their herbages, dayries, mellificiaries, fruitages; setting up of the most expedient agricolary instruments of wains, carts, slades, with their several devices of wheels and axle-trees, plows and harrows of divers sorts, feezes, winder, pullies, and all other manner of engines fit for easing the toyl and furthering the work; whereby one weak man, with skill, may effectuate more than fourty strong ones without it.*

Urquhart's equally great enthusiasm for coining new words can at times make his prose almost impenetrable, but some are memorable. Readers might care to note, for future use, his description of Scottish bankers as 'quodomodocunquizing clusterfists'.

Gaelic poetry

There have been a number of Gaelic poets from Ross and Cromarty. The work of some, such as Fear na Pairce (Mac-Culloch of Park, near Strathpeffer) and the Mackenzies of Achilty, is primarily of historical interest.

Uilleam (William) Ross (1762–91) is, however, recognised as a poet of high quality, sometimes said to have written the most beautiful of Gaelic love poetry. Sorley Maclean writes of 'the musical chiselling of words which is a marvel in his poetry'. Although born in Skye, he lived most of his life at Gairloch, and the foundations of his house can still be made out at Leas-a-Rosaich, Aird. He is buried at Badachro Cemetery. Ross is perhaps best remembered for the bare and desolate love song *Oran Eile* (Another Song), written after Marion Ross, a young woman whom he loved, married another man in the island of Lewis. An extract from the poem is given below, with a translation by Iain Crichton Smith.

Tha mise fo mhulad 'san àm,
Cha n-òlar leam dram le sunnd,
Tha durrag air ghur ann mo chàil
A dh'fhiosraich do chàchno rùn;
Chan fhaic mi dol seachad air sràid
An cailin bu tlàithe sùil,
'S e sin a leag m'aigne gu làr,
Mar dhuilleach o bhàrr nan craobh.

I am lonely here and depressed.
No more can I drink and be gay.
The worm that feeds on my breast
is giving my secret away.
Nor do I see, walking past,
the girl of the tenderest gaze.
It is this which has brought me to waste
like the leaf in the autumn days.

'S fad a tha m'aigne fo ghruaim,
Cha mhosgail mo chluain ri ceòl,
'M breislich mar ànrach a'chuain
Air bhàrraibh nan stuagh ri cèo.
'S e iunndaran t'àbhachd bhuam
A chaochail air snuadh mo neòil,
Gun sùgradh, gun mhire, gun uaill,
Gun chaithream, gun bhuaidh, gun treòir.

My spirit is dulled by your loss,
the song of my mouth is dumb.
I moan with the sea's distress
when the mist lies over the foam.
It's the lack of talk and your grace
which has clouded the sun from my eyes
and has sunk it deep in the place
from which light will never arise.

Cha dùisgear leam ealaidh air àill',
Cha chuirear leam dàn air dòigh,
Cha togar leam fonn uir clàr,
Cha chluinnear leam gàir nan òg:
Cha dìrich me bealach nan àrd
Le suigeart mar bha mi'n tòs,
Ach triallam a chadal gu bràth
Do thalla nam bàrd nach beò.

I shall never praise beauty again.
I shall never design a song.
I shall never take pleasure in tune,
nor hear the clear laugh of the young.
I shall never climb hill with the vain
youthful arrogant joy that I had.
But I'll sleep in a hall of stone
with the great bards who are dead.

Essential Reading: Hugh Miller (1802–56)

At the end of the nineteenth century many households throughout Scotland would have had an edition of one or other of Hugh Miller's many books. He was a largely self-taught stone mason from Cromarty whose wide ranging interests led him to the study of geology (particularly the exploration of local fossil beds), the collection of folklore and involvement in church affairs. In 1839 he became editor of the Witness, *a church newspaper published in Edinburgh, and over the next seventeen years he used its columns to write on a vast number of topics – often penning 10,000 words a week himself. He was a trenchant commentator on many social issues, including the Highland Clearances, and was particularly successful in involving the Scottish public in debates on creation and evolution. It was for this combination of theology and geology that he remained best remembered after he unexpectedly committed suicide in 1856.*

His reputation faded in the twentieth century but is now reviving, though with some debate as to the relative importance of his many achievements in science, journalism, literature and public affairs. In relation to local culture, however, Miller's principal achievement is clear – his record of the traditional folk tales of Easter Ross and the Black Isle. He was one of the first in Scotland to take such material seriously, and the first to gather material systematically in the north. He published this valuable remnant of an oral culture, which would otherwise have disappeared, in Scenes and Legends of the North of Scotland, *still in print almost 150 years after his death.*

Also in print, and both a readable and valuable source, is his autobiographical My Schools and Schoolmasters.

This is not simply an account of Miller's schooling, but of all the influences which shaped his mind and character during his up-bringing in Cromarty, in his first employments as a stonemason and bank clerk, and in his first writings. The book contains much information on life in the area in the first decades of the nineteenth century, including Miller's visits to Sutherland, Gairloch and Edinburgh.

Miller's fame in the late nineteenth century led to a simplistic portrayal of him as a pioneering scientist with strong religious beliefs who ultimately could not reconcile the two and so took his own life. This tragic view of Miller still has appeal – but it is complete nonsense. Although we now see that Miller's theory of creation was wrong, he cogently argued a case which took full account of the available scientific evidence of the time. Those who try to become better acquainted with his work will find that he was a more complex man, who evades simple explanation both in his life and in his death. It is this rugged and sometimes difficult individuality which is likely to ensure continuing popular interest in him. Miller's birthplace in Cromarty is in the care of the National Trust for Scotland and contains much information on his life and work.

Modern writing about the past

At Heights of Brae, above Strathpeffer, is a modern memorial to the novelist Neil Gunn (1891–1974), who lived nearby for much of his working life. Although a twentieth-century writer, and so outside the scope of this guide, his novels are important interpretations of many aspects of the history of the Highlands, including the Clearances (in *Butcher's Broom*) and the herring fishing boom (in *The Silver Darlings*). He is by far the most significant novelist to come out of the north of Scotland.

Oral tradition

Folklore

The folk traditions recorded by Miller were largely those of the Scots-speaking east coast and he gathered, in total, some 350 stories and customs. As interest in the Highlands increased the threatened culture of Scottish Gaeldom was also being sought out. The collectors included the Rev. John MacDonald of Ferintosh, on the Black Isle, in the early nineteenth century and later, Alexander Carmichael, whose *Carmina Gaedelica* is an extensive gathering of traditional 'charms and incantations'. Carmichael's work is mostly derived from the Western Isles, but there are also contributions from Ross and Cromarty.

The process of collecting folklore is not at an end. It is still possible to hear accounts of a ceremony performed about 100 years ago in Balintore, Easter Ross, where a 'cure' was attempted on a teenage girl who was suffering from epilepsy. This consisted of burying a black cock alive in a hole dug in front of the hearth. Kirk session records from Sutherland describe similar rituals in the eighteenth century, sometimes with a silver coin being placed under the bird's wing. Or, to take an example from the west, tales were being passed on earlier this century when herring boats anchored off the Crowlin Islands. The crews gathered together on one boat for evening ceilidhs, which included tales of Viking raids on Maelrubha's monastery at Applecross. Much similar material from Ross and Cromarty, both east and west, can be found in Alexander Polson's *Our Highland Folklore Heritage*, published in the 1920s and long out of print.

There was, however, a third tradition which went largely unnoticed until the 1950s, when the School of Scottish Studies began to record among the travelling people of the north. Hamish Henderson, a prominent folklorist, considered their tales and songs to be 'the most substantially ancient and the most vital of Scotland's various, towering folk traditions – traditions which are of crucial national importance here at home, and matchless gems in the crown of international folk music'. *The Summer Walkers* (Canongate, 1996) is a fascinating account of the travelling people of Sutherland and Ross and Cromarty, and of Henderson's involvement in recording their tales and songs.

Sculpture

It is in two other art forms that the area has excelled – the stone carving of the Pictish period and the pipe music of the seventeenth and eighteenth centuries. Details of Pictish stones have been given in earlier sections and a fuller guide is available in Elizabeth Sutherland's *The Pictish Guide* (Birlinn, 1997). The precise importance of the school of carving, which seems to have focused on Rosemarkie, and the extent of its influence on the southern Pictland is a topic on which views are still developing. There is also a fascination in detecting the possible influences on local Pictish art from elsewhere, including styles and motifs transmitted from Byzantine culture through the Columban church.

The four great cross slabs of Rosemarkie, Nigg, Hilton and Shandwick are supreme examples of the stone carver's craft. We should now, perhaps, add Tarbat to the list, since recent finds seem to confirm the existence of a similar stone, later broken into fragments. The great skill which was required to make these stones should encourage us to assess them not only as feats of technical brilliance, but also as works of art. A part of their artistic success is the fluidity of their complex forms. Inter-weavings, which might seem foreign to the hard material, emerge gracefully from the sandstone – a sign, for their creators, of the redemption of the material world. The tools of the carver, directed by faith and intelligence, transformed the raw material – just as, for the Church, the world was transformed by God's grace. Art mirrored and served Faith. The wholeness and wholesomeness of what was newly made in this way is embodied in the unity of the cross, a simple shape formed from the controlled intricacies of spirals, interlacings and key-patterns. It is possible to share in the appreciation of this vision, in the combination of medium and message, without sharing the faith in which it originated.

Music and song

Church music and the traditions of psalm singing
Visits to churches in the area can be enhanced by an awareness of the music which would have been heard in them – and as this is available on tape and CD it can also be played *in situ*. The work of the sixteenth-century Scots composer Robert Carver has recently been rediscovered, studied and performed. His church music is of the highest quality, and it is entirely possible that it was once heard in the Collegiate Church of

Tain when the shrine of St Duthac was visited by his patrons
James IV and James V.

A quite different tradition is to be found in Gaelic psalmody,
which was the common method of singing in church in the
Highlands until the eighteenth century. Each line of the psalm
was 'given out' by a precentor and then taken up by the congregation, with each person adopting their own tempo and
embellishments. The style, technically known as free hetero-
phony, has its closest parallels in the Middle East, and it is an
uncanny sound. When sung in the now ruined churches of
the west, it must have seemed to echo the swell of the sea.

Essential Listening: Ceol Mor

Some of the greatest Scottish art is to be found in ceol mor,
or piobaireachd, *a form of music for the Highland bagpipe
consisting of a set of variations on a theme or* urlar *(ground).
After some development of the* urlar, *a more limited set of
notes is isolated and elaborated by more and more complicated
ornamentation, before returning at the end to a restatement
of the theme.* Ceol mor *('big music') is so called to distinguish it from* ceol beag *('little music'), that is, airs and
dance tunes. The bagpipe is such that the loudness of the
note cannot be varied, the flow of sound is continuous and
there is the constant background of the drones.* Ceol mor
*works within these limits to create haunting effects. The music
is truly of European significance and widespread ignorance
of it, both within and furth of Scotland, is a matter of regret.*

The best remembered composers of ceol mor *were the
MacCrimmons, hereditary pipers to the Macleods of
Dunvegan on Skye, but the Mackays of Gairloch, pipers to
Mackenzie of Gairloch, were of similar calibre. Ian Dall
Mackay (1656–1754) composed over thirty pieces, including
one of the greatest* piobaireachd, *the* Lament for Patrick
Og MacCrimmon, *written when he heard of the death of
his teacher – who was, in fact, still alive and later played
the tune himself. Ian Dall's only son, Angus Mackay (1725–
1805), was also a composer and notable piper, but his
grandson John Roy (1753–1835) emigrated to Canada
about 1800 bringing the line in Scotland to an end.*

A number of MacCrimmon piobaireachd *have associations with Wester Ross and Kintail. Donald Mor MacCrimmon's brother, Patrick, was murdered in Glenelg about 1610. Donald subsequently took revenge by burning several houses in Kintail and then fled to Sutherland where he remained for several years.* A Flame of Wrath for Patrick Caogach *('squinting Patrick') is a fierce musical expression of his anger. Gentler emotions are to be found in a simpler* piobaireachd, The Glen is Mine, *composed by Iain MacPhadruig MacCrimmon, piper to Mackenzie of Seaforth. It is said to have been played for the first time as Seaforth passed through Glen Shiel.*

Conclusion

In both of the supreme artistic achievements of the area, in the art of the Pictish stones and in the music of *ceol mor*, complexity and gracefulness emerge from what might have seemed limiting and unpromising raw material. Indeed, the austerity of the material enhances the value of what is created. This may serve as a fitting symbol for what has been achieved by the people of Ross and Cromarty at their best. And, as with the interlacings of Pictish design or the variations of the *piobaireachd*, it is appropriate to return to the beginning and the quotation from Edwin Muir which appears in the preface:

This is a difficult country, and our home.

POSTSCRIPT

By the 1860s there had been dramatic changes in the area. Earlier sections of this guide have described the transformation of farming in the lowland areas and the sweeping away of the traditional *baìle* settlements of the Highlands, both leading to their own forms of clearance of the population. There were two other changes, both so important as to amount to revolutions.

First, the attitude to the Highlands which had prevailed in the eighteenth century was overturned. The very areas which had been regarded as savage and barbarous, which had been pillaged by government troops and whose culture had been derided, were now idealised in poetry and in prose. The romantic Highlands were born, wild landscapes were sought out and, from genuine local traditions of weaving patterned cloth, the myth of clan tartan was invented. Queen Victoria's passion for all things Highland furthered the process, while Prince Albert's love of hunting made the Highland sporting estate fashionable among the aristocracy and the *nouveau riche*.

There is an interesting local connection in all this. Demand for 'ancient' clan tartan designs was fuelled by the visit of George IV to Edinburgh in 1822, for which the monarch, on the advice of Sir Walter Scott, wore Highland dress, though with flesh-coloured tights to preserve royal dignity. In 1829 this demand was largely satisfied by the publication of *Vestiarum Scoticum* by the Sobieski Stuart brothers. This pair of con-men, who let it be assumed that their father was the illegitimate son of Charles Edward Stewart, took up residence and held court in Eilean Aigas House, near Beauly. The one piece of evidence produced to support their work on Highland dress was a forged document, known as the Cromarty Manuscript, which it was claimed had been written by one of the Urquhart family. They conveniently provided detailed descriptions of numerous 'traditional' clan tartans.

As the Highlands rose in popular esteem, railways opened up the area to visitors, hotels and shooting lodges were built, and deer forests and grouse moors were created, all further transforming the landscape. Public interest in the Highlands helped bring an end to the worst excesses of the clearances. Of particular note from this period are the buildings of Victorian Strathpeffer which flourished as a spa (Gazetteer 23).

But as this happened, the second revolution was underway – in landownership. Between 1820 and 1860, around 70 per cent of Highland land passed from the hands of the traditional owners to a new elite of wealthy southern businessmen. This was not a new phenomenon. In the east of Ross and Cromarty, southern money (or the influence of money) gave possession of Inverbreakie to the London financier Sir Adam Gordon as early as 1700. Now this process affected vast western estates, principally those of the Mackenzie earls of Seaforth, who had sold almost everything by 1844.

Two of the largest of the new landowners were Sir James Matheson and his nephew, Sir Alexander, both of the Hong Kong based trading company Jardine-Matheson. Sir Alexander bought estates in the west, building Duncraig Castle on the Loch Alsh estate in 1866, but his principal house in Ross and Cromarty was Ardross. The improvement of the Ardross estate and the building of Ardross Castle in the late 1840s brought much needed work to the area, but ironically, it was financed by the profits of the opium trade. The Mathesons were, in effect, drug barons operating with government support. Britain fought the shameful opium wars with China to protect their interests.

Change in landownership has continued. The Mathesons were succeeded at Ardross by a family whose fortunes were based on a decidedly more wholesome product – the Perrins, manufactures of Worcester sauce – and in the last twenty-five years over half of the estates in Ross and Cromarty have again passed to new owners. Understanding this more recent past, and planning for the future, requires a realisation that the history of Ross and Cromarty is, and has been for some time, caught up with much wider trends of European and global history.

FURTHER READING

History is a sacred kind of writing, because truth is essential
to it; and where truth is, there God Himself is, so far as truth
is concerned: notwithstanding which, there are those, who
compose books, and toss them out into the world like fritters.

MIGUEL DE CERVANTES (*Don Quixote*, Part II, Chapter 3)

With the above quotation in mind, a short list of suggestions
for further reading is given below. The list contains no 'fritters'
but omits many valuable and relevant works.

General

Scotland's pre-history is well covered in Caroline Wickham-
Jones' *Scotland's First Settlers* (London, 1994) and A. and G.
Ritchie's *Scotland: Archaeology and Early History* (Edinburgh,
1991). Audrey Henshall's two volume *The Chambered Tombs
of Scotland* (Edinburgh University Press, 1963 and 1972) is a
key reference work available in many libraries. G. Ritchie's
Brochs of Scotland (Shire Archaeology, 1988) has detailed
descriptions of Dun Telve and Dun Troddan brochs. Ian
Armit's *The Archaeology of Skye and the Wester Isles* (Edinburgh
University Press, 1996) is both an excellent account of another
part of northern Scotland and provides clear summaries of
much current thinking in archaeology.

For general Scottish history from AD 80 to the present the
six-volume *New History of Scotland* (Edinburgh University
Press) or Michael Lynch's one-volume *Scotland: A New History*
(Century, 1991) are both available in paperback. T. M.
Devine's *Clanship to Crofters' War* (Manchester University
Press, 1994) is an accessible history of the Highlands from
the eighteenth century, with clear overviews of key issues such
as the clearances, land ownership and emigration.

Ross and Cromarty

Marinell Ash's *This Noble Harbour* (Cromarty Firth Port
Authority, 1991) is an accessible and wide-ranging history of

the area around the Cromarty Firth. Copies can be obtained from the Cromarty Firth Port Authority (01349 852308). Monica Clough and Eric Richard's *Cromartie: Highland Life: 1650–1914* (Aberdeen University Press, 1989) gives a detailed account of the fortunes of one large estate, with property on both east and west coasts, and of the people who lived on it.

Firthlands of Ross and Sutherland and *People and Settlement in North West Ross* both edited by John Baldwin (Scottish Society for Northern Studies, 1986 and 1994) are valuable collections of essays on a variety of topics and Ian Mowat's *Easter Ross: The Double Frontier* (John Donald, 1981) although out of print is worth looking out for. Douglas Willis' *The Black Isle* (John Donald, new edition 1997) is a guide to one part of Ross and Cromarty, admirable for its combination of geology, natural history and history.

For further information on the architecture of the area Elizabeth Beaton's *Ross and Cromarty: An Illustrated Architectural Guide* (Rutland Press, 1992) is highly recommended. W. J. Watson's classic *Place Names of Ross and Cromarty* (1904, re-issued by Highland Heritage Books, 1996) is a mine of information, not only on place-names. A number of museums, including Cromarty, Dingwall and Groam House, have published booklets on various aspects of the area's history including the Dingwall Canal, the Resolis Riot and the art of the Pictish stones. Details are available from the museums.

Art and culture

Hugh Miller's *Scenes and Legends of the North of Scotland* (Edinburgh, 1994) is both a key work in Scottish folklore and easy to dip into. His autobiographical *My Schools and Schoolmaster* (Edinburgh, 1991) is harder going but well worth the effort. J. H. Dixon's *Gairloch and Guide to Loch Maree* (1886, reprinted by Gairloch Heritage Society) contains many traditional tales from the west and Timothy Neat's *The Summer Walkers* (Canongate, 1996) is a fascinating account of the travelling people of Sutherland and Ross and Cromarty.

Sir Thomas Urquhart's translation of Rabelais' *Gargantua and Pantagruel* was reprinted a number of times, almost always without acknowledgement of Urquhart's contribution. It is worth looking out for the 1931 edition (Navarre Society), extensively illustrated by Heath Robinson – the trio of Rabelais, Urquhart and Heath Robinson being difficult to match for exuberance.

The *Lament for Patrick Og MacCrimmon* played by Donald MacPherson is available on compact disc (Lismore LCOM 9013). The same CD has the great *Lament for the Children* and the mesmeric *Lament for Mary MacLeod*. Gaelic psalm singing can be heard on the School of Scottish Studies *Gaelic Psalms from Lewis* (Greentrax Recordings CDTRAX 9006) or on a series of tapes produced by Lewis Recordings.

George Bain's *Celtic Art: The Methods of Construction*, a pioneering work in the 1950s which showed how the designs of the Pictish stones were achieved, is still in print. For a comprehensive guide to the stones, see Elizabeth Sutherland's *The Pictish Guide* (Birlinn, 1997).

GAZETTEERS

GAZETTEER 1: MESOLITHIC SITES

There are two Mesolithic sites, neither with visible remains. Those interested in the sites should refer to the descriptions and excavation reports in the Sites and Monuments Record.

1 Redpoint   NG 726685: OS19 or 24

Two 'chipping floors' on which stone tools had been made were discovered.

2 Shieldaig   NG 816523: OS24

A detailed excavation was carried out in 1973.

GAZETTEER 2: NEOLITHIC SITES

CHAMBERED CAIRNS

This gazetteer lists all identified chambered cairns and Neolithic long cairns and notes (a) the type of cairn according to standard classifications as either Orkney–Cromarty (O–C), Clava, Hebridean or long; (b) the shape of the chamber (square or polygonal); and (c) the shape of the cairn over the chamber (round, trapezoid, square, heel-shaped, short or long horned). Where the cairn material has been mostly removed it is not always possible to identify the shape of the cairn. In some cases where the cairn is intact it is not possible to identify the shape of the chamber still sealed within the cairn – or indeed to determine whether or not there is a chamber.

1 Ardross Mains   NH 615747: OS21

O–C type, rectangular chamber. Only stones of a chamber (5.8 m × 1.5 m) remain.

2 Ardvannie   NH 681874: OS21*

O–C type, polygonal chamber, round cairn. In scrub on the north side of old A93, 25 km north-west of Edderton, beside

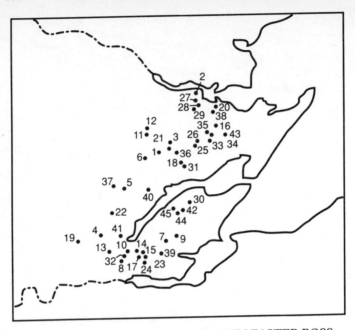

NEOLITHIC CHAMBERED CAIRNS IN EASTER ROSS
AND THE BLACK ISLE

track to Ardvannie. The cairn, 30 m above sea level, is partially
robbed of cairn material. It is 21 m in diameter and several of
its main features survive. Near its centre the tops of slabs are
visible, indicating a polygonal chamber (3.3 m × 1.8 m). The
entrance passage was from the east, where what was probably
the lintel can be seen near the edge of the cairn.

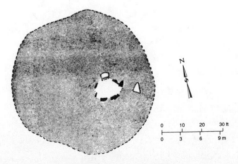

FIGURE 8. *Ardvannie – plan*

3 Baldoon

NH 633759: OS21

O–C type, rectangular chamber. At over 260 m above sea level, this is one of the highest-sited cairns. Little cairn material remains but large stones show a chamber 5 m long with two compartments.

4 Ballachnecore

NH 488566: OS26

O–C type, polygonal chamber. The cairn material has been cleared, apart from some traces around the chamber, the main stones of which remain.

5 Balnacrae

NH 533646: OS20

O–C type. The cairn, 240 m above sea level in rough pasture, has had its material almost entirely removed but was probably about 23 m in diameter. The chamber was very large (7 m × 4.3 m) with the entrance from the north-east. The surviving stones lean at precarious angles.

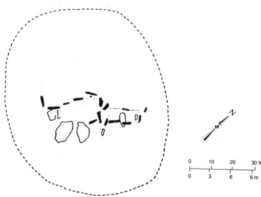

FIGURE 9. *Balnacrae – plan*

6 Balnagrotchen

NH 581735: OS21★

O–C type, polygonal chamber, possibly short horned. In the valley of the River Alness, the cairn is 210 m above sea level on a terrace above the river, close to two other cairns at Boath. The cairn material has been largely removed and it is crossed at its east side by a dyke. The chamber was large and oval, with an entrance at the east.

7 **Balnaguie**   NH 628547: OS26*

O–C type, rectangular chamber, round cairn. The cairn stands
105 m above sea level. Cairn material has been almost entirely
removed but the diameter seems to have been about 28 m.
The chamber, of particularly large slabs, measures 5.4 m ×
2.3 m, and is divided into two compartments. There may have
been a concave façade at the entrance of which two uprights
(.75 m high) survive.

8 **Balvaird**   NH 539519: OS26*

O–C type, polygonal chamber. Beside a ruined cottage. The
cairn lies 95 m above sea level and, severely robbed of cairn
material, stands to a height of only 1 m. It is also truncated by
a stone dyke and overgrown with whins. The chamber is 1.8 m
long.

9 **Belmaduthy**   NH 644559: OS26*

O–C type, rectangular chamber, oval cairn. The cairn lies
130 m above sea level on the top of a low ridge. It is severely
robbed of cairn material and partly ploughed. The original
was oval, about 20 m × 14 m, but this shape is not now visible.
There is a rectangular chamber (5.2 m × 4.6 m) of large slabs
with its entrance at the south-east. There was probably a
forecourt façade and one stone may be cup marked.

10 **Bishop Kinkell**   NH 543531: OS26

O–C type, polygonal chamber, round. The cairn, 75 m above
sea level, is unusually on a sloping site. Cairn material has
been almost entirely removed and it is truncated by a dyke.
Nine stones remain of the oval chamber (3.4 m × 2.3 m).

11 **Boath Long**   NH 581738: OS21*

O–C type, long horned. The cairn lies 195 m above sea level
on a flat terrace above the River Alness. The cairn material
was used as building material c.1820 and it is now difficult to
discern the shape. It was originally 60 m long (excluding the
horns) and 20 m wide at the east, from where two horns project,
4.6 m and 6.1 m long. Slabs show the site of the chamber.
This appears to be an extension of an earlier, smaller cairn. A

leaf-shaped flint arrowhead, now lost, was found either here or at Boath Short cairn (see below).

12 Boath Short NH 583739: OS21*

O–C type, polygonal chamber, short horned. The cairn is 180 m above sea level, north-east of Boath Long cairn. The centre, virtually undisturbed, is 3 m high with a fine intact oval chamber (5 m × 2.5 m), with the entrance at the east. The passage is blocked by rubble.

13 Brahan Wood NH 504552: OS26

O–C type, rectangular chamber. The cairn material has been entirely removed. The two part chamber is 7.8 m × 2.6 m.

14 Cairnside, Newton of Kinkell NH 561526: OS26

Long cairn. The cairn is depleted but clearly visible.

15 Carn Glas, Kilcoy NH 578520: OS26*

O–C type, rectangular chamber, round cairn. This unusually large cairn, 120 m above sea level, stood at a height of 6.5 m in 1881 and was about 37 m in diameter but is now reduced to a little over 1 m in height and 21.5 m diameter. The chamber (2.8 m × 1.4 m) has two compartments. Excavations in 1955 produced two arrowheads, sherds of beaker and Neolithic pottery and a single fragment of burnt bone in the outer chamber. The arrowheads are of two different kinds: one with a barbed and tanged head and the other with a broad leaf-shaped head.

16 Carn Liath, Morangie Forest NH 729798: OS21*

Long cairn. The cairn lies 180 m above sea level in an un-planted area in surrounding woods. It is trapezoid-shaped, 37 m long and rising to height of 7.7 m, and shows signs of being an extension of a smaller, earlier cairn.

17 Carn Urnan NH 566523: OS26*

Clava-type passage grave. 4 km south-east of Conon Bridge. The cairn lies 150 m above sea level. Cairn material has been entirely removed but the kerb of large boulders, 30 m in diameter, is almost complete. Two lintels of the entrance passage, at the south-west, can be seen. The cairn stands in a circle of large stones (monoliths), 22.5 m in diameter. Four of these stones remain upright, the tallest 1.8 m high. The most recent evidence suggests that Clava-type cairns are in fact Bronze Age monuments dating from *c.*2000 BC.

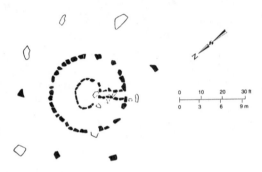

FIGURE 10. *Carn Urnan – plan*

18 Cnoc Navie   NH 656722: OS21*

O–C type, polygonal chamber, round cairn. The cairn is below the summit of a flat-topped hill north of Alness at 225 m above sea level. Cairn material has been entirely removed. It was about 23 m in diameter and the chamber, entered from the SE, was 8.6 m long, divided into three or four sections.

19 Preas Maree, Contin Mains   NH 460558: OS26

O–C type, rectangular chamber. Situated within a private burial ground. Only stones of the chamber remain, with three large cup marks on the single stone which survives from the outer compartment.

20 Edderton Hill   NH 734834: OS21

Long cairn which is 61 m long with a maximum width of 14 m.

21 Glaich   NH 635744: OS21

Round. 18 m diameter.

22 Heights of Brae
NH 514615: OS20*

O–C type, polygonal chamber, round cairn. At 240 m one of the highest-situated cairns. Cairn material has been removed but the diameter seems to have been about 22 m. The stones suggest two chambers: one off-centre with a rectangular outer compartment and a polygonal inner compartment; the other, of which only two stones remain, nearer the centre of the cairn. The arrangement of stones suggests a lengthening of the original entrance passage and it is probable that this cairn is an enlargement of an earlier structure.

23 Kilcoy North
NH 570517: OS26*

O–C type, polygonal chamber, round cairn. The cairn lies 120 m above sea level in the middle of a field. Although denuded it is still over 1 m high and about 18.5 m in diameter. Stones protruding in the centre suggest a chamber of two compartments, the inner 2.4 m × 2.8 m and the outer 2.8 m × 1.5–2 m.

24 Kilcoy South
NH 569516: OS26*

O–C type, polygonal, short horned. The cairn, 120 m above sea level, has been reduced by farming and is crossed by a dyke. It now measures 15 m × 18 m and there are remains of a funnel-shaped forecourt at the south-east. This is one of the two cairns in the area to have been scientifically excavated. Excavation revealed that the ground near the cairn slopes away and a flat area for the forecourt had been created by building an earth and stone platform. A patch of charcoal was found in the forecourt, near the entrance to the tomb. The walls of the passage (1.2 m × 1.2 m) are each made from a single upright stone and a flat sill stone in the passage covered a pit in which were charcoal and burnt bones. The outer compartment (1.8 m long) is built with one large stone on each side and dry walling. There were two patches of charcoal and burnt bone on the floor.

The lintel to the inner chamber is still in place. The opening to this chamber had been carefully blocked, with patches of charcoal, burnt bone and a sherd in the blocking stones. The central compartment (3 m × 2.8 m) is polygonal and on the floor there was a large patch of charcoal and burned bone, covered with a layer of clean sand, above which were remains of six pots. A further small circular compartment lies off the north corner of the central compartment.

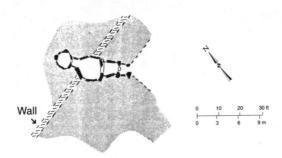

Wall

FIGURE 11. *Kilcoy South – plan*

It is possible that there are three phases of building here. The small chamber, off the central compartment, may be the original chamber of a small cairn. This was then extended by building the central compartment, with the outer chamber as the passage entrance in this phase. Finally the outer passage and funnel-shaped forecourt were added.

25 King's Head cairn   NH 697751: OS21*

O–C type, polygonal chamber, round cairn. The cairn lies 165 m above sea level. Cairn material was almost entirely removed in 1887 but the edge is distinct, measuring about 28 m east-west × 23 m north-south. The chamber of large slabs is 6.8 m long, divided into two compartments, almost intact but choked with debris. Four slabs, from a cist burial, lie 2 m north-west of the chamber. The off-centre chamber and short passage suggest that this is an enlargement of an earlier cairn.

26 Kinrive West   NH 699753: OS21*

Long or possibly heel-shaped cairn, 45 m from above. The cairn is over 30 m long and between 2.7 m and 18.8 m wide. There are no convincing traces of horns. This appears to be an expansion of an earlier cairn. A skull, now in Inverness Museum, may come from this or one of the previous two sites.

27 Leachonich   NH 682859: OS21★

Round cairn which is 11 m in diameter, with two slabs at the centre.

28 Lower Lechanich North   NH 684858: OS21★

O–C type, polygonal chamber, round cairn. The cairn is on a small knoll on open hillside, 120 m above sea level. It is 15 m in diameter, with a chamber 5.4 m in diameter, divided into two compartments.

29 Lower Lechanich South   NH 685851: OS21

O–C type, round. The cairn is rather strangely sited on a slope on the side of a small rounded hill. It measures 21.5 m in diameter. The chamber is not visible but is possibly intact under the cairn.

30 Mid Brae   NH 661628: OS21★

O–C type, rectangular chamber, long cairn. The cairn, 135 m above sea level, is severely robbed of material and surrounded by ruins of croft houses. It appears to have been about 70 m long and 12.5–15 m wide. A chamber survives at the west end and there may have been another at the east. This is an example of the elongation of an earlier cairn.

31 Millcraig   NH 658710: OS21★

O–C type, round cairn. The cairn lies 60 m above sea level, in gently sloping arable ground, north of Alness. It was originally 34 m–40 m in diameter but the cairn material was removed in 1854. The remaining stones suggest a very large chamber.

32 Muir of Conon   NH 546524: OS26★

O–C type, rectangular chamber, round cairn. The cairn, 20 m in diameter, lies 120 m above sea level in a field and is ruined and heavily overgrown with broom. Some slabs are visible, suggesting an entrance passage leading to a chamber, divided into two compartments.

33 Scotsburn House   NH 715761: OS21

O–C type. The cairn lies 120 m above sea level. Its dimensions are uncertain but the stones suggest some form of chamber.

34 Scotsburn Wood
NH 726768: OS21*

O–C type, round cairn. The cairn, 165 m above sea level, had an original diameter of about 15 m. The chamber (4.5 m long) was divided into two compartments, with a 3.3 m entrance passage.

35 Scotsburn Wood West
NH 721767: OS21*

O–C type. The cairn, 180 m above sea level, is almost completely destroyed. Stones suggest a chamber, divided into two compartments, with a 1.4 m entrance passage.

36 Sittenham
NH 649743: OS21*

O–C type, polygonal chamber, round cairn. The cairn, situated in a pine wood on the 80 m contour above the River Alness, has had much of its material removed. It was originally 12.5 m in diameter, with a circular chamber of 2.5 m diameter and a 1.5 m entrance passage

37 Swordale
NH 518661: OS20

O–C type. Only three stones remain.

38 Redburn
NH 727834: OS21*

O–C type, heel shaped. A fairly complete cairn, 135 m above sea level, rising to a height of 4 m and 22 m in diameter (but has been 3 m wider). Three slabs and a lintel from the entrance passage are visible and the chamber is probably intact inside the cairn.

39 The Temple, Tore
NH 617526: OS26*

Possibly O–C type. About 25 m in diameter, the cairn stood to height of 2.5 m in 1882 but has been robbed almost flat. Three large slabs survive.

40 Upper Park
NH 589665: OS21*

O-C type, possibly a polygonal chamber, round cairn. The cairn, on a ridge at a height of 105 m, has been much robbed and disturbed. Its original diameter was about 24 m and it had an unusually large chamber (3.4 m × 4.6 m).

41 Ussie   NH 530565: OS21*

O–C type, polygonal chamber. The cairn, 120 m above
sea level, is very denuded. Seven stones of the chamber
survive.

42 Wester Brae   NH 656613: OS21*

Long cairn. The cairn is 165 m above sea level and lies in a
field of small cairns. It is 26 m long and the width varies
between 11.5 m and 14.8 m. The ends appear to be intact but
it has been robbed of stone in the middle.

43 Wester Lamington   NH 747779: OS21*

Long cairn. The cairn, 32 m long and from 14.8 m to 19 m
wide, is surrounded by conifers and consists of bare stones
piled up to 5.7 m high.

44 Woodhead Long   NH 653607: OS21*

Long cairn. In conifers and cut by drainage ditch. The cairn,
180 m above sea level, is 40 m long, 12.3 m wide and up to
2.5 m high.

45 Woodhead Round   NH 650610: OS21*

O–C type, rectangular chamber, round cairn. The cairn,
180 m above sea level, has been much robbed but was
probably about 25 m in diameter. Side and end stones of
chamber (3.7 m × 1.3 m) remain. A capstone has slipped
but is still in position. There is a report from 1816 of a cist
burial.

46 Glenelg   NG 845166: OS33*

Square cairn of Hebridean group. The cairn lies in a former
field at the upper end of Glen Beag and has been much robbed.
It was almost 15 m square, with its edges marked by dry-stone
walling. The chamber was about 1.8 m square with a 1.8 m
entrance passage. Excavation produced sherds of Neolithic
and beaker pottery, lignite beads, a leaf-shaped arrowhead and
a stone spindle whorl.

LOST SITES

47 Clachan Biorach   NH 562617: OS21

Possibly an O–C type cairn with a polygonal chamber, destroyed before 1839.

48 Heights of Docharty   NH 52 61: OS20

Long cairn.

49 Priest's Sepulchre   NH 60 65: OS21

A description in 1791 suggests a denuded rectangular chamber.

50 Ardmeanach   NH 701608: OS21

A long cairn is marked here on the 1816 map of the Mulbuie Commonty. Some cairn material may remain but further investigation is required.

GAZETTEER 3: HENGES
(marked 'earthwork' on OS)

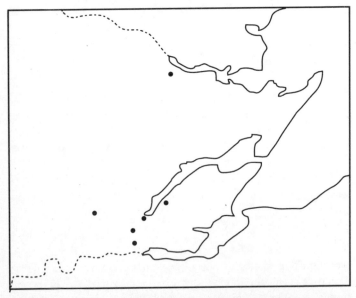

HENGES AND STONE CIRCLES IN EASTER ROSS AND
THE BLACK ISLE

1 Muir of Ord

NH 527497: OS26

On golf course at the south-west end of Muir of Ord. Check at Clubhouse before visiting. This Class II henge has found a new ritual use as a green on the golf course. The central area measures 25.5 m × 19.5 m, with a ditch up to 5.4 m wide and 1.3 m deep. Part of the ditch at the NW has been filled in.

2 Crochar, Culbokie

NH 594578: OS26*

180 m to north of B9169. A Class I henge with an 8 m wide ditch enclosing a central area of *c*.15 m diameter. The single entrance is to the east. The bank opposite the causeway has been disturbed by a field boundary.

3 Dugary

NH 523526: OS26*

Little can be seen of this Class I henge lying in a field 400 m south-east of Dugary farmhouse.

4 Cononbridge

NH 543551: OS21*

At the south end of Cononbridge. The central area is 23 m in diameter.

5 Contin

NH 441569: OS26*

The central area is 21.5 m in diameter.

6 Carriblair

NH 709851: OS21

A possible stone circle near Edderton. Four stones are visible and a central cist burial, with a food vessel, was discovered.

7 Shiel Bridge

NG 930186: OS33

This is the smallest henge in Ross and Cromarty, its central area only 8 m in diameter, and is included in the gazetteer as an example of a west coast henge. It is a Class II structure.

NOTE: the 'stone circle' marked on the OS Landranger map at Arcan (NH 503535: OS26*) is a Bronze Age cairn from which the cairn material has been taken, leaving only the large kerb stones.

GAZETTEER 4: BRONZE AGE SITES

There are a large number of reported cist and urn burials, cairns, hut circles and field clearance cairns, and a number of cup marked stones. The gazetteer covers those which appear on the OS Landranger series maps and one or two others of particular interest.

BURIAL SITES

1 Croftcrunie   NH 610520: OS26

An enclosed cremation cemetery (19 m × 16.4 m) with a 3 m wide stoney bank.

2 Cairn a'Chat   NH 716804: OS21★

A cairn of 16 m diameter and 1.5 m in height, with a later boundary marker on top since it was once of the marches of the burgh of Tain.

3 Cnoc Duchaire   NH 62 71: OS21★

Two cairns, one 16 m diameter with a kerb and the other 8 m, both 1.2 m high but difficult to see in dense woodland. A cist burial was discovered in the first cairn in 1874.

4 Dalreoch Wood   NH 631718: OS21★

A 10 m diameter cairn, 1 m high, with a surrounding bank. Difficult to see in dense woodland.

5 Callachy Hill   NH 738605: OS21★

A 13.8 m diameter cairn which had cremation burials within it. Now in dense woodland.

6 Muir of Conon   NH 544520: OS26

12.5 m diameter and 1m high.

7 Arcan   NH 503535: OS26★

Marked on the OS map as a stone circle, this is a 16 m diameter Bronze Age cairn from which the cairn material has been taken, leaving only the large kerb stones.

CUP MARKED STONES

Stones and boulders decorated with shallow hollows known as cup marks are found in many places, including chambered cairns. The meaning or function of the marks is unknown. The only cup marked stones to be identified on the OS Landranger maps are at Blackhill.

8 Blackhill   NH 573637: OS21*

Two boulders, one with forty cup marks and the other with fifteen.

HUT CIRCLES AND FIELD SYSTEMS

9 Craigiehowe   NH 679517 and NH 680514: OS26

10 Coille Cnoc na h'Eirachd   NH 619498: OS26*

Stone foundations of six Bronze Age huts, each about 16 m diameter, with a related field system nearby.

11 Drumderfit   NH 658521: OS26

Hut circle with nearby field system

12 Sand   NG 773802: OS19*

West of Poolewe. There are a number of hut circles on the site, which was later re-used as a shieling with some of the shieling huts constructed inside the remains of the hut circles. There are also later rectangular enclosures and field boundaries. More hut circles, shielings and field systems are scattered over a wide area to the east of this map reference. *The Sand River Trail /Slighe Abhainn Shannda*, a bi-lingual guide published by the Highland Archaeology Service provides a valuable guide to this area.

13 West shore of Loch Ewe   NG 87 86: OS19*

Remains of three huts.

14 Strathbeag, Dundonnel   NH 12 85: OS19*

Remains of three huts.

15 Achtertyre   NG 84 27 and 84 29: OS33*

There are four huts on the first site, with evidence of later cultivation; two on the second, with a Bronze Age field system and re-use of the site for shielings.

16 Pollagharrie   NH 67 84: OS21*

A field system over an area of 7.5 hectares, most cairns being 1-2 m diameter.

17 Strathrusdale   NH 578769 and NH 59 75: OS21*

The first site has two circles and the second, Bog Ban, has seven. Both have associated field systems.

18 Hartmount   NG 765775: OS21*

Five hut circles but in dense vegetation.

19 Polintack   NH 66 82: OS21*

On Struie road north of Altnamain. Six hut circles, in two groupings, and numerous clearance cairns.

20 Glen Goibhre   NH 45 50 and NH 46 50: OS26*

A total of twelve huts, nine being circular and three oval.

21 Strath Sgitheach   NH 51 62: OS20*

Six huts, with remains of others not marked on the OS map in the area surrounding.

22 Wester Brae   NH 655615: OS21*

Hut circles within an extensive cairn field, marked as cairns on OS21.

23 Lochcarron   NG 88 38: OS25*

Appears on the OS map but may not be a hut circle.

STANDING STONES

24 Edderton   NH 708850: OS21*

In field on left of minor road to Ardmore. 3 m high and carved with later Pictish symbols (*see* Gazetteer 6:3).

25 Clach a'Mheirleich   NH 681690: OS21★

Near Rosskeen old church. A 1.8 m high stone incised with later Pictish symbols (*see* Gazetteer 6:4).

26 Windhill   NH 531484 and NH 533483: OS26★

South of Muir of Ord, a group of three standing stones, two east of the road (one only a stump) and one west of it.

27 Inchvannie   NH 500593: OS26

A standing stone 1.6 m high with a second smaller stone 60 m to WSW.

28 Kildonan, Little Lochbroom   NH 081915: OS19★

A stone 1.4 m high near Kildonan Farm.

29 Cill Fhearchair   NG 938187: OS33

There is a standing stone in this burial ground near Shiel Bridge.

LOST STANDING STONES

30 Highfield   NH 521518: OS26

A standing stone was removed in 1955.

BURIAL SITES

31 Burial mound, Auchtertyre   NG 850294: OS33★

Marked as a 'tumulus' on the OS. Consists of a circular bank of 27 m diameter with an inner 7 m ditch, enclosing a central platform of 13.5 m diameter. At the centre is a low mound 6.5 m in diameter. Without excavation it is impossible to date this.

GAZETTEER 5:
FORTS, DUNS, BROCHS AND CRANNOGS

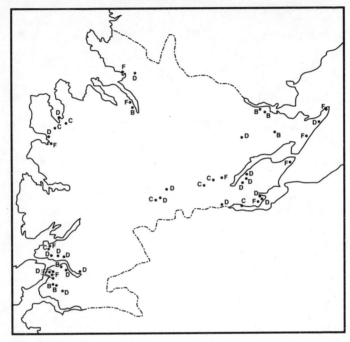

HILL AND PROMONTORY FORTS, BROCHS, AND DUNS

F = fort; B = broch; D = dun; C = crannog

HILL AND PROMONTORY FORTS

1 Ord Hill   NH 664491: OS26★

Can be approached from parking area off A9(T) east of
Kessock Junction. The route is marked on an interpretive panel
in car park. The stone ramparts, originally timber-laced and
vitrified in parts, enclose an area 265 m long and 115 m wide.
The entrance is at the south-west with an additional protecting
wall beyond.

2 Knockfarril   NH 504585: OS26★

The single stone rampart of the fort, on a grassy top of the
hill, is heavily vitrified. The plan of the fort is confused by

three later ditches, of unknown date, and by unusual lines of vitrified rampart running out from the east and west ends, possibly as part of extended defences for the entrances. A pond within the fort is probably a rock-cut cistern. The site has not been excavated.

3 Castledownie, Eathie   NH 779640: OS21

A promontory fort with ramparts to landward enclosing an area 30 m by 17 m.

4 Castlehaven   NH 929872: OS21

Only a few traces remain.

5 Easter Rarichie   NH 843736: OS21*

A multi-period fort of which the inner enclosure may be a dun. There are three ramparts and two defensive walls.

6 Carn na Buaile   NH 412567: OS26*

A hill fort overlooking Strath Conon.

7 Cnoc an Duin   NH 696769: OS21*

A fine and clear example of an unfinished hill fort. A single wall was originally intended to enclose an area 220 m × 75 m but was abandoned when little more than half the circuit was complete. Two further lines of unfinished rampart, with external quarry ditches, can be traced at the west.

8 Dun Canna   NC 111008: OS15*

A promontory fort 1 mile north of the mouth of the River Kanaird, looking west over the bay to the Summer Isles. The main defence is a massive wall across the narrow promontory. A further wall defends an inner section. The defences may have been timber laced.

9 Dun Lagaigh   NH 149913: OS19*

On the west shore of Lochbroom. The earliest structure on the site is a fort (90 m × 35 m) occupying the whole of the west end of the hill, defended at the west by a large timber laced rampart, now vitrified. There is another section of rampart at the east end, but none on the steep north and south slopes.

The entrance was at the east, where there is also an outer defensive wall.

A later dun occupies the highest part of the site. The entrance, now blocked, was at the east. On the west are stairs which ran up inside the thickness of the wall. Stones cleared from the interior of the dun are piled outside and should be disregarded when trying to understand the structure. The site was again occupied in the twelfth century when a simple castle was constructed.

10 Creagan Fhamhair   NG 823726: OS19

A fort south east of Gairloch on a hill above the River Kerry. Cliffs to the north and west provide natural defences, while a wall up to 2 m thick defends the other two sides. The central area is *c.*30 m across.

11 Loch Acaidh na h-Inich   NG 818314: OS24★

A galleried fort measuring 30 m × 28 m on high ground above the loch.

12 Am Baghan Bublach   NG 831200: OS33★

In Glenelg. An oval fort, 57 m × 30 m, with two opposing entrances.

BROCHS

Essential Viewing

Dun Telve is the best preserved broch on the Scottish mainland and, with nearby Dun Troddan, illustrates the key features of broch building.

13 *Dun Telve*   *NG 829172: OS33★*

Dun Telve is not only a well-preserved broch, standing in to a height of 10 m, but also, having had some parts removed, has become a three-dimensional cut-away illustration of the principal features of broch architecture. The hollow wall construction, with inner and outer dry-stone walls bonded by cross slabs, is clearly visible, as is the wide solid base.

1. Clach a'Mheirleich
(The Thief's Stone):
a Bronze Age
standing stone.

2. The Clootie Well, Munlochy.

11. Scots twelve shilling piece of Charles II, found in Cromarty.

12. Silver penny of Edward II, found in Cromarty.

9. Applecross cross fragment.

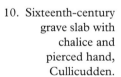

10. Sixteenth-century grave slab with chalice and pierced hand, Cullicudden.

11. Scots twelve shilling piece of Charles II,
found in Cromarty.

12. Silver penny of Edward II, found in Cromarty.

7. Fourteenth-century grave slab with ornamental cross, Cullicudden.

8. Applecross cross-shaft.

5. Fourteenth-century grave slab with ornamental cross, Cullicudden.

6. Fourteenth-century grave slab with ornamental cross, Cullicudden.

1. Clach a'Mheirleich (The Thief's Stone): a Bronze Age standing stone.

2. The Clootie Well, Munlochy.

3. Kirkmichael, Resolis.

4. Statue of St Duthac,
Tain Collegiate Church.

13. Cromarty fisherwomen.

14. Bernera Barracks.

15. The Fyrish Monument, reputedly a replica of the gates of Negapatam.

16. The gates of Ardross Castle and the arms of the Perrins family.

Four internal galleries remain intact with part of the fifth. In the inner wall of the broch there are two ledges, one at a height of 2 m and the other at 9 m, almost certainly designed to support timber structures. Although ledges are found elsewhere, this double ledge is unique. There are also two sets of openings in the inner wall, one above the entrance passage, probably intended to reduce the weight of stone over the entrance. Both would have allowed air and light into the upper galleries, which may have been used for storage.

Dun Telve is entered by a passage from the south side, checked for a timber door and with one bar hole remaining. As one goes through there is a guard chamber to the right in the thickness of the wall. Once inside, the entrance to the staircase is to the left. A section of seventeen steps survives within the thickness of the wall, stopping where it runs into the fallen part of the broch. At the bottom of the stairs is a small cell with a corbelled roof.

Outside are remains of other structures which may have been in the form of an enclosure, with houses, around the broch. A rectangular building to the left of the entrance may be of a much later date.

FIGURE 12. *Dun Telve Broch*

14 *Dun Troddan*   *NG 833172: OS33**

*Dun Troddan is only 500 m from Dun Telve and it is
unusual, though not unique, to find brochs so close to each
other. One-third of the broch still stands to a height of 7.6 m
making it the third best preserved broch. The basic method
of construction is as in Dun Telve. When the broch was
cleared out in the 1920s a ring of post holes was found which
would have supported a wooden floor running around the
inner wall supported on a ledge. There was also a central
stone hearth which seems to have continued in use after part
of the broch had fallen.*

*The entrance is checked for a timber door and has a guard
chamber to the left, now only partly roofed. The stairs have
nine steps leading to a 5.5 m passage, before beginning a
second flight. There may have been a door from this passage
to the internal wooden floor, as at Caisteal Grugaig.*

15 Caisteal Grugaig   NG 866251: OS33*

The broch is on a rocky knoll above Loch Duich and has the
uneven rock as its internal floor. It was cleared of rubble in
the nineteenth century and, as a result, many of its features
are visible. The entrance has a large triangular lintel stone
which helped to spread the weight of the structure above. There
are door-checks, a long bar-hole and a guard chamber, now
blocked, on the left. As at Dun Troddan a short flight of stairs
leads to a passage from which there is a high door on to what
would have been an internal wooden floor supported on an
internal ledge and wooden uprights. There are three other cells
within the base wall, mostly blocked by fallen stone but still
visible.

16 Rhiroy   NH 149990: OS20*

The broch stands on the edge of a low cliff on the south-west
side of Lochbroom. On the side away from the cliff it stands
to a height of 3.5 m but has fallen on the other side. Excavations
revealed a ring of post holes as at Dun Troddan and there is
an internal ledge. Parts of the broch have been blocked after
excavation to preserve the structure. There is some dispute as
to the original form of this broch, with competing claims that

it was D-shaped (with a very thin wall on the precipice side) or, alternatively, that a section of cliff, on which a wide wall would have stood, has fallen away.

17 Dun Alascaig   NG 657868: OS21*

The broch, which was solid based with a diameter of over 9 m, was largely destroyed in 1818. The large triangular stone which acted as a lintel is still on the site.

18 Leachonich   NH 682855: OS21*

Only a mound of tumbled stones remain.

19 Scotsburn   NH 715762: OS21*

A pile of tumbled stones, marked on the OS as a dun, but probably a broch.

DUNS

On the east coast

20 Findon   NH 609603: OS21*

To the north of the B9169, overlooking the Findon Burn. A single stone rampart enclosing an area 7.5 m in diameter.

21 Creag a'Chaisteal   NH 669506: OS26*

On the ridge west of Loch Lundie above Kilmuir. Access by footpath from Kilmuir Church. The dun is about 20 m in diameter with dry-stone walls standing four courses high.

22 Glascairn, Culbokie   NH 603587: OS26*

A dun about 15 m in diameter now cleared from trees and with interpretive board. Inner dry-stone rampart and two outer walls of turf and stones.

23 Drumondreoch   NH 583576: OS26*

An enclosure about 20 m in diameter surrounded by a much-robbed stone wall, with two outer ramparts and ditches.

24 Castle Corbet   NH 904803: OS21

Near Tarrel. Only scant remains.

25 Cnoc na Sroine   NH 584748: OS21*

A few remains of a dun above the valley of the River Alness.

26 Dun Mor   NH 512471: OS26*

While the dun itself is badly mutilated the outworks of double ramparts and ditches are well preserved. There is a cup marked stone on the inner side of the north arc of the inner rampart.

27 James's Temple, Drumderfit   NH 660521: OS26

A heavily overgrown dun.

On the west coast

The dun within the earlier fort on Dun Lagaigh is described above. At Eilean Donan Castle, until the 1920s, there were traces of an earlier vitrified fortification.

28 An Dun   NG 802753: OS19*

Near Gairloch. The dun on the headland of An Ard is on a narrow rocky promontory with good natural defences. The approach is by a narrow and rocky path from the shore and from this side the dun is protected by two walls, with a small enclosed area between them. The inner area, beyond the second wall, is small. This is said to have become a stronghold of the Macbeaths and then of the Macleods.

29 Strathcanaird   NC 165019: OS15*

Severely robbed so that no useful plan can be made.

30 Dunan, Poolewe   NG 863833: OS19*

This dun incorporates natural cliffs in its defence with an entrance reached over stepping-stones and a narrow isthmus.

31 Sgurr Mor, Balmacara   NG 828277: OS33*

A dun on a spur projecting from a steep hill slope.

32 Nostie, Auchtertye   NG 851277: OS33*

An oval dun measuring 23 m × 13 m.

33 Dunan Diarmid   NG 939207: OS33*

An oval dun enclosing an area 17 m × 7.5 m on the summit of an isolated rocky knoll on a little promontory.

34 Torran a'Bharraidh   NG 884229: OS33*

On west shore of Loch Duich with a defensive wall on one side of a steep-sided knoll.

35 An Dun, Bernera   NG 824198: OS33*

Thoroughly robbed of stone.

36 Caisteal Mhicleod, Glenelg   NG 815202: OS33

A galleried D-shaped dun on the edge of a precipice behind Galldar, using the cliffs as part of its defences.

37 Am Baghan   G 821207: OS33*

A dun 20.5 m × 22.5 m on the summit of a knoll.

38 Dun Grugaig, Glen Elg   NH 852159: OS33*

A galleried dun sited on the side of a narrow and steep-sided gorge. A wall over 4 m thick and still standing to a height of almost 2.5 m encloses a D-shaped area. There are traces of chambers within the wall and of an entrance passage with door-checks and a bar-hole.

39 Bards Castle   NG 898279: OS33

A timber-laced and vitrified dun.

CENTRAL ROSS

40 Creag Ruadh   NH 287535: OS25*

In Glen Meig. An oval dun on a rocky spur.

41 Carnoch   NH 252507: OS25

A galleried dun.

CRANNOGS

There are crannogs in the following lochs, some of which continued in use until a late date. The crannog at Redcastle has been recently excavated, revealing evidence of Iron Age occupation.

42 Loch Kernsary NG 882803: OS19*

Near Poolewe.

43 Loch Tollaidh NG 842797: OS19

Later a Macbeath stronghold and subsequently held by the Macleods.

44 Loch Achilty NH 431564: OS26*

Later a Mackenzie stronghold.

45 Kinellan NH 473578: OS26*

Later a Mackenzie stronghold.

46 Redcastle NH 586489: OS26

Currently the subject of archaeological investigation. This has revealed a series of wicker-lined pits which may have been used for soaking animal skins or salting meat – or may have a different function. Over this is a structure of interlocking wooden beams. Water levels have risen in this area and this may originally have been closer to shore or even a quay for log boats. There is no causeway between the crannog and the present coastline.

47 Loch Achaidh NG 811309: OS24

48 Loch Beannachan NH 243508: OS25

183 m from the shore only visible when water is low.

MISCELLANEOUS

49 Easter Rarichie NH 841736: OS21*

A fortified homestead which may have been occupied at later dates.

50 Tarradale NH 548485: OS21

The presumed Roman camp at Tarradale is apparent only from aerial photography. The remains are of a timber box rampart and a corner tower.

GAZETTEER 6: PICTISH SCULPTURED STONES AND EARLY CHRISTIAN SITES

The most useful distinction in considering sculptured Pictish stones is between those with Pictish symbols only (Class I) and those with Christian crosses or other iconography, whether or not combined with a continued use of Pictish symbolism (Class II and Class III).

CLASS I PICTISH SYMBOL STONES

At or near their original sites:

1 Eagle Stone, Strathpeffer   NH 485585: OS26*

Follow signs from the main street. The upright slab is carved with a horseshoe shape and a realistic eagle with detailed feathers, beak and talons. The Gaelic name for the stone is *Clach Tiompan* ('sounding stone'). Stone gongs or ringing rocks are known in many ancient cultures and were used by some early Christian communities before the introduction of bells.

2 St Clement's Dingwall   NH 549589: OS26

At the gate of the kirkyard. In addition to double-disc, crescent, circle, Z- and V-rods this stone has six cup marks, indicating that it is a stone of an earlier period re-used by the Picts.

3 Edderton   NH 708850: OS21*

In a field on the minor road to Ardmore. A tall 3 m Bronze Age pillar later carved at the top with a fish and below a double disc and Z-rod, set vertically to fit on to the narrow stone. The carving, particularly of the fish, is worn and is best seen in early light.

4 Clach a'Mheirleich   NH 681690: OS21*

In a field near old Rosskeen parish church. A Bronze Age pillar, 1.8 m high, later incised with a crescent and what is possibly a pair of tongs. The name means 'the thief's stone'.

5 Londubh   NG 860809: OS19

Near Poolewe. A stone later used as a grave slab with part of a crescent and V-rod.

IN MUSEUMS

6 Ardross Stone

Two fragments carved with a powerful wolf and a non-realistic but gentle and elegant Pictish beast are displayed in Inverness Museum (Castle Wynd, Inverness).

7 Torgorm   NH 559549

A fragment of the Class I stone, carved with two double-disc and Z-rod symbols, is in Inverness Museum.

8 Nonikiln   NH 662712

A symbol stone found here was lost but a copy had been lodged with the National Museums of Scotland.

9 Gairloch

A symbol stone found in the area, carved with an eagle and salmon, is on display at Gairloch Museum.

PICTISH CROSS SLABS

The high quality of the craft exercised in these sculptures should be seen in the context of other skills, such as metal-working and the production of illuminated manuscripts, whose products have not survived in the area.

Essential Viewing

10 The Nigg Stone   *NH 804717: OS21*

In Nigg Old Church, open during the summer months. This magnificent cross slab, which stood outside the church, has been moved inside for protection. It has also been cleaned and repaired. The side carved with an ornamented cross has, at the top, the figures of St Paul and St Anthony on the desert. Between them is a raven, which was said to have fed St Paul – there is a piece of bread in its beak – and two animals which may be lions. The cross itself is carved with key-pattern and interlace and surrounded by bosses around which are entwined the bodies of snakes. The back of the stone is carved with an eagle and, in a worn section, representations of David as shepherd, warrior, king and musician. The harp shown has been reconstructed and can be seen, and played, at Groam House Museum. Part of the missing section of the stone, carved with a mythical 'Pictish beast', has recently been found.

11 Shandwick   NH 855747: OS21*

In a field beside the road south-west of Shandwick, now protected within a glass box. This stone, known as the *Clach a'Charridh* is one of the most impressive of Pictish monuments. It fell in a storm in 1846, broke and was re-erected. The side towards the sea is carved with a cross consisting of bosses decorated with interlocking spirals. Below the arms of the cross are two angels and, on either side of the shaft, are beasts, snakes and interlacing creatures. The other side is divided into five panels carved, from top to bottom, as follows: double-disc; Pictish beast and other animals; men on horseback, a man with a drinking horn, a deer hunt, two armed men fighting and a kneeling man with a crossbow shooting at a stag; and, finally, a partly hidden pattern of interlocking spirals.

12 Hilton of Cadboll   NH 873768: OS21

The cross from the chapel site is now in the National Museum of Scotland. It is notable for its hunting scene.

13 Rosemarkie   NH 737576: OS27

Rosemarkie has an ornate cross slab, which had been built into the floor of the church but is now in Groam House Museum, and fragments of fourteen other stones. The cross, 2.6 m high, has its top, and possibly bottom, missing. There are crosses carved on both sides but they are smaller than on the Nigg, Shandwick and Cadboll stones, and it has instead a remarkable display of Pictish symbols – three crescent and V-rods, a double-disc and Z-rod, comb and two mirrors. The triple crescent and V-rod is unique.

In addition to the other fragments from Rosemarkie, the museum has copies of other Pictish carvings and much reference material.

FIGURE 13. *Nigg cross slab (front) with sculpture partly incised and partly in relief*

FIGURE 14. *Nigg cross slab (back) with sculpture partly incised and partly in relief*

14 Tarbat   NH 914840: OS21

See below Gazetteer 6:21.

15 Edderton   NH 719842: OS21

In the kirkyard of Edderton old parish church, beside the old
A9, with easy parking. The slab is carved with crosses on both
sides. On the east a simple cross is set above a curved frame in
which is an unarmed rider on horseback; below, and partly
hidden, are two riders with shields, spears and swords. The
west face has a large ring cross on a tall stem. Three fragments
from another cross slab have been recovered from the kirkyard
and are held by Highland Council's Museums Service.

16 Applecross   NG 713458: OS24

See below.

EARLY CHRISTIAN SITES

Essential Viewing

17 Site of the monastery of Applecross
                         NG 713458: OS24*

*The importance of the site is not so much in what can be
seen as in its significance since this was, like Iona, a cradle
of Christianity in Scotland and, after Columba, Maelrubha
is the early saint most widely commemorated in church
dedications and place-names. The best way to approach
Applecross is by the spectacular winding road from Kishorn
over the high pass of Bealach nam Bo ('The Pass of the
Cattle'). Until recently this was the only way to reach the
settlement and it is still a reminder of the difficulties of
overland travel and of the importance of sea routes in the
west. Although the sea was in a sense a highway, journeys
could be dangerous, and in AD 737 Maelrubha's successor,
Failbe mac Guaire, was shipwrecked off Applecross and
drowned with twenty-two companions.*

*The present church on the site was built in 1817 and
remains of its predecessor, possibly from the fifteenth century,
stand nearby. In the kirkyard note the traces of the wall*

which surrounded the circular monastic settlement. There
were once more extensive remains of the enclosing wall as
shown on the map below.

A wider area around the monastery was a girth – a place
of sanctuary – whose bounds were marked by crosses, one of
which survived until the late nineteenth century, when it
succumbed to the hammer of a puritanical mason.

Inside the church are three fragments of carved stones.
The largest is part of a cross slab carved with whirling spirals
and, on the edge, interlace and the figure of a naked man,
possibly Adam ashamed of his nakedness after the Fall. The

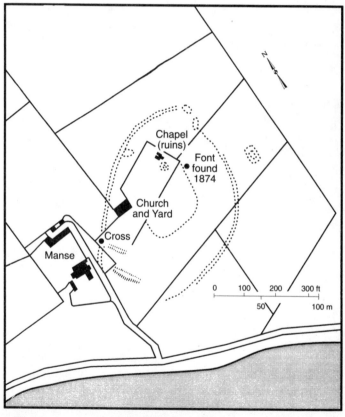

FIGURE 15. *Applecross Churchyard – details of early seventh-century
enclosure from ground and aerial surveys*

decoration is similar to that in illuminated gospels of the period. Two other pieces, with interlace, also come from cross slabs. At the entrance to the kirkyard is a stone, almost 3 m high, simply carved with the outline of a large, plain ringed cross.

It is likely that the monastery was abandoned c.AD 800 after a series of Viking raids. The office of hereditary abbot remained with a local family and the 1st Earl of Ross, Farquhar Mactaggart (i.e. Farquhar, 'son of the priest') is said to have stemmed from this line, though there is no firm evidence for this.

There was clearly an active Pictish Christian church in Easter Ross and the Black Isle, with sculptured stones of the highest quality found on several sites. It is not clear which place was the centre of this culture or, indeed, if it had a single centre.

18 Rosemarkie   NH 737576: OS27

The church of Rosemarkie later emerged as the cathedral of the diocese of Ross, perhaps because of some earlier pre-eminence

19 St Duthac's, Tain   NH 78 82: OS21

Duthac of Tain may be an early Christian saint and his shrine may pre-date the eleventh century.

20 Old Fearn   NH 63 87: OS21

The monastery established here in the thirteenth century may have been a development of some earlier community.

Essential viewing

21 Tarbat   NH 914840: OS21

Like Rosemarkie, Tarbat may be a Pictish monastic settlement. The area around the redundant eighteenth-century church is the focus of continuing archaeological investigation by the University of York. The importance of Tarbat lies in what these excavations may reveal. The site is

open to the public during the summer months and will be developed as a permanent interpretive centre.

To date (1999), aerial photography and excavations have revealed an extensive area surrounded by a ditch, which has been dated by radiocarbon analysis to the second to the fourth century. Within the enclosure are remains of what appears to be a large oval house site, probably of the same date, offering the possibility of insights into this little known period of local and Scottish history.

The evidence for this being a later Pictish monastic site lies with the many fragments of Pictish Christian sculpture recovered over the past 100 years. The most recent was found built into the stone work of the pre-Reformation crypt below the church. Pieces of a Pictish cross which once stood in the kirkyard are in the National Museums of Scotland (Edinburgh). Of particular importance is a stone with the only carved Latin inscription from Pictland: IN THE NAME OF JESUS CHRIST, THE CROSS OF CHRIST IN MEMORY OF REODATIUS . . .

The site is of special interest in the wide period it covers. The National Museums hold a hoard of Viking-period silver from the kirkyard wall – the only material remains of Norse settlement to be recovered in Ross and Cromarty – and recent excavation has uncovered what appears to be the medieval settlement of Tarbat, with evidence of extensive iron working.

22 Chapelton Point, Newhall   NH 708670: OS21

Recent excavations have revealed a Christian cemetery with burials dating from the tenth to the fourteenth century. No trace of a chapel has been found.

23 Isle Martin   NH 097989: OS19*

An early grave stone on Isle Martin may be of a similar date.

PLACE-NAME EVIDENCE FOR EARLY CHRISTIAN SITES

The map of dedications to Maelrubha and Donnan identifies what are probably early Christian sites. These, though not necessarily founded by the saints themselves, are likely to be associated with their followers. Since the reputations of Maelrubha and Donnan within Pictland were later eclipsed by Columba, it is unlikely that churches of a significantly later date would have such dedications.

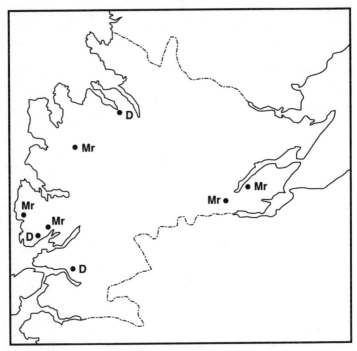

DONNAN AND MAELRUBHA – DISTRIBUTION OF
CHURCH DEDICATIONS AND PLACE-NAMES

D = Donnan; Mr = Maelrubha

The place-name element *annaid* may indicate an early church site:

24 Annat, Nigg   NH 827704: OS21
Near here is *Port an Druidh* ('the druid's port' – not *Port an Righ*, 'the king's port').

25 Annat, Strathconon   NH 35 54: OS26
On the south shore of Loch Meig.

26 Annat, Contin   NH 287530: OS25

27 Annat, Lochcarron   OS25
Named in census returns in 1841. On the opposite shore of
the loch to Lochcarron but not otherwise identifiable.

28 Annat, Torridon   NG 898546: OS24
This site has an old cemetery which suggests a church site,
although no visible traces remain.

29 Annat, Lochbroom   NH 078909: OS19
On the north side of the Scoraig peninsula and possibly
associated with the early church site of Kildonan on the south
side.

30 Camas na h-Annait   NG 698348: OS24
On the island of Crowlin, off Applecross.

The place-name element *neimhidh* suggests a pre-Christian
sacred grove:

31 Daluavie   NH 646735: OS21

32 Cnocnavie   NH 66 71: OS21

33 Inchnavie   NH 65 73: OS21

34 Navity   NH 78 64: OS21

EVIDENCE OF NORSE SETTLEMENT

There are numerous place-names containing Norse elements,
but it is those derived from *bólstadr* (farmstead), which most
clearly indicates Norse settlement. These are found at **Arboll**
(NH 878820: OS21) in Tarbat parish, **Cadboll** (NH 879776:
OS21) in Fearn parish, **Culbo** (NH 638605: OS21) in Resolis
parish and, possibly, on the west coast in the name **Ullapool**.
The Norse *thingvollr* ('assembly place') at Dingwall was
probably at Greenhill.

GAZETTEER 7:
CASTLES AND FORTIFIED HOUSES

Because buildings were adapted and extended the gazetteer covers a wider period than 1100–1600. Church sites, including the important medieval religious foundations of Fearn, Tain and Chanonry, are described in a later section, which also identifies links between the landed families and particular parish churches. The medieval royal burghs (Dingwall, Cromarty, Tain and Fortrose) are also described in later sections (Gazetteer 23: 1-4).

EARLY MEDIEVAL CASTLES AND CASTLE SITES

1 Site of Eddirdowyr (Tarradale/Redcastle)
NH 553487: OS26

The castle of Eddirdowyr, fortified by William the Lion in 1179, was almost certainly well to the west of the later Redcastle. There are no substantial remains but there are traces of a motehill earthwork above the narrowest part of the firth, a suitable ferry crossing. The castle was one of the strongholds of the Lordship of Ardmeanach (the 'middle height' – probably an early name for the Black Isle). It reverted to the crown in 1455, along with Ormond Castle.

2 Site of Dunskaith   NH 807689: OS21*

This castle, also fortified by William the Lion in 1179, is a promontory earthwork on the side of the North Sutor overlooking the Cromarty Firth. It is protected on the landward side by a ditch and there are traces of defensive banks. The site is disfigured by remains of First World War gun emplacements, but still impresses by the site's commanding view over the firth and out to sea.

Essential viewing
3 *Site of Ormond Castle*   *NH 696536: OS26**
Within easy walking distance of Avoch. Park at west end, take side road and then Craigton farm road. The path to the castle starts from just before the farm itself. The site of

the castle has recently been cleared of trees and it is once more possible to gain an impression of its commanding position. A deep well cut into the rock survives and care should be taken since the water is over 2 m deep and is, at the time of writing, uncovered.

Ormond Castle was held by the de Moravias, passing to the Douglas family until their forfeiture in 1455. Andrew de Moravia was the principal commander of Scottish forces in the north during the Wars of Independence, and he is commemorated by a cairn and plaque at the castle site (erected by the Scottish Patriot Movement in 1980). It was a substantial castle with a double system of curtain walls around the summit, creating two outer and an inner courtyard (c.47 m × c.30 m) with towers and buildings. There is no evidence that it was occupied after it became crown property in 1455.

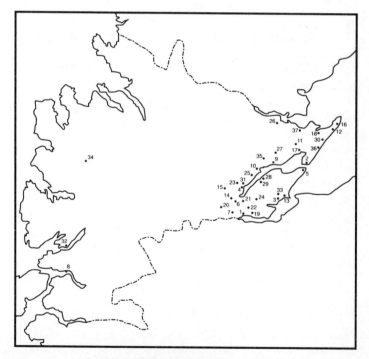

CASTLES AND FORTIFIED HOUSES

4 Site of Dingwall Castle   NH 553590: OS26

The site is now occupied by a private house. This was originally a royal castle and subsequently a principal centre of the earldom of Ross, reverting to the crown in 1476. It occupied a low-lying site beside the River Peffery, surrounded by a wet ditch connected to the river. Part of a ditch survives and there are traces of medieval masonry and a vaulted underground chamber. The tower-like building on Castle Street is a doocot (dovecote).

5 Cromarty Castle   NH 792691: OS21

The royal castle was built in the thirteenth century, and in 1470, permission to erect a stone castle was granted to the Urquharts, who were hereditary sheriffs. Plans drawn in the eighteenth century show it to have been a very substantial L-plan tower, more sophisticated than any surviving late medieval structure in the area. It was extended in 1643 but demolished in 1770 and replaced by Cromarty House, slightly to the east of the castle site. The only remains of the castle are a bottle well 2.7 m deep in the grounds of Cromarty House and two carved stones (the Kinbeachie stone in the National Museums of Scotland and a sixteenth-century stone now in Cromarty House). It is possible that the original castle was where the later Chapel of St Regulus was built (NH 795671) – a site with much better natural defences.

6 David's Fort   NH 539533: OS26*

Near Conon Bridge, marked as 'homestead' on the OS map. Now in densely planted woodland and difficult to see the site well. This low earthwork (29 m × 26–30 m) is surrounded by a wet ditch (4.6 m deep) fed by water from a dam 100 m to the east. It is probably not a castle but a moated homestead, perhaps of the thirteenth century. If so, it is the most northerly recorded example of this type of structure.

7 Muir of Ord motte   NH 525498: OS26*

Marked as 'earthwork' on the OS map. This oval mound is now 4.7 m high and the flat top, measures 13 m × 7 m. It is surrounded by a ditch, originally fed by a watercourse, and there is a further outer defensive bank. Nothing more is known of its history but it probably dates from the twelfth or thirteenth century.

Essential viewing

8 *Eilean Donan*   *NG 881258: OS33**

At the head of Loch Duich, just S of Dornie. Open to the public May to September.

   There were traces of vitrified stone at the site earlier in this century, indicating that it was a fortified site in the Iron Age. From the late thirteenth century it was held by the Mackenzies as constables for the Earls of Ross, but an attempt by the earl to repossess it in 1266 led to a crushing defeat. In preparation for a visit by royal officials in 1331, the severed heads of fifty convicted wrongdoers were displayed on the battlements. The Mackenzies lost possession at about this time, re-acquiring the castle in their own right sometime before 1509. It was occupied by a small Spanish garrison as part of an unsuccessful Jacobite rising, supported by the Mackenzies, in 1719 and shelled by three government frigates. After this it lay in ruins until restored between 1912 and 1932.

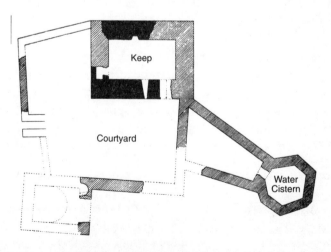

FIGURE 16. *Eilean Donan Castle – plan*

The main tower was built in the late fourteenth century, with its entrance on the first floor reached by external wooden stairs. The doorway was well-protected by wooden bars and an additional iron yett. On this level was the great hall with a large canopied fireplace and a wooden ceiling, supported by heavy timber beams. The ground floor was reached only by internal stairs. An unusual surviving structure in the courtyard, near the bridge, is a hexagonal cistern for storing rain water. The bridge linking the castle to the shore is modern, and it would originally have been accessible only from the water.

OTHER SITES

9 Teaninich   NH 659690: OS21*

Traces of a motte.

A number of other east coast castles, such as Foulis and Delny, have thirteenth-century origins but there are no remains from this period. On the west, at Dun Lagaigh (Gazetteer 6:9), there is a twelfth-century fort built with lime mortared masonry on an earlier dun. There is a suggestion that there may have been an early MacNicol, and later Macleod, castle in Ullapool's Castle Street. Flowerdale House replaced an earlier moated dwelling of uncertain date, but which is on record as being there in the sixteenth century.

LATER CASTLES AND FORTIFIED HOUSES

The simplest form of fortified house was a rectangular tower, often with the entrance on the first floor reached by wooden stairs or removable ladders. By the late sixteenth century the L-plan tower was common, now with a ground floor entrance and the stair to the first floor usually in the shorter arm of the L. A further development was the addition of square or round towers at opposing corners of the central tower, creating a Z-plan. An advantage of the Z-plan was that it allowed gunfire from defenders in the towers to cover all of the external walls of the central section. All these types of tower might be further defended by outer walls. From the early seventeenth century the need for a defensive structure became less, and many fortified houses were given more elegant additions, a process which continued in the following centuries, often obscuring the original form.

THE EARLS OF ROSS

The sparse remains of Dingwall Castle have been described above.

10 Delny   NH 734723: OS21

There was a residence of some kind here in the fifteenth century, and probably before, but nothing survives.

11 Site of Balconie Castle   NH 615660: OS21

This was also an early Ross residence. Parts of an earlier structure were incorporated in a new building by Fraser of Inchcoulter in the early nineteenth century but the building was destroyed by fire and demolished in 1966. The rubble was used for the foundations of the Invergordon aluminium smelter.

ROSS OF BALNAGOWAN

12 Balnagowan   NH 762752: OS21*

No public access, but visible from the A9 when there are no leaves on surrounding trees. The castle, occupying a site protected on two sides by steep slopes running down to the Balnagowan River, is first recorded in 1490, but probably dates from earlier in that century. It was extended in 1593 and again in 1668 to make it an L-shaped building. A barn near the castle dates from c.1700. The original line of the Rosses of Balnagowan died out in 1711. Later owners transformed the building with substantial works in the 1760s and again from the 1810s to the 1840s. Balnagowan Castle has the distinction of having been considered part of the USA. In the early part of this century the owner, Sir Charles Ross, was pursued by the Inland Revenue for unpaid tax. He took up residence in the USA, had the castle declared a ward of the Delaware court, ordered the stars and stripes flown from the battlements and announced that any action by the Inland Revenue against it would be considered an act of war.

13 Little Tarrel   NH 910819: OS21*

A mid-sixteenth-century L-plan fortified house built by a branch of the Rosses of Balnagowan. Now restored, it retains many original features including a vaulted kitchen on the ground floor. Below the first floor window is a stone with the date 155(?) and the initials of Alexander Ross and his wife Elizabeth, for whom it was built.

THE MACKENZIES

At least two crannogs, at Kinellan and Achilty, were used as Mackenzie strongholds in the sixteenth century (Gazetteer 6:44, 45). There were also houses on natural islands in Loch Maree – on Eilean Ruairidh (NG 89 73: OS19) recorded in 1619 and possibly also on Eilean Sùbhainn (NG 92 72: OS19).

13 Site of Castle of Chanonry   NH 728568: OS27

Seaforth or Chanonry Castle, which stood at the corner of modern High Street and Church Street, was a fortified house built c.1500 by Bishop Fraser and acquired by the Mackenzies at the Reformation. It was extended by Colin Mackenzie after 1623 and he lived there 'in great state and very magnificently' until his death in 1633. The castle was besieged and taken by the covenanting General, John Middleton in 1646, and English troops were later garrisoned there. Some later building took place and a weathered stone built into the gable of a single storey warehouse in Station Road, with a worn coat of arms and the initials 'C B S' (Countess Barbara of Seafield) may be from the castle.

14 Site of Brahan castle   NH 511545: OS26

This castle, built in the seventeenth century, became the seat of the earls of Seaforth, the principal line of the Mackenzies. The original tower house was extended and remodelled in the eighteenth and nineteenth centuries but later demolished.

Some fragments of masonry lie near the farm buildings and stables. It was described in 1808 as an 'awkward and ugly mass of building', but its great hall was apparently notable.

15 Castle Leod   NH 486593: OS26*

Occasionally open to public. The castle was built for Sir Rorie Mackenzie, founder of the Tarbat branch of the Mackenzie family, on land acquired in 1585. Sir Rorie married a Macleod heiress in 1605 and had gained royal favour by being active in imposing authority in the west. He was also tutor (guardian) to the young chief of Kintail in the 1610s. His character was recorded by a Gaelic saying to the effect that there were three

FIGURE 17. *Castle Leod – view from the north-east* c. *1880*

things which brought disaster to the small farmer: frost at seed
time, mist at harvest . . . and the Tutor of Kintail.

The five-storey tower probably completed in 1616, a date
which appears carved above the dormer windows along
with the initials of Rorie Mackenzie and his wife, Margaret
Macleod. There were, however, additions soon afterwards with
the building of an elegant stair to the first floor. The castle
retains its original L-shape, although this is less pronounced
as a result of the seventeenth-century additions. In the first-
floor hall is an unusual painted fireplace lintel of the seventeenth century but the internal appearance is otherwise
predominantly Georgian. The grounds of Castle Leod include
some fine trees including sweet chestnuts planted in the
sixteenth century.

16 Ballone   NH 928837: OS21*

In private ownership but easily seen from the shore by parking
at Rockfield and taking the coastal path north. Ruined but in
the process of being restored.

The site of the castle was in the hands of Dunbar family
from the fifteenth century but the castle itself seems to date
from the late sixteenth. After a brief period in the hands of the
Munros of Meikle Tarrel it was acquired in 1623 by the

FIGURE 18. *Ballone Castle – view from the south-west c.1880*

FIGURE 19. *Ballone Castle – plans*

Mackenzies, who added the north-east range of buildings. The original building is Z-plan with a round tower at the north and a square tower at the south. The whole of the first floor of

FIGURE 20. *Ballone Castle – view from the north-east c. 1880*

the central portion is occupied by the great hall, with service stairs running down to the kitchens and cellars below. The tower is well protected with plentiful gun-loops, splayed so as to allow a wide angle of fire. The castle was abandoned as the Mackenzies moved on to build more elegant houses and was ruinous by the eighteenth century.

17 Site of Milton castle   NH 772737: OS21

Like Ballone, this castle was acquired by the Mackenzies from the Munros. It had been burned in 1642 by a fire started in a jackdaws nest in a chimney and, although bought by George Mackenzie in 1656, it was soon abandoned and replaced by a mansion house at nearby New Tarbat (Gazetteer 14:1). No traces remain – though the ruins of an icehouse are sometimes mistaken for part of the castle.

18 Site of Lochslin castle   NH 849806: OS21*

This sixteenth-century castle, first mentioned in 1590, was built by the Vasses of Lochslin, who had held the land from the previous century but were declared rebels in 1603. It passed

FIGURE 21. *Redcastle – view from the south c.1880*

to Munros and then to Cuthbert of Drakies before being acquired by the Mackenzies of Allangrange in 1624. It was a L-plan tower, similar to Castle Leod, with the kitchen on the ground floor. The ruins stood by the side of Loch Eye until the last part fell in 1953.

19 Redcastle
NH 586495: OS26

In dangerous condition and so surrounded by a high chain-link fence.

The twelfth-century castle of Eddirdowyr was sited farther west and the move to this site may have taken place after 1455, when it reverted to the crown as part of the Lordship of Ardmeanach. It was acquired by the Mackenzies in 1623. The later site is in a commanding position and well protected on the edge of a ravine. The building is an L-plan sixteenth and seventeenth century tower with extensive later additions and alterations. It was inhabited until the present century.

20 Fairburn Tower
NH 469524: OS26*

FIGURE 22. *Fairburn Tower – view from the south-east* c. *1880*

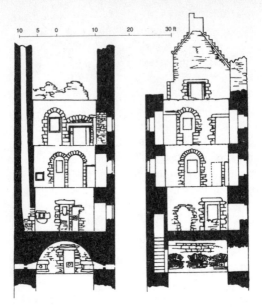

FIGURE 23. *Fairburn Tower – section*

Built shortly after 1542 for a Murdoch Mackenzie, the plain tower is striking because although five storeys high it is only 8.2 m × 7.9 m square. The entrance was on the first floor, originally with a wooden stair or ladder but replaced by a stair tower in the seventeenth century. The ground floor is vaulted and had no external access when built. There are remains of a single storey, cruck-framed kitchen annexe.

21 Kinkell Castle   NH 554544: OS26*

Private house. Restored from ruin in 1969–70.

A Z-plan tower, once known as Kinkell Clarsach, built around 1590 for Mackenzie of Gairloch. The central section was probably originally one floor higher, lowered in the 1770s when additions (removed during recent restoration) were made. The building is now of three storeys. It is well protected with numerous gunloops and notable features include a fireplace lintel with the date 1594 and, above the door in the stairtower, an empty frame for an armorial panel.

FIGURE 24. *Kinkell – view from the south-west* c.*1880*

22 Kilcoy   NH 576512: OS26*

Private house.

A four-storey Z-plan tower built shortly after 1618, restored in 1890, by which date it was very ruinous, and again in 1968. Many original features survive including carved dormer heads

FIGURE 25. *Kilcoy Castle – view from the south-west* c.*1880*

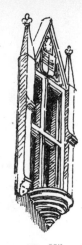

FIGURE 26. *Kilcoy Castle – plans*

FIGURE 27. *Kilcoy Castle – enlarged view of dormer*

above a number of windows and a fine fireplace lintel, dated 1679, with harp-playing mermaids, commemorating the marriages of three successive Kilcoy lairds. In 1687 Rorie Mackenzie, a son of the last marriage commemorated, attacked

FIGURE 28. *Kilcoy Castle – view in hall c.1880*

FIGURE 29. *Kilcoy Castle – view from the north-east* c.*1880*

the castle with a hundred armed men and imprisoned his mother, holding her until she was freed by the Sheriff of Ross.

23 Dochmaluag   NH 521601: OS20

A seventeenth-century L-plan tower formerly of three storeys, of which only ruins remain, with a date stone inscribed 1687.

24 Tore   NH 61 54: OS26

There was a Mackenzie house or castle at Tore, shown on maps of the 1720s and 1790s, probably north of Mains of Tore. It was owned by the same family as nearby Belmaduthy and probably allowed to decay since they required only one residence.

THE MUNROS

Milton Castle (NH 772737) noted above, was built by the Munros in the face of strong opposition from the Rosses of Balnagowan.

25 Foulis Castle   NH 589641: OS21*

Private house occasionally open to the public. For details contact Foulis Estate Office. The Munros held Foulis from the thirteenth century and there would probably have been an early castle of which no trace remains. The present castle was extensively remodelled from the 1740s but there are earlier features within the building. A vaulted chamber with gunloops in one of the courtyard buildings is probably of the sixteenth century, and there are features of a similar date incorporated in the basement and in the rear walls. The high walls which surround the courtyard date from 1792 and the front and internal arrangements are elegantly Georgian, with a gazebo projecting from the roof.

26 Meikle Daan   NH 689845: OS21

A late Munro house of 1680 on an earlier site. The door lintel, with this date and the initials A M and M F (Alexander Munro and Margaret Forrester), is matched by an ornate fireplace lintel with the same initials and date now in Balnagowan Castle. The building is of two storeys, with a rear projection containing an old stair.

27 Newmore   NH 680719: OS21*

Although ruinous this is the only Munro house to remain in its original form. The vaulted ground floor contained kitchens and cellars, with access to the hall on the first floor level (which does not survive) by a corner stair tower. The entrance is surrounded by gunloops and was designed to take an iron gate. The house probably dates from the late sixteenth century.

THE URQUHARTS

Cromarty Castle is described above.

28 Castle Craig   NH 631638: OS21*

A substantial tower built before 1551 on a small promontory on the Cromarty Firth, protected by steep drops to the shore on three sides and originally by a wall on the landward side, with gun loops, battlements and round towers. There are also gunloops in the tower, which is of four storeys with an elegant cornice, and a door in the gable on to what was a wooden parapet walk linking the corner turrets. The stone vaulting survives on each floor, with a large kitchen fireplace on the ground floor. A later extension to the west, with wooden floors,

FIGURE 30. *Castle Craig – view from the north-east* c.*1880*

has fallen. The early history of the castle is obscure, but it was in Urquhart hands from 1561, and marks the western boundary of the old sheriffdom of Cromarty. Nearby Cullicudden kirkyard has many fine fourteenth-century gravestones.

29 Site of Kinbeachie NH 628622: OS21*

Little remains of this fortified house of the Urquharts of Kinbeachie. A magnificent stone from Cromarty Castle, originally carved for Sir Thomas Urquhart of Cromarty, was re-used here as a chimneypiece. The Kinbeachie Stone is now in the National Museums of Scotland. The graves of the Kinbeachie Urquharts are in Cullicudden kirkyard.

OTHER

30 Cadboll NH 878776: OS21*

The castle is Z-plan with the main block of two storeys above a blocked basement, a round tower at the north-west and a bartizan at the south-east. A later stair tower, with a panel for a heraldic crest, was added at the north-west around 1600. The vaulted rooms show no signs of any fireplace. In the south-east corner of the walled garden are remains of another building, possibly medieval.

The lands of Cadboll were held in 1540 by the family of Innes and the castle was probably built for Innes or his predecessors, the MacCullochs. It was acquired in 1587 by the Sinclairs of Mey, in Caithness, who took up residence there after a dispute with the Earl of Caithness. In 1595 the eldest son, fourteen-year-old William Sinclair, shot and killed an Edinburgh baillie during a riot at the High School over the shortening of the school holidays. In 1616 the same William broke into the castle by scaling the walls at night with ladders – all this to drive out his mother who had the life-rent of the property.

It passed into the hands of Macleods c.1680, after which the adjoining Cadboll House was built. There are Macleod arms and crest on the west skewputts – that is, the bottom stones of the gable. There is also a re-used stone with Macleod arms and initials built into the wall of the garden. The castle appears to have continued in use for some time, since in 1770 the owner, Roderick Macleod, was noted for his extensive library and collection of coins kept in four vaulted rooms with arched roofs on two floors, two of the rooms pavemented with marble. Roderick Macleod also built the artificial 'mount' (10 m high) to the north of the castle and house.

31 Tulloch Castle   NH 547603: OS20

A tower built shortly after 1542 and extended around 1700. The original tower was square with a stair tower at the north-west corner. In the 1760s the estate was acquired by Henry Davidson of Tulloch, a prosperous London sugar merchant originating from Cromarty. He refashioned the castle and also built the folly, Caisteal Gorach ('Fool's Castle'), on the hill above, in 1790. Extensive grounds were laid out around the castle including, by 1827, a race course.

32 Strome Castle   NG 862354: OS24*

In the care of the National Trust for Scotland and open at all times. The castle on a rocky promontory consists of a rectangular hall with a tower at the east end. The castle was in existence by 1492, passed into the hands of the MacDonalds of

Glengarry and was destroyed by Kenneth Mackenzie of Kintail in 1602. This was part of a continuing feud, with the Mac-Donalds reputedly burning the church of Gilchrist, with its Mackenzie congregation inside, in 1603. Excavations at the castle in 1994 revealed the foundations of the tower and a well.

33 Arkendeith Tower   NH 696560: OS27

The remnant of a small tower house only 6 m square, probably of the sixteenth century. Only the vaulted basement survives.

34 Eilean Grudidh   NG 952693: OS19★

On an island on the west side of Loch Maree. Remains of a fifteenth or sixteenth-century castle, probably of the Macleods of Gairloch.

35 Contullich   NH 637705: OS21

Demolished in 1826 but a seventeenth-century door surround and window pediment were incorporated in later buildings.

36 Site of Old Shandwick Castle   NH 858742: OS21

Said to date from 1460. Removed in 1942 during construction of Second World War defences.

37 Site of Tain Castle   NH 781822: OS21

On Castle Brae, Tain. Nothing is known of what was probably a fortified town house.

GAZETTEER 8: BATTLE SITES

The following were decisive battles of some importance:

1 Mam Garvia, 1187

The site of the battle of Mam Garvia at which Donald Mac-William was defeated cannot be identified. It was probably on moorland somewhere to the north of Dingwall.

2 Site unknown, 1266

Defeat of the Earl of Ross by the MacIver, MacAuley, Mac-
Bollan and Talach clans, all allies of the Mackenzies.

3 Bealach nam Bròg, 1369   NH 421712: OS20

'The Pass of the Shoes', so called because the men hung their
shoes round their necks, dangling in front of them, to provide
some protection in place of shields. In this battle the Mackenzie
allies (Maclennans, MacIvers and Macleays) were finally
defeated by the earls of Ross and their supporters (Munros
and Dingwalls). There is a pipe tune associated with the conflict
which, if composed close to the time of the battle, is remarkably
old.

4 Ford of the Conon, 1481   NH 535541: OS26

Below Logie Wester church, allegedly the site of the defeat of
the army of Earl of Atholl and Alexander Mackenzie of Kintail
by Angus Og Macdonald.

5 Blar na Pairc, 1491

Possibly near Dingwall. Defeat of Alexander MacDonald of
Lochalsh.

There were numerous smaller skirmishes between feuding
clans including:

6 An Garbhaidh, 1596   NG 03 13: OS15

A battle between the Macleods of Lewis and the Macleods of
Coigach, towards the end of a thirty-year feud which ended
when the Mackenzies took over Macleod lands in Lewis.
Nearby Loch na Claidheichean is said to be named after the
swords thrown into the water after the battle.

7 Lochan an Fheidh, 1610

Defeat of Gairloch Macleods by Mackenzies.

GAZETTEER 9:
PRINCIPAL MEDIEVAL CHURCH SITES

Many parish churches are on the site of medieval buildings and incorporate fabric from this period. Details are included in a survey of church sites later in this chapter.

Essential Viewing
1 The Shrine of St Duthac, Tain

NH 781822: OS21

The history of Tain is intertwined with the shadowy figure of St Duthac (Duthus is the latinised form of the name), around whose shrine a sanctuary developed and whose relics were, by the fifteenth century, of sufficient importance to make this one of the principal places of pilgrimage in Scotland. It remains important as the only medieval church in Ross and Cromarty whose fabric is virtually complete.

Attempts have been made to identify Duthac of Tain with Dubhtach Albannach, who died at Armagh in 1065, but the evidence is inconclusive and the notion that relics were transferred from Armagh to Tain in 1263 is an invention of the nineteenth century. The historical Duthac – assuming that there was such a person – may have lived in any period from the seventh to the eleventh century. It is clear that the sanctuary was well established by 1306, when the wife and daughter of Robert Bruce sought refuge there. By 1439, it was a firmly held local tradition that as a result of its importance as a religious centre, the town's trading rights had been granted by Malcolm Canmore. Malcolm reigned 1058–1093, but the date of 1066, displayed at the entrances to Tain, is over-precise. It is equally clear that the shrine was of great personal importance to James IV, who visited it in most, if not every, years of his reign (1488–1513), the last time shortly before his death at Flodden. The saint's relics, which James and many others had venerated, included Duthac's head and breastbone, shirt, cup, bell and staff. They were all dispersed at the Reformation, and four girth crosses which marked the boundaries of the sanctuary around the town are now also lost. However, the town has three surviving medieval religious buildings.

On the links, between the town and the shore, is a ruined church (14m × 4m) with narrow windows, a door on the southern side and a broken stone bracket in the east wall, possibly for a statue. This may be the chapel which, in the time of James IV, housed a hermit.

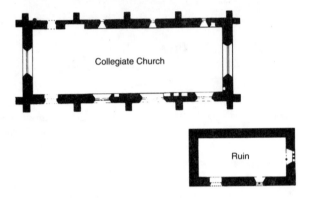

FIGURE 31. *St Duthus' Church – plan*

There is a second ruined building (10m × 5.5m) in the grounds of the larger collegiate church. This has a triple window in the east wall, above where the altar would have stood, and a double window in the south wall, both with checks for shutters. The door in the south wall dates from c.1450, and to the east of this doorway is the earliest stonework in any of the buildings, possibly from before 1200. It is not certain whether this, or the church by the shore, is the original parish church. In the kirkyard close to this building are three stone grave covers with coped (rounded) tops, which are likely to be of the thirteenth century or before.

The third and most important building is the collegiate church itself, probably completed by the 1460s. The tracery of the windows, although restored, is consistent with a date in the first half of the fifteenth century. On the south wall of the chancel is a triple sedilia (seat) and opposite this three aumbries (wall recesses), all checked for doors or grills. It has been suggested that the upper recess may have contained a relic, as indeed may the others. There are two piscina (water stoups) in the north and south walls. Other fittings from the medieval church include a tomb recess on the north wall and the gravestone of a priest. A number of external structures, including stairs, a porch and vestry, have been demolished, but traces of them remain in the masonry. An unusual survival is a statue of a bishop, probably Duthac, shown in the drawing below in a niche high on the west wall. It has now been moved to inside the church and a replica placed in the niche.

After the Reformation, the building served as the parish church for the burgh until 1815. During this period a series of lofts (galleries) were erected and the front of one survives, the Trades' Loft, decorated with the symbols of the incorporated trades of Tain. With some care the visitor should be able to match the emblems with weavers, cordiners (shoemakers), tailors, masons, carpenters and hammermen. The pulpit is a nineteenth-century replica but, if accurate, it suggests that the original may have been constructed from pieces of the medieval choir stalls and rood screen.

A new parish church was built in 1815 and the old collegiate church building lay derelict until restored, sensitively and to a high standard, by architects Andrew Maitland and

FIGURE 32. *St Duthus' Church – view from the south-east c. 1880*

*Robert Mathieson, in the 1860s and 1870s. The appeal for
funds for the restoration was on a non-sectarian basis with a
view to it being used for monumental purposes – a 'Ross-
shire Valhalla'. The gate lodge for this restored building now
houses* Tain Museum *which, with the collegiate church and
interpretive displays in another building within the grounds,
make up* Tain Through Time, *where more information
can be had on the buildings and on Tain's history.*

2 Fearn Abbey   NH 837773: OS21

The abbey of Fearn, the most northerly medieval religious
foundation in Scotland, was established in the 1220s by
Farquhar Mactaggart, 1st Earl of Ross. This was a house of
the Premonstratensian order, founded in 1120 in Prémontre
in the north of France, and its members were known from the
colour of their habits, as 'white canons'. The size of the original
community is not known, but later there were seven or eight
canons, all priests, ruled over by an abbot. There were five
other monasteries of white canons in Scotland, including
Whithorn, from where Farquhar Mactaggart brought both the
original members of the Fearn community and relics of St
Ninian. Fearn retained close links with Whithorn until the

FIGURE 33. *Fearn Abbey – view from the north-east* c.1880

Reformation, and the election of the abbot required Whithorn's approval.

The monastery's original location was farther north, in Edderton parish, but it was moved to this site after about fifteen years. It was substantially rebuilt between 1338 and 1372. Much of the building is lost, but it is still possible to see the canopied tomb and effigy of Abbot Finlay McFaed (d.1485) and the tomb of his successor, Abbot John. The original fittings of the church may have been impressive, since in 1485 the abbot bought an organ and other furnishings for the church from Flanders.

As with most religious houses, by the sixteenth century the principal revenues were diverted into private hands in the form of individuals appointed as commendators. Although commendators had usually taken some form of religious vows, they had no role in the religious community from which they derived their income. One of the last commendators of Fearn was Patrick Hamilton, a protestant burned for heresy at St Andrews in 1528. He is commemorated by a large memorial in the collegiate church of Tain – something of an irony, since his only connection with the area was his income from the lands of Fearn Abbey, an example of the very abuses to which, as a reformer, he was opposed.

FIGURE 34. *Fearn Abbey – monument to Abbot Finlay McFaed*

After the Reformation, the building was used as a parish church, with parts of the medieval structure adapted as burial aisles. In 1742 the roof of the church collapsed during a Sunday service, killing thirty-six people. Earlier in the day, according to a local tradition, a young woman had seen a mermaid wash bloodstained shirts in the waters of nearby Lochslin. The church was disused until 1772, when it was repaired. It continues in use as the parish church.

Essential viewing

3 Cathedral Church of St Peter and
St Boniface, Fortrose   NH 726565: OS27

The cathedral of Ross was moved from Rosemarkie c.1240 by Bishop Robert. Only two parts of the building remain, the south aisle and the chapter house, but the outline of the rest of the church, revealed by excavations in 1873, is marked out allowing the visitor to see the original ground plan.

The main structure of the original church consisted of a long choir and nave, 64 m long with no aisles or transepts. A sacristy, perhaps with a chapter house above, was on the north side. This was an ambitious building for the Highlands,

FIGURE 35. *Fortrose Cathedral – view from the south-east c.1880*

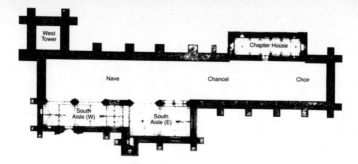

FIGURE 36. *General plan of Fortrose Cathedral*

much larger than the cathedral of Dornoch. It may have been complete by the end of the thirteenth century, or work may have been interrupted by the beginning of Wars of Independence in 1296. Since all of this building (except the sacristy) was later destroyed, the only clue to its appearance is in the small chapel of St John at Allangrange, the sole thirteenth-century church building in the area to survive in its original form (Gazetteer 9:4).

Construction began again in the late fourteenth century and the plans were adapted to include the remarkable south aisle, which was intended to provide a fitting setting for the commemoration of the church's chief benefactors, the earls of Ross. Although not completed until after 1420, its foundation can probably be attributed to Countess Euphemia (d. 1394) or her son, Earl Alexander (d. 1402). There is an irony in the fact that Countess Euphemia's second husband was Alexander Stewart, the 'Wolf of Badenoch', who ordered the burning of the great cathedral of Elgin in 1390.

Fortrose is one of the outstanding examples of late medieval architecture in Scotland. There is work of a similar date in the collegiate church of St Duthac at Tain, at Pluscarden Abbey and in Elgin Cathedral, all of which must have allowed for the development of a thriving tradition of mason work along the Moray Firth. Working in sandstone allowed them to create slender and complex traceries in the windows and fine detail in their carvings. The same skills are evident in the number of decorated fourteenth-century grave slabs in the kirkyards of Easter Ross and the Black Isle.

The masons at Fortrose adopted what was, at that time, a rather old-fashioned style, presumably in order to blend the new aisle with the existing cathedral nave and choir. A similar approach was taken at Pluscarden.

The south aisle is best considered as two distinct chapels, and it is possible that the narrower and lower west chapel was an afterthought. The east chapel has two tombs along the north side, the most easterly traditionally said to be the burial place of Countess Euphemia. The second tomb is that of a bishop (said to be Bishop Cairncross 1539–45, but there is no evidence for this). When opened in 1797, it was found to contain a crozier and robes. The ceiling of the west chapel is carved with two heraldic bosses; one is probably that of Earl Alexander and the other is of Bishop John Bulloch (1420–39). The tomb on the north side is late medieval and .

FIGURE 37. *Fortrose Cathedral – east end of south aisle*

FIGURE 38. *Fortrose Cathedral – west end of south aisle*

is traditionally said to be that of Bishop Fraser (1498–1507) – but again there is no evidence to confirm this. The cathedral was also the burial place of Alexander Macdonald, Earl of Ross and Lord of the Isles (d. 1449).

On the north side of the missing choir is the sacristy, which also served as a chapter house for meetings of the cathedral clergy. The vaulted room on the lower floor has stone seats backed by arches. This work is probably part of the original thirteenth-century cathedral. The upper floor, now reached by seventeenth-century external stairs (though originally by an internal staircase), was much altered in the late eighteenth century.

Use of the cathedral ended at the Reformation. The bishop's palace was occupied by Mackenzie of Kintail, and his brother occupied and strengthened the cathedral. The destruction of the building came in the 1650s when stone was taken to build the Cromwellian fort in Inverness known as the Citadel or 'Oliver's Fort'. The south aisle owes its survival to its having been adapted as the burial place of the Mackenzies of Seaforth and of Coul.

Like all cathedrals, that of Ross was governed by the bishop and a chapter of clergy (canons). The principal clergy (the dignitaries) were the chancellor, dean, treasurer and precentor, and the remainder were known as prebends (many had other titles such as archdeacon, sub-dean, chanter and sub-chanter). They were all supported by parish revenues (teinds) appropriated by the cathedral. At the time of the Reformation in 1560, the cathedral clergy in Fortrose consisted of the bishop, four dignitaries and twenty prebends, receiving income from thirty parish churches. The revenues of Avoch were appropriated to the Abbey of Kinloss, whose abbot was a canon of Fortrose. The remaining six parishes of the diocese were common, that is, their income was diverted to the cathedral clergy as a whole. The dignitaries and prebends, in addition to appointing poorly paid vicars to

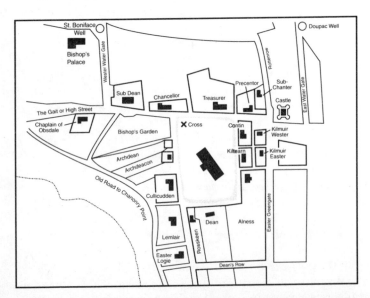

FIGURE 39. *Fortrose – plan of pre-Reformation cathedral and manses*

serve in the parishes, might absent themselves from the cathedral and appoint substitutes there as well.

The cathedral also received an income from lands throughout the diocese which had been given to support chaplains, whose role was to celebrate daily masses for the souls of the benefactors and their descendants. These endowments were known by the name of the lands which supported them, for example the Chaplainry of Fyrish. This sometimes leads to a confusion in local histories, with the assumption being made that there were chapels on these lands.

Each of the cathedral canons had a residence (a manse) in the grounds around the cathedral. This was the Canonry or Chanonry – a name often applied to Fortrose as a whole, since the town was originally a bishop's burgh, governed by the church. The prebends and their manses were named after the parishes from which they derived their principal income. It is possible to take a circular route through the streets surrounding the cathedral, passing the sites of many of the manses. It is not possible to identify the residences of all the canons, but the sites of sixteen of the twenty-five, together with the bishop's palace and the residence of the chaplain of Obsdale, are marked on the map above.

Although most of the buildings date from after the Reformation, there are some traces of earlier structures. In the garden of The Deanery, on the corner of Rose Street, there is a moulded panel for a coat of arms, possibly from the Manse of Rosskeen. Also on Rose Street is the moulded stone arched entrance to Angel Court and Rose Court. In the front doorway of St Katherine's, Union Street, are a skewputt (bottom stone of the gable) with the Burnett arms and a stone inscribed 'M R Burnett Ad 1558' – Master Robert Burnett occupied the manse of Contin.

4 St John's Chapel, Allangrange   NH 625514: OS26*

The thirteenth-century chapel of St John on private ground is contemporary with the first cathedral at Fortrose. Only the east gable, with a narrow triple window, and parts of the south and north walls remain. The Templars' Cross on top is a

Victorian addition, on the assumption that the chapel had a connection with the Knights Templar.

5 The first monastery of Fearn, Mid Fearn
NH 63 87: OS21

Na Claignean (NH 472898), meaning 'the skulls', above Amat Lodge is canvassed as a possible site for the first monastery of Fearn, since the place-names *Amat na h-eaglias* ('Amat of the church') and *Amot Abbott* are also found in Kincardine. This is, however, likely to be an area of highland ground, principally for grazing cattle, attached to the low-lying estate in the parish of Fearn known as the Abbacy – so the place-names suggest Amat belonging to the church or abbacy rather than the site of a church. A more likely site for the original abbey is in the parish of Edderton at Mid Fearn.

GAZETTEER 10: HOLY WELLS

Many wells have dedications to particular saints and were once associated with cures for particular illnesses. It is possible that some are pre-Christian sites which were given a Christian significance by the early Church. Some are still visited and the tradition continues of hanging clooties (cloths) at some wells. The following is a selective list of holy wells.

Essential Viewing

1 The Clootie Well, Hurdyhill   *NH 641537: OS26**

Dedicated to St Curidan. This is an eerie site and a vivid reminder of how folk traditions survive or are revived. It is located beside the A832 between Tore roundabout and Munlochy, and is unmistakable. The trees around the well are festooned with rags. In the 1870s it was recorded that there had been a tradition of leaving sick children here overnight – if they recovered it was attributed to the power of the well. There was, of course, no cure for death.

2 Craiguck Well   NH 679532: OS26

Another clootie well but less commonly used, on the north
shore of Munlochy Bay.

3 St Bainan's, Navity   NH 792651: OS21*

Below the site of the chapel dedicated to the saint. Used as a
clootie well until the nineteenth century.

4 St John the Baptist's Well, Knockfarril

NH 514588: OS26*

The feast of St John the Baptist (Johnsmass) being near to
midsummer's day often became a Christian substitute for
earlier midsummer festivals.

5 Tobar na Slainte, Shandwick   NH 855737: OS21

Meaning the well of health, is reached by a path along the shore.
The well, close to the high-water mark, is still cared for.

6 St Mary's Well, Tain   NH 776831: OS21*

Notable in being below the high-water mark and only exposed
when the tide falls.

7 Doupac Well   NH 726568: OS27

In Fortrose. The name a corruption of Duthac.

8 St Boniface   NH 724566: OS27

In Fortrose.

GAZETTEER 11: LATE MEDIEVAL STONE
CARVINGS IN KIRKYARDS

These stones should not be uncovered or disturbed, and this
listing is simply to indicate the extent of their use and survival.
Stones of this type are displayed inside Contin and Cromarty
churches.

1 Edderton   NH 719843: OS21

One stone recorded in 1911 but now buried.

2 Tarbat   NH 914840: OS21

One worn stone.

3 Urray   NH 507532: OS26

One fragment of a Gothic cross.

4 Kirkmichael   NH 705658: OS21

Four stones.

5 Urquhart   NH 649650: OS21

Five stones.

6 Cullicudden   NH 649650: OS21

Six stones.

7 Nigg   NH 880471: OS21

Two stones, one with carving not now visible.

8 Killearnan   NH 576495: OS26

One stone.

9 Contin   NH 456557: OS26

Three stones including two displayed in the church.

10 Kilmuir Wester   NH 676501: OS26

Several noted in 1904 but not now visible.

11 Cromarty   NH 791673: OS21

One now in the west porch of the church.

12 Avoch   NH 576495: OS26

Stones noted in nineteenth century.

13 Kiltearn   NH 576614: OS21

Stones noted in nineteenth century.

14 Rosskeen   NH 688692: OS21

One stone.

GAZETTEER 12:
PARISH CHURCHES (PRE-1800) AND
PRE-REFORMATION CHAPELS

The gazetteer is arranged according to the medieval parishes of the diocese of Ross, with indications where parishes were merged. Thirty-three parishes are described, with Kincardine lying outwith the scope of this guide and three parishes (Ardersier, Kilmorack, Convinth) disjoined from the diocese. The parish of Fearn was separated from Tarbat at the Reformation and its church is the monastery of Fearn, described above.

There are ruins in burial grounds which can be visited at most times (though some are in poor and, in some cases, dangerous condition) as follows: Tain (chapel/possibly early parish church on links), Alness, Kiltearn, Dingwall (but in dangerous condition and can be viewed only from outside),

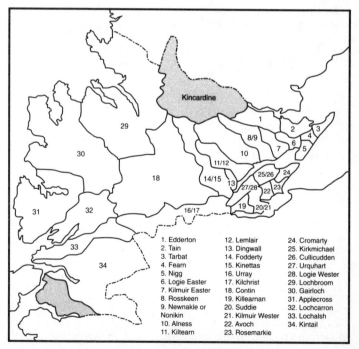

1. Edderton	12. Lemlair	24. Cromarty
2. Tain	13. Dingwall	25. Kirkmichael
3. Tarbat	14. Fodderty	26. Cullicudden
4. Fearn	15. Kinettas	27. Urquhart
5. Nigg	16. Urray	28. Logie Wester
6. Logie Easter	17. Kilchrist	29. Lochbroom
7. Kilmuir Easter	18. Contin	30. Gairloch
8. Rosskeen	19. Killearnan	31. Applecross
9. Newnakle or Nonikin	20. Suddie	32. Lochcarron
10. Alness	21. Kilmuir Wester	33. Lochalsh
11. Kiltearn	22. Avoch	34. Kintail
	23. Rosemarkie	

PARISHES OF THE DIOCESE OF ROSS

Suddie, Urray, Fodderty, Kilmuir Wester, Kirkmichael, Cullicudden, Urquhart, Rosskeen, Gairloch, Lochcarron (fenced off because of its condition), Kintail and Applecross. There are ruins on private ground at: Marybank Chapel (original Logie Easter parish church), Lemlair and Logie Wester.

The following are in use as parish churches: Fearn (open at regular times), Kilmuir Easter, Contin, Killearnan, Avoch, Rosemarkie and Lochbroom. The following are not in use for regular worship but are regularly open to public: Kincardine, Tarbat, Cromarty and Nigg. The following are disused and normally closed: Edderton, Rosskeen. Kilchrist has been converted to a mausoleum.

There are substantial eighteenth-century parish churches on new sites with associated manses in Urquhart, Resolis and Urray.

1 Parish of Edderton
Parish church   NH 719843: OS21

The site is medieval, or possibly earlier, given the Pictish cross in the kirkyard. The present church, which is disused, dates from 1743 and the attractive, low building has scarcely been altered since the eighteenth century. Ruins of a burial aisle with the date 1637, to east of present building, may be part of an earlier church. A carved Pictish stone stands in the kirkyard and fragments of another stone or stones have recently been recovered from another part. There is also a thirteenth-century carved stone, recorded in 1911, but the location is now uncertain. An unusual survival in this parish is a wooden preaching tent or booth used for preaching outdoors to the large congregations who gathered for communion services.

For the site of the first Abbey of Fearn *see* Gazetteer 8:2.

2 Parish of Tain

The medieval collegiate church and its associated buildings are described in Gazetteer 8:1. In the 1790s there were said to be remains of a chapel beside Lochslin and traces remain of a chapel at **Newton** (NH 845814: OS21*).

3 Parish of Tarbat
Parish church NH 914840: OS21

Dedicated to St Colman. The fabric of the church is mainly seventeenth and eighteenth century, including a combined belfry and doocot (dovecote), but much older remains and recent discoveries by archaeologists at the church make this one of the most interesting sites in the area – see Gazetteer 6:21.

There are a number of chapel sites in the Tarbat/Fearn area. At **Teampul Eraich** (NH 926834: OS21) on the shore below Ballone Castle is a single broken gravestone dated 1682 from a chapel and burial ground. There was a nearby well dedicated to St Mary. The site of the chapel at **Hilton of Cadboll** (NH 873768: OS21*) is in the care of Historic Scotland. The Hilton of Cadboll stone, a Pictish cross slab, was removed from here to the National Museum of Scotland. The remains of the chapel can be traced in the grass, and there is a broken font in what was the burial ground immediately to the north.

The chapel dedicated to St Barr at **Mid Geanies** (NH 897792: OS21) and the chapel of St Mary at **Cadboll** (NH 883791: OS21) near Cadboll Mount are well documented. There may also have been remains of chapels on **Chapel Hill** (NH 916845: OS21) at Portmahomack; at **Wester Arboll** (NH 864829: OS21) dedicated to St John the Baptist; and at **Alhansallach** (NH 92 84: OS21) dedicated to St Bride.

4 Parish of Fearn

The parish of Fearn was separated from Tarbat c.1625. Its parish church, the former monastery of Fearn, is described in Gazetteer 9:2. Other sites in the parish are included under Tarbat, above.

5 Parish of Nigg
Parish church NH 880471: OS21

The site is medieval, or earlier. The present church is no longer used for regular services but is well cared for by Nigg Old Trust and open to the public (details at entrance). A leaflet detailing its history is available. The present building dates from 1626, with substantial changes from the 1720s and the addition of a north aisle in the 1780s. The magnificent Pictish

Nigg stone is housed within the church (Gazetteer 6:10). The kirkyard has two very worn medieval grave slabs, probably fourteenth century, and some fine carving from the late seventeenth century. The mort bell (death-bell) from Nigg is preserved in Tain Museum.

On Nigg Hill, **Annat** (NH 827704: OS21) may be the site of an old church or land which belonged to the church at Nigg.

There was a chapel and graveyard at **Old Shandwick** (NH 858747: OS21) now destroyed but the walls were complete in the eighteenth century. A burial ground at **Shandwick** (NH 855747: OS21) around the Shandwick stone was ploughed *c.*1885 and there was an area known as the **Grave Field** (NH 842746: OS21) in the late eighteenth century, possibly the site of the Chapel of Culiss.

6 Parish of Logie Easter
Original parish church   NH 749761: OS21*

This ruin, on the site of the original parish church at Marybank on the side of the River Rory, has been disused since 1767. The earliest legible stone in its walled burial ground is dated 1593. The manse, built in 1759, is now Marybank Lodge. This was replaced by a later **parish church** (NH 777761: OS21) on top of a small hill and surrounded by a graveyard. This, too, is now disused.

7 Parish of Kilmuir Easter
Parish church   NH 757731: OS21

The church, still in use, was built in 1798 and incorporated the round tower of an earlier structure as a belfry and possibly retaining it as a useful navigation mark for vessels entering the firth. The upper part of the tower is dated 1616 but the lower part is much older. This older section is used as a burial vault for the earls of Cromartie and contains some remarkably well preserved painted seventeenth-century mural monuments. There is no public access to the vault.

There are ruins of a plain rectangular chapel at **Balnagowan** (NH 757759: OS21) and there was a chapel dedicated to the Virgin Mary at **Delny** (NH 734723: OS21). Both were probably endowed by the Rosses of Balnagowan.

8 Parish of Rosskeen
Parish church   NH 688692: OS21

The main building (1832) is disused and the ruins of a thirteenth- or fourteenth-century building, re-used as a burial aisle, stand in the kirkyard, which also has a grave slab with a calvary cross and longsword of similar date.

Obsdale may take its name from a medieval **hospital** (a lodging house for travellers, especially pilgrims) although there are no surviving records of hospitals in the diocese. Land at Obsdale later supported a chaplain in the cathedral of Ross.

Also within the parish is the **Covenanters' Memorial** (NH 665689: OS21) to the ministers Thomas Hog of Kiltearn, John McKillican of Alness and Hugh Anderson of Cromarty who were arrested after holding a conventicle at Obsdale. This memorial is on an old stretch of the A9, now within the perimeter of Dalmore Distillery but accessible.

9 Parish of Newnakle or Nonikiln (subsumed within Rosskeen parish)
Parish church   NH 662712: OS21*

All that remains is the west gable with a door and arched window, incorporated in later farm buildings. A Pictish stone was found on the site in the nineteenth century and, although the original was lost, a cast was presented to the National Museums of Scotland.

10 Parish of Alness
Parish church   NH 644690: OS21

The roofless T-plan church, on a medieval site, has a date stone on a skewputt (bottom stone of the gable) with 1775 and two stones marked 1625 at the base of the belfry. A blocked-up arched opening in the inside north-east wall is probably a medieval tomb-recess. The parish manse beside the church dates from 1797.

At **Kildermorie** (NH 522722: OS20*) at the head of Loch Muire, are the ruins of Cille Mhuire, a chapel (12.3 m × 5.5 m) dedicated to the Virgin Mary, with a cemetery attached. This was also known as the Chapel of Tollie, named after the lands which supported the chaplain. A stone font survives. Also in the parish is **Cladh Churadain** (NH 585673: OS21*). Little is visible of what may be an early chapel site dedicated to Curitan.

11 Parish of Kiltearn
Parish church   NH 576614: OS21

Much of the structure of this large roofless T-plan church is of the eighteenth century, reflecting the patronage of the Munros of Foulis, but it is built around an earlier medieval structure, parts of which are visible in the bare stonework. In the kirkyard is one possibly late medieval gravestone, but others were noted in the early nineteenth century: 'The old church yard had older tablets, grey and shaggy with the mosses and lichens of three centuries with battle axes and double handed swords' (Hugh Miller, *My Schools and Schoolmasters*, ch. XXV).

There are some visible remains of the Chapel of Wester Foulis at **Cnoc an Teampoill** (NH 588637: OS21*), and fragments of two well-carved grave slabs from this site are now in Foulis Castle. They are probably of the mid-seventeenth century, suggesting that the chapel was used as a burial place after it went out of use at the Reformation. There was reputedly a chapel of St Monan at Balconie and a chapel at Culnaskeath, but no trace remains of either.

12 Parish of Lemlair (subsumed within Kiltearn parish)
Parish church   NH 576614: OS21*

Dedicated to St Bride. Excavations in the 1960s at the ruined site (on private ground) revealed a font, part of an altar and arms of a decorated cross. The cemetery surrounding the site is suffering from coastal erosion.

Along the shore, nearer to Dingwall, was the site of the **Chapel at Kilchoan** (NH 563604: OS21) dedicated to St Congan, destroyed during the building of the railway.

13 Parish of Dingwall
Parish church NH 549589: OS26

Dedicated to the Virgin Mary and to St Clement. The present church, still in use, dates from around 1800. Part of the earlier church, re-used as a burial aisle, stands in the kirkyard. There is a fifteenth-century grave slab under the blocked south arch. The dedication of the church to St Clement may indicate a Norse influence. There is a Pictish symbol stone in the kirkyard (*see* Gazetteer 6:2).

There was a chapel dedicated to St Lawrence in or near the lost castle of Dingwall.

14 Parish of Fodderty
Parish church NH 513593: OS26

A few remains of the church can be seen in the burial ground. A **new parish church** (NH 502564: OS26) was built in the eighteenth century and has since been converted to a hotel, Kilvannie Manor.

An early chapel at **Inchrory** (NH 512596: OS26) by the River Peffery is lost.

15 Parish of Kinettas (subsumed within Fodderty parish)
Parish church NH 480581: OS26

Thought to have been within the surviving burial ground.

16 Parish of Urray
Original parish church NH 507532: OS26

The burial ground contains a fragment of a fourteenth-century Gothic cross. The nineteenth-century burial enclosure may incorporate stones from an earlier structure.

The later **parish church** (NH 509525: OS26), on a new site, dates from 1780, but there was a church on this site before that date. Nearby is the eighteenth-century manse with its crow-stepped barn, described in 1750 as 'the best in the synod'.

17 Parish of Kilchrist (subsumed within Urray parish)
Parish church NH 539492: OS26*

Marked as 'mausoleum' on the OS map. The seventeenth-century building, on a medieval site, incorporates earlier stonework including a pre-Reformation sacrament house in the north wall. It was adapted as a burial place for the Gillanders of Highfield family in 1870. There is no access to the inside of the building. The church was reputedly the site of a massacre of Mackenzies by Macdonalds of Glengarry in 1603. The Mackenzies were burned alive inside the church while the Macdonald piper marched around the building.

18　Parish of Contin
Parish church　　　　　　　　　NH 456557: OS26

Dedicated to St Maelrubha. The church, still in use, is on its original island site in the River Blackwater, but is easily accessible by a road bridge. The structure of the building is in part medieval and includes a medieval sacrament house (c.1490) and a tomb recess in the north wall. A carved fourteenth-century grave slab and a fragment of a wheel cross of similar date are preserved in the church and another wheel cross remains in the kirkyard. Also in the church is the parish mort bell (death-bell). The nearby manse dates from 1794.

Preas Mairi (NH 460558: OS26) is a private cemetery with remains of a neolithic burial cairn. Its name links it with St Maelrubha (Preas Ma-Ruibh), but there is no trace of a church building. At or near **Killin** (NH 399609: OS20) there is likely to have been a church dedicated to St Fionn and nearby Loch Garve is, in Gaelic, Loch Maol-Fhinn ('loch of the follower of St Fionn'). **Annat** (NH 287530: OS20) may be an early church site or church land.

19　Parish of Killearnan
Parish church　　　　　　　　　NH 576495: OS26

The church, rebuilt after 1800, is on a medieval site and incorporates earlier fabric, including a blocked arched doorway in the south wall. There is a recumbent medieval effigy inside and a calvary cross with an ornamental head, probably fourteenth century, immediately to the south of the church.

There was a chapel dedicated to St Andrew at or near Redcastle, and at Spittal there may have been a **hospital** (NH

54 50: OS26) for travellers, perhaps connected with the nearby medieval ferry crossing.

20 Parish of Suddie (joined with Kilmuir Wester in 1756 to form the parish of Knockbain)
Original parish church   NH 665547: OS26*

The east gable and part of north wall, with an aumbry, remain standing.

21 Parish of Kilmuir Wester (joined with Suddie in 1756 to form the parish of Knockbain)
Original parish church   NH 676501: OS26*

Dedicated to St Mary. The east and west gables, and some other low walls, survive. A number of carved stones, described as 'late Celtic' were recorded in the early part of this century but are not now visible. They are likely to be ornamental crosses of the fourteenth century, similar to those in a number of other kirkyards in the area. There is said to have been a chapel at Haudach or Haldach, in the parish.

The church of the united parish of **Knockbain** (NH 646522: OS26) was built in 1754, with an aisle added in 1816. It has been disused since 1933 and is now ruined.

22 Parish of Avoch
Parish church   NH 702552: OS27

The present church, still in use, is on a medieval site and the building incorporates a rare pre-Reformation sacrament house of c.1500. Early carved stones were noted in the kirkyard in the nineteenth century.

There was a chapel dedicated to the Virgin Mary at Ormond Castle (Gazetteer 7:3) and possibly a chapel and early burial ground at **Killen** (NH 672568: OS26). **Bennetsfield** (NH 678536: OS26), with a holy well below on the shore, may be associated with an early chapel.

23 Parish of Rosemarkie
Parish church   NH 738577: OS27

The church, rebuilt in 1735 and again in 1821, is on the site of the first cathedral of the diocese of Ross. During the first of these re-buildings, stone coffins were apparently found in a vault. The cathedral probably stood on or near the site of an earlier Christian community, as evidenced by the Rosemarkie cross slab in Groam House Museum. The cathedral was moved to Fortrose *c.*1240. After the Reformation, Fortrose and Rosemarkie had, for some time, separate ministers, but after *c.*1650 it was served by one. This continued until 1838, when a minister was appointed to Fortrose and a chapel of ease, later used as the town hall, was built (1839–41).

Rosemarkie is associated with an early saint known both as Curitan or Boniface. There is a further dedication to this saint west of Rosemarkie at Kincurdy (NH 73 58: OS27), which was described in 1436 as the chapel of St Boniface at 'Cuthyl Curitin'. The exact site is not identifiable.

24 Parish of Cromarty

Essential viewing

Parish church   *NH 791673: OS21*

Probably dedicated to St Mary. The present church dates substantially from the seventeenth century but incorporates medieval fabric. There is an aumbry at the east end of the south wall and a fourteenth-century carved grave slab in the west porch. The church was extended in 1739 with the addition of the north aisle, built with money from the poor fund. On the front of the gallery in this aisle are the initials of some of those who rented pews, and some of the pews themselves are made from sections of earlier painted pews. The laird's loft was built in the mid-eighteenth century to provide accommodation for the landowner, his family and servants. The church is open every day and a guide to the church and its history is available.

The roofless **Gaelic Chapel** (NH 788674: OS21) was built by the laird, George Ross, in 1784 to provide services for Gaelic speakers who had moved into the town from the surrounding parishes – and not, as is sometimes claimed, from the west coast. Another church, possibly of an early date, may have stood on the shore to the east of the town, on an area now eroded by the sea (NH 795673). Some remains were visible in the eighteenth century. (The 25″ OS map is in error in placing this church in front of Cromarty's Shore Street.)

Little remains of the fourteenth-century **Chapel of St Regulus** (NH 795671: OS21) except a few traces of walls and an underground vault, altered in the nineteenth century, but the setting and the fine carved stones of the late seventeenth and early eighteenth century make it worth a visit. At Navity is the site of the **Chapel of St Bainan** (NH 791651: OS21), incorrectly interpreted as St Bennet in the nineteenth century. On the shore below the site is St Bainan's Well, once visited as a holy well. A well, and possibly a chapel, dedicated to **St Duthac** (NH 779645: OS21) survived west of Navity until c.1800.

25 **Parish of Kirkmichael** (joined with Cullicudden in 1662 to form the parish of Resolis)
Original parish church   NH 705658: OS21*

Part of ruins of the early church were converted in the eighteenth century to a mausoleum for the family of Gordon of Newhall and Braelangwell, and later for the Munros of Poyntzfield. The verse epitaph on the memorial to William Gordon of Newhall is by the Scottish author Henry Mackenzie (1745–1831). A section of what is probably the original north wall of the medieval church runs west, projecting from the north-west corner of the mausoleum. There are a number of fourteenth-century grave slabs in the kirkyard, one with the symbol of a hammer beside an ornamented cross.

26 **Parish of Cullicudden** (joined with Kirkmichael in 1662 to form the parish of Resolis)
Parish church   NH 649650: OS21

It seems likely that this was the original parish church. The best preserved part is a south aisle with a date of 1609 marked above the door. There are a number of well preserved fourteenth-century grave slabs in the kirkyard and a later stone carved with a chalice and a pierced hand, a piece of Roman Catholic symbolism whose survival is unusual.

The site of the **Chapel of St Martin** (NH 645626: OS21) can be identified but nothing remains of the building or the burial ground which was ploughed up before 1825. A large annual fair was held here until 1641.

Resolis Church (NH 678655: OS21) was built in 1767 to serve the united parish. The nearby manse dates from 1830. This was the site of the Resolis Riot of 1843, when the congregation, having seceded to the Free Church, attempted to stop the induction of a new parish minister.

27 Parish of Urquhart
Original parish church   NH 581585: OS26*

The church is ruined but there are a number of fourteenth-century carved stones in the kirkyard, some fine late seventeenth-century carving and, most unusually, an early eighteenth-century stone with a carving of Christ crucified. The site was traditionally the place where St Maelrubha was martyred in 722 (this despite the fact that Maelrubha died in Applecross of old age in this year), and a chapel of oak reputedly stood on the site. The church stands within a large oval enclosure (80 m × 60 m), a feature sometimes taken to indicate an early Christian site. It was abandoned in 1795 when a **new parish church** (NH 578579: OS26) was built a mile to the west.

In the oak wood of Drumondreoch, to the south of the later parish church, is the **Ferintosh preaching site** (NH 581576: OS26) – an open-air amphitheatre used by the noted Gaelic preacher Rev. Dr John MacDonald between 1813 and 1849.

28 Parish of Logie Wester (subsumed within Urquhart parish)
Parish church   NH 535541: OS26

The ruins of the church are in a graveyard on a wooded knoll within the grounds of Conon House, above what was once a ford on the River Conon. A folktale tells of the appearance of a water wraith which prophesied a death by drowning. A man, who was determined to cross the Conon, was locked in the chapel by his friends to ensure his safety – but was found dead a few hours later. He had stumbled and drowned in the shallow water of the font.

29 Parish of Lochbroom
Parish church   NH 177846: OS20

The present church at Clachan at the head of Lochbroom, still in use, was built in 1817 on an earlier site. It is unusual in being still very much in its original state internally, with two long communion table pews running down the centre of the church.

A number of burial grounds in the parish are on the sites of earlier chapels, including **Ullapool** (NH 132942: OS19) and, on the Scoraig peninsula, **Kildonan** (NH 078911: OS19). There may have been a chapel in the burial ground at **Badenscallie** (NC 037062: OS15) near Achiltibuie.

30 Parish of Gairloch
Parish church   NG 804761: OS19

The church dates from 1792 with remains of a medieval church across the road in the burial ground.

There are remains of chapels at Laide (NG 902920: OS19*) and at Londubh (NG 860809: OS19), where the kirkyard has an incised Pictish symbol stone. The church at Londubh, measuring approx 12 m × 6 m, was converted to a burial aisle in 1689. There are also burials on **Isle Maree** (NG 93 72: OS19) in Loch Maree, where there was a well dedicated to St Maelrubha and a 'wishing tree' studded with coins. Two of the burials, in local legend associated with a Norwegian prince, are marked by stones carved with crosses which may be late medieval. The other graves may be of ironworkers. **Claod nan Sasganach** (NH 006569: OS19) near the end of Loch Maree is also said to be a place where English-speaking (though not necessarily English) ironworkers buried their dead.

31 Parish of Applecross
Parish church   NG 713458: OS24*

On the site of the monastery founded by Maelrubha in AD 673. Dates from 1817, with remains of an earlier church, possibly of the fifteenth century, in the kirkyard. The nearby Old Manse was built in 1796. For details of the early Christian site see Gazetteer 6:20.

At Torridon is **Annat** (NG 895545: OS24), with a cemetery which, together with the place-name, suggests an early chapel site.

32 Parish of Lochcarron
Parish church   NH 914414: OS25

The ruins of a church built in 1751 and known as the 'great church of Lochcarron' stand in a burial ground on or near the site of an early Christian church dedicated to St Maelrubha. To the east is a later church built in 1834, still with long communion tables.

At Kishorn is **Seipeil Dhonnáin** (NH 830406: OS24) an early chapel site dedicated to Donnan of Eigg.

33 Parish of Lochalsh
Parish church   NG 829272: OS33

On the east shore of Loch Alsh. The church was dedicated to St Congan (died *c.*600) and reputedly built by his nephew, St Felan. A newer building, now ruined, was erected in 1641.

34 Parish of Kintail
Original parish church   NG 947211: OS33*

Dedicated to St Duthac. The medieval church, at the head of Loch Duich, was shelled by Hanoverian ships during the abortive Jacobite rising in 1719. Although later repaired, it is now ruined. This is the traditional burial place of the chiefs of Clan Macrae.

There is a burial ground and early chapel site at **Cill Fhearchair** (NG 938187: OS33) with a standing stone; and possibly a lost **chapel site** (NH 906204: OS33). A church was built at **Glenshiel** (NG 933192: OS33) in 1758.

OTHER PARISHES

The parish of Kincardine now lies in Sutherland. Its parish church (NH 605894: OS21), now disused but recently restored, is on a medieval site, and there is an early chapel at Kilmachalmag (NH 503982: OS20). The parishes of Ardersier, Kilmorack and Convinth, and the priory of Beauly, were all at one time within the diocese of Ross.

GAZETTEER 13:
OTHER CHURCHES AND SITES

THE EVANGELICAL REVIVAL

A leading early force in the revival, credited with creating the body of lay spiritual leaders known as 'The Men', was Rev Thomas Hog of Kiltearn, commemorated by his burial stone at Kiltearn Church and by a nineteenth-century memorial in the collegiate church building in Tain.

The parish of Nigg was a centre of the evangelical revival of the mid-eighteenth century, a movement which led to most of the congregation seceding to form their own church. When the seceders' chapel near Ankerville was pulled down and the stone used to build Old Shandwick House (NH 798753: OS21), one of 'The Men' cursed the stones and the 'Curse of Shandwick' is still remembered in local folklore. The Secession congregation subsequently built their church at **Chapelhill** (NH 825736: OS21), but the present building dates from 1871.

Other secession congregations were formed in Evanton in 1824, where the chapel is now converted to housing, and at Tain in 1839, where the King Street chapel is still in use as a Free Presbyterian church.

Where the evangelical revival was contained within the established church it produced such notable figures as Rev. Dr John Macdonald of Ferintosh. In 1843, the inability of the established church to respond to the demands of the evangelical party led to the Disruption and the formation of the Free Church. Early Free Church buildings can be found as follows:

1 Urquhart and Ferintosh   NH 57 56: OS26

1843, notable and well worth visiting for the late nineteenth-century cast iron urinal in its grounds.

2 Castle Street, Dingwall   NH 55 58: OS26

1844, later converted to other uses and, more recently, gutted by fire.

3 Jemimaville   NH 72 65: OS21

1844, now a ruin on the shore behind the village.

4 Mill Street, Ullapool   NH 13 94: OS19

1844, now used as the Church of Scotland parish church.

5 Applecross   NG 71 41: OS24

1845, now used as the Church of Scotland parish church.

6 Lochcarron   NG 89 39: OS24

1846.

7 Achiltibuie   NC 01 09: OS15

1843, now with a corrugated iron roof.

8 Alness   NH 64 69: OS21

1843, now used by the Church of Scotland as the parish church.

9 Nigg   NH 80 72: OS21

1844, now Nigg village hall.

10 Innes Street, Plockton   NG 80 33: OS24

1845, now disused.

11 Maryburgh   NH 54 56: OS26

A mission church, built by the Mackenzies of Seaforth in 1840–41, was made over to the Free Church after the Disruption.

Before these churches were built a number of open-air preaching sites were used, such as:

12 Am Ploc   NG 894562: OS24

Near Plockton. Stone seats can still be seen.

Many parts of Easter Ross and the Black Isle were strongly episcopalian in the seventeenth century. Episcopalianism declined after presbyterian government of the Church of Scotland was established in 1690, but some congregations remained.

13 Episcopalian chapel   NH 525506: OS26

Muir of Ord. An eighteenth-century chapel nestling in a hollow, now converted to a private house (Ord Cottage).

14 Arpafeelie Church
NH 610505: OS26

Built in 1810–16 and extensively remodelled in 1876.

After the Reformation there were no Roman Catholic chapels within the area until the late nineteenth century.

In the early nineteenth century a number of churches were built with government funds to serve remote areas. These are known as parliamentary churches, and were built according to standard designs by Thomas Telford and William Thomson.

15 Ullapool
OS 19

1829. Now houses Ullapool Museum.

16 Plockton
OS 19

1827.

17 Poolewe
OS 19

1828.

18 Strathconon
OS 26

1830.

19 Kinlochluichart
OS 20

1825.

A parliamentary church in Shieldaig was destroyed by fire and replaced by a later building.

GAZETTEER 14:
LATER BATTLES AND MILITARY SITES

1 Battle of Glenshiel
NG 991133: OS33*

Fought on 10 June 1719. 300 Spaniards were defeated by government troops. The hill above is *Sgùrr na' Spainnteach* ('peak of the spaniards').

Essential Viewing

2 Bernera Barracks   *NG 815196: OS33**

Designed in 1718 and completed by 1723, the fort is rectangular (30 m × 37 m), with two projecting towers whose gun loops allowed the entrance to be protected by musket fire. One tower contains a bakehouse, the other a guardroom. The east wall of the enclosure has fallen but the west wall stands. On the north and south sides are identical three-storey barracks, roofless and without floors.

3 Langwell House   NH 174028: OS20

Ransacked by government troops in 1746 as part of the systematic terrorising of the west Highlands.

MILITARY ROADS

Military road building to link the Highland forts was carried out between 1724 and 1740 by General Wade, and from 1740 to 1767 by General Caulfield. The military road from Bernera follows, with occasional deviations, the line of the modern road through Glen More, over the Bealach Ratagain pass to Shiel Bridge and on through Glenshiel.

4 Little Garve Bridge   NH 396628: OS20

A two-arched hump-backed bridge built *c.*1762 under the direction of General Caulfield, as part of an incomplete military road along the north side of Loch Garve which was planned as a link between Contin and Poolewe.

GAZETTEER 15: MANSION HOUSES

This section describes the principal new mansion houses of the late seventeenth, eighteenth and early nineteenth centuries. A number of principal residences were earlier castles (described in the gazetteer of castles) which were enlarged and restored. Some earlier castles and fortified houses were demolished, fell into ruin or were incorporated into farmhouses. It is possible that many of the houses described below are on the sites of earlier buildings and may incorporate part of the earlier fabric.

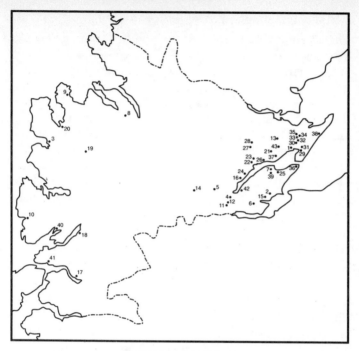

MANSION HOUSES

THE MACKENZIES

1 New Tarbat House   NH 769736: OS21

The 1st Earl of Cromartie, George Mackenzie, set about building himself a new mansion house a short distance from Milton
Castle, which he had acquired in 1656. At least part of it was
ready for occupation in 1670, when ceilings were plastered,
but work on the original building, or on alterations, continued
until about 1712. During the period when the Cromartie
estates were forfeited to the crown (1747–84), the building
decayed and was used both for storing grain and, for a time,
as a linen factory. The building was pulled down in 1784 and
replaced by the present house, designed by James McLeran
and completed by 1787 It is now sadly in ruins, but the gaunt
shell is sufficient to show that it was once one of the most
elegant houses in the north. The east side incorporates some
stonework from the earlier building.

2 Site of Rosehaugh House and grounds   NH 68 55: OS26

The original Rosehaugh House was the home of George Mackenzie of Rosehaugh (1636–91), a cousin of the 1st Earl of Cromartie. He became Lord Advocate, founded the Advocates' Library in Edinburgh (subsequently the National Library of Scotland) and, among other achievements, wrote *Aretina*, the first Scottish novel. He is remembered as 'Bluidy Mackenzie' for his role in prosecuting Covenanters, but was also instrumental in bringing to an end trials for witchcraft in Scotland. The house was acquired by Mackenzie of Scatwell, who remodelled it in 1798. It was substantially rebuilt, most ambitiously, in 1898–1903 for its new owners, the Fletchers, to produce one of the largest mansions in the Highlands. Rosehaugh was demolished in 1959, but a number of houses in the grounds, built *c.* 1900 to designs of the English Arts and Crafts Movement, survive.

3 Flowerdale   NG 814754: OS19

The house was built in 1738, beside an earlier moated site, for the Mackenzies of Gairloch. Its crow-stepped double gable in the shape of an 'M' is similar to that of Applecross House. The style is peculiar to Wester Ross and Sutherland, and possibly shows the influence of the military architecture of Bernera Barracks in Glenelg. The initials of Alexander Mackenzie and his wife Janet are on the skewputts (the bottom stones of the roof gable). At the nearby Mains Farm is a barn with the same initials, Mackenzie arms and a date stone inscribed 1730 – making it the oldest dated barn in Ross and Cromarty. It was originally thatched but is now roofed with corrugated iron.

4 Conan House   NH 534538: OS26

This was built for the Mackenzies of Gairloch (see Flowerdale above) in 1790–99 to replace their earlier residence of Kinkell Castle. Kinkell may, in turn, have replaced an earlier moated homestead at David's Fort (Gazetteer 7:6). All are linked with the early parish church of Logie Wester, now within the grounds of Conan House. It is a handsome, two-storey white building, with later extensions, described in 1808 by Sir George

Steuart Mackenzie of Coul as 'one of the best houses I ever saw'. For no important reason, Conan House has a different spelling from the river Conon and Conon Bridge. Beside the farm buildings is a ruined eight-sided doocot (dovecote), probably contemporary with Conan House itself.

5 Coul House   NH 463564: OS26

Built in 1819–21 for the Mackenzies of Coul, this is the third house on the site. The first may be the castle depicted on the Mackenzie of Coul mausoleum in Fortrose Cathedral. This was ruinous by 1746 and was replaced by a second house. An Alexander Mackenzie of Coul made money serving in the East India Company in the eighteenth century, restoring the family's fortune and allowing his son, Sir George Mackenzie, to erect the present building. Sir George had the house designed to an unusual plan, based around two octagons. Half-octagons are used in the porch and in the entrance lodge at the foot of the winding drive. The internal work is to a high standard with ornate plasterwork.

The farm buildings of Mains of Coul are of 1795 and the grounds also contained an extensive orchard in which Sir George, a keen agricultural improver, developed at least two varieties of apple, now unfortunately lost.

6 Old Allangrange   NH 625514: OS26

A two-storey mansion built in 1760 by George Mackenzie, second laird of Allangrange. The house had bow-fronted windows which were removed in 1907 and added to the present Allangrange House to the east. There is also an earlier date stone of 1730 under a first floor window, with the initials of Simon Mackenzie of Allangrange and his wife Isobel Mackenzie. Unlike many small estates of the late eighteenth century, Allangrange was noted for its improvements. A considerable amount of land was drained and reclaimed, and new breeds of cattle and sheep were introduced.

7 Newhall   NH 698656: OS21

The present Newhall House was built in 1805–07 for Donald Mackenzie of Newhall. It incorporates an earlier house begun in 1725 for Alexander Urquhart of Newhall, but which passed to the Gordon family shortly after completion. Urquhart's house had, in turn, replaced an earlier building, possibly nearer to the present entrance gates. Newhall is a fine classical mansion.

8 Dundonnell   NH 112860: OS19

Built for the Mackenzies of Dundonnell in 1767, it may incorporate parts of an earlier residence. The house is a tall two-storey building with narrow windows and later dormers in the attic rooms. By the early nineteenth century the Dundonnell estate was noted for its improved farming, orchards, garden and the planting of 'millions of fir and hard wood trees'.

9 Udrigle   NG 896936: OS19

Built in 1745 for William Mackenzie of Gruinard, whose initials, with those of his wife, are on a marriage stone inside. This is a fine example of the house of a small laird from the mid-eighteenth century. The staircase is inside against the front wall. This accounts for the 'dropped' central window on the house front, which lights the stairs. It was restored from a ruin in the early 1990s.

10 Applecross House   NG 719459: OS24

A three-storey house built for the Mackenzies of Applecross *c.*1730–40 with a re-used date stone of 1695 from an earlier residence. The house, like Flowerdale (Gazetteer 15:3), has double gables in the shape of an 'M' and, like Udrigle, a dropped window in the front to light the stairs. The front porch is a later addition using a lower stair window to replace the original entrance, at the rear.

At nearby Applecross Mains is a mid-nineteenth-century farm square. Sited on an exposed spot to catch the prevailing wind are two creel barns, which were used to dry hay and unthreshed grain in the wet climate of Wester Ross.

11 Ord House   NH 515505: OS26

Built *c.*1810 for the Mackenzies of Ord who had owned the land since 1637.

12 Site of Highfield House NH 52 51: OS26

This was the seat of the Mackenzie Gillander family, built in the mid-nineteenth century and now demolished. There are surviving gate lodges and a dower house of *c.*1800.

13 Scotsburn NH 723762: OS21

A laird's house of *c.*1800–10 for a small estate also known in the eighteenth century as Ulladale.

14 Scatwell House NH 399569: OS26

The Mackenzies of Scatwell were, by the mid-eighteenth century, one of the largest landowning families in the county. Their main residence was at Rosehaugh (Gazetteer 15:2). This shooting lodge on their original estate of Scatwell is of the 1890s, but incorporates an earlier house of unknown date.

15 Roskill House NH 661546: OS26

Clearly visible from the main road below, this was built for the Mackenzies of Suddie in 1784. It was later heightened, making it unusually tall, but is still a good example of the house of a small laird, dominating the surrounding farmland.

16 Mountgerald NG 571615: OS21

An eighteenth-century Mackenzie house, originally named Clyne.

17 Inverinate NG 922216: OS33

The original house was built for Kenneth Mackenzie in 1801. It was remodelled or replaced *c.*1850 with a larger house for Sir Alexander Matheson and substantially changed in the twentieth century.

18 Attadale NG 926392: OS25

The house is dated 1755 but has earlier features. It was probably a Mackenzie house but was in the hands of Mathesons by 1808.

19 Letterewe NG 95 71: OS19

A late eighteenth-century Mackenzie laird's house with many later additions. Converted to a shooting lodge. It is accessible only by boat or by many miles of footpath. Close to the house are two creel barns.

20 Strondubh   NG 862813: OS19

Probably a Mackenzie house of *c.*1730–40, with earlier parts. A two-storey white-harled house, with a long low barn beside the road.

21 Kincraig House   NH 692710: OS21

Now a hotel. Built in 1800 for the Mackenzies of Kincraig, with additions in the 1870s. The Mackenzie stag and the initials of John Mackenzie and his wife Mary can be seen above the original south entrance. John Mackenzie of the Redcastle Mackenzies inherited Kincraig in 1760, at the age of nine.

THE MUNROS

The principal Munro residence was Foulis, described in Gazetteer 7.

22 Novar   NH 614679: OS21

The central section of the house, a plain two-storey building with wings running back to enclose a rear courtyard, dates from *c.*1720, although it incorporates a date stone of 1634. Two side-wings were added *c.*1770 by Colonel Hector Munro, who had made his fortune as a soldier during the conquest of Bengal for the East India Company in the early 1760s. From 1765 he spent considerable sums in landscaping his property, including enclosure of fields, planting of trees, the creation of a walled garden and the erection of several obelisks, statues and Indian-style mini-temples. He returned to India in order to replenish his capital, returned with further spoils of war from the capture of Negapatam and completed his programme of improvements. Fyrish Hill was replanted and topped by a replica of the gates of an Indian city, possibly Negapatam. It is said to have been originally painted white to contrast the green of the surrounding woods, but even without this it is an imposing monument. It can be reached by a path running from the road to Boath.

23 Fyrish   NH 618690: OS21

An early eighteenth-century Munro mansion with crow-stepped gables.

24 Ardullie Lodge   NH 586623: OS21

The house, of two storeys with a steeply pitched roof, incorporates seventeenth-century date stones with the Munro eagle, but it is substantially of the early eighteenth century.

25 Poyntzfield   NH 12642: OS21

The estate of Ardoch was owned by Alexander Gordon, whose wife was Ann Munro, a daughter of the laird of Foulis. This fact may account for some similarities between this house – built before 1757 by their son Adam Gordon – and the Munros' castle at Foulis. Adam Gordon sold the estate shortly afterwards to George Gun Munro, who renamed it Poyntzfield in honour of his wife, Anna Maria Poyntz, the widow of Stephen Poyntz of Cowdray House, Sussex. George Gun Munro was a descendant of the Munros of Lemlair.

The house front is of three storeys with a regular five-window-wide front, topped by a pediment with the date 1757 at its base. From the rear of the roof an eight-sided outlook tower or gazebo projects, similar to that at Foulis. The Poyntzfield estate was small, but noted for its improvements in the late eighteenth century. In the early nineteenth century it was associated with the planned village of Jemimaville, named after the wife of a later Munro owner.

In the grounds of Poyntzfield are two carved window heads dated 1673 with the initials of Revd Hugh Anderson and his wife Grizel Rowe. Anderson was the presbyterian minister of Cromarty, ousted after the re-establishment of episcopacy in 1663 and re-instated after 1690. He is one of the covenanting ministers commemorated at Obsdale.

26 Teaninich House   NH 651689: OS21

The house of the Munros of Teaninich, built in 1784, is encased in a later nineteenth-century frontage. Like the estate girnal of 1774, on the shore below Alness, it was built by Captain James Munro. His son, Captain Hugh Munro, having been blinded at the siege of Njemingen in 1794, devoted his energies to improvements on the estate, including the straightening of the River Alness to prevent flooding and the establishment of Teaninich Distillery.

27 Lealty   NH 609733: OS21

Lealty is a small Munro house of the eighteenth century now standing abandoned in the middle of fields.

28 Ardross   NH 611741: OS21

The Munro properties of Lealty and Ardross were bought up by the rich opium trader Alexander Matheson in 1846. Ardross Castle stands on the other side of the valley from Lealty, a stark contrast between old and new wealth. The original Munro house of Ardross stood by the river, a mile downstream. The Duke of Sutherland had already built a shooting lodge on the present castle site, and parts of this may have been incorporated in Matheson's castle, completed by the mid-1850s. There were further additions and alterations in 1880–81. For another Matheson's house, see Inverinate (Gazetteer 15:17).

There were important cadet families of the Munros at **Culcairn** (NG 659667: OS21) and **Culrain** (NG 672716: OS21). (Culrain is misnamed Culcairn on some editions of the Ordnance Survey.)

THE ROSSES

29 Pitcalnie   NH 808722: OS21

The Rosses of Pitcalnie fought a long and unsuccessful legal battle after 1711 to claim the succession to the estate of Balnagowan after the death of the childless last laird, David Ross. They lost their case to the better-financed family of Rosse of Halkhead who, although their claim was dubious, gained Balnagowan, while the chiefship of Clan Ross went to the Pitcalnie family. The costs crippled the Pitcalnie Rosses, whose estates were gradually reduced. The present house at Pitcalnie may incorporate some earlier fabric.

Other Ross properties in the parishes of Nigg, Fearn and Cromarty typify various forms of 'new money' in the eighteenth century.

30 Old Shandwick
NH 788754: OS21

The estate of Easter Kindeace was acquired in 1721 by 'Polander' Ross, formerly a Scots merchant in Krakow. He was renowned for his capacity for drink – an ability he claimed to have exercised in drinking bouts with the King of Poland. He changed the name of his estate to Ankerville, an anker being a 10-gallon cask of wine. It was inherited by David Ross, who became Lord Ankerville, a judge of the Court of Session. The estate included lands in Strathoykell in Sutherland and a number of farms in the parishes of Nigg and Fearn, including Shandwick. The last laird, Hugh Ross of Shandwick, was killed in a duel in London in 1790 and the property then passed to Cockburn Ross of Berwickshire, who had married the laird's niece. The original house at Ankerville had long since disappeared.

Cockburn Ross brought farmers from the Lowlands and created larger farms. His house at Old Shandwick was originally designed as farm buildings, with the plan altered mid-way through construction when Ross decided to take up residence in Easter Ross. For an account of the cursing of the house, see Gazetteer 13.

31 Bayfield
NH 811729: OS21

Formerly Mickle Kindeace. Bayfield was built *c.*1790 by Hugh Rose of Glastullich, with the remains of an earlier house incorporated in the nearby farm steading.

32 Arabella House
NH 799754: OS21

Bayfield was superseded *c.*1800 by Arabella House, built for and named after Hugh Rose's first wife Arabella Phipps, who died young in 1806. According to tradition, she was murdered by her husband's West Indian mistress, and her ghost, the 'White Lady', haunts Bayfield House. There is no evidence for this account of her death, though her husband did make his money supplying the British Fleet in the West Indies. Hugh Rose, through a second marriage and a complex legal case, inherited the Cromarty estate and took the name Hugh Rose Ross.

33 Phippsfield   NH 786764: OS21

Hugh Rose Ross (see above) was a prominent improver, particularly in developing drainage schemes for farmland. He built his own brick and tile works here to produce drainage materials.

34 Calrossie   NH 804776: OS21

Another property of Hugh Rose Ross.

35 Glastullich   NH 792765: OS21

A Ross property originally belonging to MacCullochs.

36 Cromarty House   NH 793670: OS21

George Ross of Pitkerrie, in the parish of Fearn, was born c.1708/09, trained as a solicitor and made his fortune in London as the representative of various Scottish bodies and as an army agent, supplying British regiments with arms and stores. He acquired the Cromarty estate in 1767 and set about numerous improvements, which included demolishing the fifteenth-century castle and replacing it with a Georgian mansion. The house is notable for its servants' tunnel, providing underground access from the road for tradesmen and others.

Nearby are the stables, of similar date to the house, now restored as part of the Cromarty Centre. The horses were housed under a fine arched plaster ceiling rising above Tuscan columns.

OTHER

37 Site of Inverbreakie/Invergordon Castle
                    NH 715700: OS21

The date of the original castle of Inverbreakie is unknown. The estate and its castle were acquired by Adam Gordon of Dalpholly, who had made money mostly through financial speculation in London. The castle was rebuilt by his grandson, Sir John Gordon, in the 1750s. The estate passed to the Macleods of Cadboll in the 1780s. The castle was destroyed by fire in 1801, was subsequently repaired and finally demolished in the 1920s. It is still possible to detect some of the regularly laid out landscape around the castle site.

38 Geanies
NH 893792: OS21

This is another Macleod house, the oldest surviving part being the east wing, built in 1742. The central section is probably of the 1760s, replacing an earlier seventeenth-century house. An heraldic stone in set in the east face of this section, with the date 1650 and arms and initials of John Sinclair, a younger son of the Sinclairs, who owned adjoining Cadboll. The walled gardens, cliff-top walk and summerhouse overlooking the Moray Firth are all of the 1760s to 1780s.

39 Braelangwell
NH 695643 OS21

Built in the late eighteenth century by David Urquhart, the 4th Laird of Braelangwell. Substantial changes, which re-oriented the house, were made between 1839 and 1844. David Urquhart carried out substantial improvements to the estate, including the planting of a 13-acre orchard, the largest in the north of Scotland. Built into walls below the house are two seventeenth-century window pediments with the initials of Thomas Urquhart, the first owner, presumably from an earlier residence. David Urquhart's son was a linguist and diplomat who served for many years in Constantinople and was responsible for the introduction of Turkish baths to Britain.

40 Courthill House
NG 832406: OS24

A tall roofless mansion, probably of the 1840s, with additions made in 1883. Built on the site of an earlier house for a Macdonald family. The court-hill and early chapel site below the house give this place a much longer, if largely unknown, history.

41 Balmacara
NG 801276: OS33

The Balmacara estate is in the care of the National Trust for Scotland and easily visited. It is substantially of 1861 and later, though there was an earlier house built for Sir Hugh Innes *c.*1800. Innes carried out many clearances on the estate.

42 Ryefield   NH 568565: OS26

The principal house of the Ferintosh estate belonging to
Forbes of Culloden, and part of Nairn-shire until 1889.
The seventeenth-century house was extended in the 1770s
and largely remodelled in the Victorian period. Much of
the Victorian building was damaged by fire and rebuilt in
the 1940s. The house probably incorporated a much older
tower house of unknown date.

43 Kindeace   NH 726734: OS21

Built *c*.1800 for the Robertsons, a family of Inverness
merchants who had bought the property in the late seventeenth
century. Altered in 1869 to the baronial style of the time.

GAZETTEER 16:
SITES RELATING TO AGRICULTURE,
INCLUDING CLEARANCES

GIRNALS

Girnals were grain stores used to receive both rents paid in
kind and the produce of the estate farms. They were often
sited near the shore for easy access to shipping.

Essential Viewing
1 Foulis Ferry   *NH 599636: OS21*

*The girnal for the Munro of Foulis estate is a substantial
three-storey building built in 1730 and now developed as the
Clan Munro Centre. Of the grain girnals which were built
around the Cromarty Firth and Easter Ross, this is the most
easily seen.*

2 Ferryton   NH 680669: OS21

This was the girnal for the small Newhall estate, built in the
mid-eighteenth century as a single-storey building and later
heightened, with external stairs to the first floor. In 1773 the
laird, William Gordon, wrote of having spent two days here
'morning to night, accounting with my tenants, without any
assistant, writing, figuring, entering in Compts Book . . . and

now half crazed and half asleep'. The girnal is now converted to a private house.

3 Invergordon
NH 709685: OS21

The long Invergordon estate girnal (38.8 m × 6.4 m) lies between Shore Road and Mill Street, with crow-stepped gables and three unusually long windows in the rear wall (now part of the adjoining garage).

4 Alness Point
NH 656679: OS21

The girnal of the Teaninich estate built in 1774 for Captain James Munro, whose initials, with those of his wife Margaret Mackenzie, can be seen on the north-east gable.

5 Nigg
NH 796687: OS21

The Dunskaith estate girnal (22 m × 6.4 m), with crow-stepped gables, was built in 1712 and now is incorporated as part of the Ferry Inn. Loadings of grain were made onto ships beached on the Nigg sands.

6 Ankerville
NH 818744: OS21

The Ankerville estate girnal, an eighteenth-century building, was converted to a row of cottages c.1900. It lies farther from the shore than the other girnals.

7 Portmahomack
NH 915846: OS21

The girnal of the Tarbat estate, built in the 1690s for George Mackenzie, is the smaller of the two buildings close to the harbour. It is a simple, single-storeyed rectangle (119 m × 6.4 m), with a steeply pitched slated roof. Beside it is a taller store built in 1779, considerably larger (31.8 m × 5.5 m) and with two storeys and a loft. Yards behind these girnals once formed a larger complex.

LOST GIRNALS

8 Portleich (later re-named Barbaraville)
NH 750722: OS21

The girnal of the New Tarbat estate was built near the shore by William Forsyth in 1757, but only the barest trace of foundations remain.

9 Cromarty   NH 786678: OS21

Fragments of the Cromarty estate girnal, built in the 1690s, can be seen between the harbour and the lighthouse.

CREEL BARNS

Creel barns are west coast barns built with louvred walls, allowing air to pass through and so dry hay and unthreshed grain in the wet climate. Usually the roof is supported on a cruck-frame.

10 Kerrysdale   NG 823733: OS19

A long cruck-frame ventilated barn, with a later corrugated iron roof, at the rear of the house, which is *c.* 1800.

11 Letterewe   NG 95 71: OS19

On the north shore of Loch Maree. There are two long ventilated cruck-frame barns, one converted to a cottage.

12 Applecross Mains   NG 72 45: OS24

There are three barns around the Mains Farm. Crac Barn in the farm square is mid-nineteenth century, a stone barn with ventilated openings. Two earlier barns, one heather thatched, are on higher ground to catch the wind better.

13 Tullich Farm   NG 918427: OS25

Near Lochcarron. One of the longest creel barns, almost 40 m, with two pairs of opposing doors for winnowing. The cruck supports for the roof have been removed.

14 New Kelso   NG 939429: OS25

Near Lochcarron. The predominantly eighteenth-century farm square includes a byre and creel barn.

'PRE-IMPROVEMENT' FARMING

15 Fermtoun, Lower Eathie   NH 774636: OS21

When a new farmhouse was built in the mid-nineteenth century, the old fermtoun of Lower Eathie was abandoned. Unusually, it was on a site which was unsuitable for ploughing and so has only been grazed. As a result there are substantial remains of turf-built houses, yards and farm buildings, and what is probably a circular kiln for drying grain. The buildings suggest that three or more families had a joint tenancy of the farm. A later stone-built cottage on the site is now ruined.

SITES RELATING TO CATTLE DROVING

Cattle from the west were driven along the straths which converge at Muir of Ord – Strath Conon, Glen Orrin, Strath Bran and Strath Garve. The drove included cattle from the islands which were landed at Aulbea, Gruinard, Gairloch and Ullapool. The drove roads from these points are now modern roads, with the exception of the route from Gruinard along the Gruinard River and through Strath na Shellag. There are also two deviations from the modern road between Inchbae and Achterneed and from Aultguish to Garve.

For cattle from the north marts were organised in Strath Oykell, the site varying but including the *Feille Edeichan* (market of the quartz stone) in Kincardine. The route south from Kincardine included:

16 Drovers stance, Sittenham   NH 653752: OS21
On the road over the Struie Hill. Created in 1847.

17 Coire mhàileagan   NH 42 84: OS20
Reputedly the base of the eighteenth-century cattle reiver Alasdair Scolair.

SHIELINGS

There are remains of shielings to be discovered in many sheltered glens on east and west coasts, sometimes on the site of Bronze Age hut circles. The general pattern for the use of shielings seems to have been that a keeper was sent there from April to keep animals off the grass. In mid-June all the cattle from the low ground moved to the shieling, accompanied by most of the people, with groups of men returning occasionally to tend the growing crop. In August the milk cattle were taken back to the low ground, leaving horses and other cattle to graze, sometimes until Christmas. Look out for patches of green grass where the ground had been manured by cattle and outlines of temporary circular huts. Those at Lochcarron, Toscaig and Applecross are the only ones marked on the OS Landranger maps.

18 Lochcarron   NH 87 36: OS24

19 Toscaig   NG 718368: OS24

20 Applecross   NG 763438: OS24

CLEARANCES

21 Kildermorie   NH 51 77: OS20

In 1791 Munro of Novar let ground here as a sheep farm, displacing tenants from the *baile* and, probably more importantly, depriving the tenants of Strathrusdale of much of the summer grazing for their cattle. In June 1792 'straying' cattle, which had been impounded by the sheep farmer at Kildermorie, were liberated by the Strathrusdale tenants. The farmer, who had armed himself and his men and threatened the tenants, was severely beaten. A few days later tenants on a number of estates gathered and began to drive sheep south. The drove began in Strathoykell, where over 10,000 sheep were gathered. They moved south to another gathering point at **Boath** (NH 57 74: OS21). The following morning three companies of soldiers of the Black Watch arrived and eleven men were taken prisoner. The two leaders were sentenced to seven years transportation but were, it seems, allowed to escape from prison, and settled in Moray. 1792 became known as 'the year of the sheep'. At around the same time there had already been sheep farms introduced in the parishes of Kilmuir Easter in the east and Lochbroom in the west, and other landowners were advertising for farmers prepared to take over land for sheep.

22 Coigach   OS15

A sheep farm was created at **Inverpolly** (NH 069142: OS15) *c.*1810 and tenants of the *baile* were moved south to the shore near Achiltibuie and to Badenscallie (NH 036062), an ancient *baile* with a medieval chapel. The line of crofts along the coast line is a creation of the clearances.

Attempts to clear Achiltibuie and Badenscallie in 1852–53 to create both farms and a shooting estate met with resistance, largely from women. In 1853, the sheriff's officer sent to serve removal notices was stripped naked and put to sea in a boat. The coverage of events by national newspapers led to the estate abandoning its plans. This success marked a turning point in the history of clearances in the Highlands.

23 Gruinard   OS19

Gruinard passed from the Mackenzies to Davidson of Tulloch who, in the early nineteenth century, created crofts at **First Coast** (NG 92 90), **Second Coast** (NG 92 90) and **Third Sand** (NG 90 91). In 1835 the estate passed to a Mr Bankes, who cleared Little Gruinard and **Badantsluig** (NG 935906) and removed the hill pasture from many crofts, creating mounting hardship. Three hundred people are said to have left or been evicted in 1846. **Drumchork** (NG 87 88) was cleared to build a lodge in 1881.

24 Strathconon   OS26

Clearance in Strathconon began in the early years of the nine-teenth century, but the principal removals were in the 1840s after the estate was acquired by the Balfour family. They were carried out under the ownership of James Balfour, father of the future Prime Minister, Arthur Balfour. A report in the *Inverness Courier* in 1850 gave details of one eviction from the *baile* of **Blarnabee** (NH 263506), where there were five tenants, three sub-tenants and four cottars – fifty-eight people in all. Around 500 people were removed from Strathconon during the 1840s, many settling on the Cromartie estates and on the Black Isle.

25 Glenelg   OS33

There were clearances to townships along the shore in the early nineteenth century and to the village of Glenelg (NG 81 18), created in 1788.

26 Torridon   OS24

The whole Torridon estate had been extensively cleared by
the 1840s. For example, the area east and west of **Inveralligin**
(NG 84 57) was cleared in 1838 and tenants, other than a few
who remained on the fringe, moved to what is now the village
of **Torridon** (NG 89 56).

27 Scoraig   OS19

In 1840 part of the *baile* of **Scoraig** (NH 00 96) was set aside
and divided into lots (the township became knows as 'Lots of
Scoraig'). The remainder was let to two tenants.

28 Gairloch   OS19

In the 1840s Mackenzie of Gairloch pursued a policy of
creating new smallholdings with adequate housing and of a
sufficient size to support a family, if cultivated intensively. This
was in contrast to the minimal holdings provided in most new
coastal settlements, and is still apparent in the layout of crofts
at **Mellon Charles**, **Ormscaig** and **Buailualuib** (NG 84 91
and to south-east) which replaced earlier joint-tenanted farms
from 1815. The scheme also involved creating new settlements
on what had formerly been grazing ground at **Altanphadruig**
(NG 742832), **Upper Diabeg** (NG 812601) and **Opinan**
(NG 745725).

29 Glenshiel   OS33

There were many removals early in the nineteenth century.
Carndubh and Bundaloch (NG 89 27), which had been
settlements created *c.*1801, were cleared in 1852, displacing
100 people. In the same year, **Letterfearn** (NG 88 23), on
the other side of Loch Duich, was cleared.

30 Balmacara   OS33

There were clearances early in the nineteenth century when
the estate was acquired by Sir Hugh Innes, who built Balmacara
House and created the village of Innestown on the shores of
Auchtertyre Bay in 1813. In 1849, **Avernish** (NG 84 26) was
cleared.

LATE EIGHTEENTH-CENTURY FARM BUILDINGS

31 Brahan Farm Square   NH 512550: OS26

The centrepiece of the farm square is a clock tower dated 1788. It was built by David Aitken, who was both an improving farmer and an important land surveyor. He mapped and planned improvements on several estates in Ross and Cromarty between the 1760 and 1790s.

32 Mains of Coul   NH 46 56: OS26

A large hollow square of farm building, dated 1795, built for Sir George Steuart Mackenzie, a noted improver and author of *A General View of the Agriculture of the Counties of Ross and Cromarty*, published in 1810. He was a supporter of the view that Highlanders should abandon their traditional ways and adapt speedily to becoming farm servants on modernised farms, such as this one.

33 Novar Mains   NH 614685: OS21

An impressive range of buildings, probably from the 1780s, with a clock tower.

SOME LATER FARM BUILDINGS

34 Invergordon Mains   NH 705695: OS21

A group of farm buildings around a courtyard, off Strath Avenue in Invergordon. The steading is dated 1810. There is a farmhouse in the west range and an entrance arch in the north, with a tower above.

35 Conon Mains Farm Square   NH 532535: OS26

Beside Conan House are impressive farm buildings erected in 1822 and visible from the main road. They are an indication of the importance given to agricultural improvement in the early nineteenth century. The belfry and clock are signs of the greater order and regulation which were imposed on farm life. One of the masons who worked here was Hugh Miller of Cromarty, before he rose to fame as a writer.

MILLS

Increased grain production in the early nineteenth century led to the building of many new grain mills throughout the area.

36 Aldie Mill   NH 788804: OS21

Signposted off the A9 just south of Tain, the mill is restored and open to the public. The present mill dates from the 1860s and is on the site of the much older burgh mills of Tain.

37 Millnain   NH 505592: OS26

Clearly visible from the road between Dingwall and Strathpeffer.

38 Newmills   NH 678648: OS21

On a minor road at the eastern end of the Black Isle, built in the 1830s to replace earlier mills.

39 Salt mills, Munlochy Bay   NH 65 62: OS26

A salt mill is a mill driven by the tide. The millstones still lie in the mud near the high-water mark.

40 Munlochy   NH 648533: OS26

The mill in Munlochy itself has a date stone 1740, probably from an earlier mill.

41 Kirkton of Resolis   NH 704662: OS21

The farm is a model early nineteenth-century farm complex dominated by the tall brick chimney of a steam threshing mill.

COMMONTIES

A commonty is an area of ground, often extensive, in the common ownership of adjoining landowners (Scotland has no common land in the English sense of land belonging to the people as a whole). Commonties were, however, used by the people for fuel, grazing and building materials. They are found principally in the east, simply because land in the west has tended to be in the ownership of a single estate. After 1695, commonties could be divided by a legal process, allowing landowners to acquire individual portions and bring them into use for farming, pasture or planting of trees.

42 Bogallan Commonty   NH 63 50: OS26

This Black Isle commonty was divided in 1784. The line of beech trees bordering the B9161 between Munlochy and the A9 probably marks the boundary of one of the allocated portions.

43 Nigg Hill Commonty   around NH 81 70: OS21

Divided by 1770. Much of the west face of the hill is traversed by the remains of substantial turf dykes built after the division.

44 Mulbuie Commonty   OS 21 and 26

Stretching the length of the Black Isle. The commonty was divided in 1829 after a complex legal process lasting over twenty years. A walk westwards beginning at the Ardmeanach road end (NH 705611) passes a number of turf dyke systems, a farm created and later abandoned (NH 693603) and a walled nursery (NH 702608) used to raise trees for planting on the divided commonty.

45 Brenachie   NH 76 76: OS21

Logie Easter. This was not divided until 1867.

Commonties should be distinguished from the common grazings shared by tenants of a single estate. Common grazings were the possession of the owner of the estate and were often turned over to other uses.

EARLY STONE DYKES

Early dykes were mostly of *feal* (turf). The earliest stone dykes have a very broad base and look, in cross section, more like a mound of loosely piled stones. They were often built up with earth on one side, intended only to keep cattle out of areas planted with trees. Two examples of such early dykes can be seen on the Black Isle.

46 Drumsmittal Wood   NH 65 49: OS26

Beside ground planted with trees on the Drynie estate in the 1770s.

47 Henrietta Park   NH 68 65: OS21

On the Newhall estate. 1770s.

GAZETTEER 17:
WOODS AND PLANTATIONS

Essential Viewing

1 The Caledonian Forest, Ben Eighe   OS19

Remnants of native Caledonian forest can best be seen by following the trail on the **Ben Eighe National Nature Reserve (NH 001650: OS19)** *on the south shore of Loch Maree. The trail not only includes pine, some over 350 years old, but sites which have been cleared of oak for charcoal production. A guidebook is available from the Reserve Visitor Centre.*

EARLY OAK PLANTATIONS

At Lochcarron in 1808 there was a coppiced oak wood, recently enclosed, and oak and ash woods at Inverinate.

2 Drumondreoch, Ferintosh   NH 58 56: OS26

The plantation was well established by the 1720s and shows signs of coppicing.

3 Craigwood   NH 71 55: OS27

Above the road from Fortrose to Avoch. It was noted in 1795 for its oak, but is now largely beech.

EARLY PINE PLANTATIONS
4 Drumsmittal Wood   NH 65 49: OS26

The Drynie estate had the first large plantation of pine, created in the early eighteenth century, and the principal source of timber in building Fort George. The woods were replanted shortly afterwards. Drumsmittal was part of this. The enclosing mid-eighteenth century dyke still surrounds later plantations.

EARLY ORNAMENTAL PLANTINGS
The houses of all landowners had plantations of trees around. From the mid-eighteenth century onwards, more ambitious plantings were undertaken.

5 Castle Leod   NH 486593: OS26*

Impressive early trees have survived including a number of sixteenth-century sweet chestnuts.

6 South Sutor   NH 80 66: OS21

Successive lairds of Cromarty created a wooded hill, reached by a spiralling road, from the top of which avenues through the trees gave views to points of interest in seven counties. Nothing remains except a few sweet chestnuts, planted in the 1750s, on the road to the Sutor and around Cromarty House.

7 Fyrish Hill   NH 60 69: OS21

Munro of Novar created a replica of the gates of an Indian town above a plantation of pines. Footpath from car park on Boath Road (off A836).

8 Dundonnell   NH 112860: OS19

Noted for its millions of pine and hardwood trees in 1808 and still a beautifully wooded area.

9 The Fairy Glen (formerly St Helena)   NH 72 58: OS27

A wooded den, named St Helena in 1815 and enhanced in the 1840s, which included weeping willows from Napoleon's grave. Good public access from Rosemarkie.

GAZETTEER 18:
SALMON FISHERY

FISH TRAPS (yairs and stake nets) can be seen between high and low water in the Cromarty, Beauly and Dornoch Firths, and in Lochbroom. The remains are either of wooden stakes, preserved in the sand, or of the low stone walls which protected the stakes. In both cases seaweed is often attached and what is most clearly visible from the shore is the dog-leg pattern of the yair or the straight line of the stake net. Yairs can also be clearly seen at low tide on the north side of the Cromarty Firth in the mudflats between the Cromarty Bridge and Dingwall. On the north side of the Beauly Firth there were stake nets and yairs at Redcastle and Kessock.

1 Udale Bay NH 72 65: OS21

Remains of a complex yair can be found well preserved in the sand.

2 Lochbroom NH 177862 and NH 172858: OS19

There are remains of substantial yairs on both shores of the loch.

3 Conon NH 53 54: OS26

Fishing on the Conon was by salmon cruives, which can still be seen on either side of an island in the river opposite Conan House. These box traps are built into walls across the river and were extremely effective.

Nineteenth-century ice houses in which ice gathered from ponds was stored. Ice could be preserved until August or September.

4 Cromarty NH 789676: OS21

The roof is still covered with an insulating layer of turf.

5 Chanonry Point NH 747558: OS27

The double compartment store has had this layer removed.

6 Dalmore NH 665687: OS21

7 Portmahomack NH 91 84: OS21

8 Teaninich NH 651681: OS21

9 Milton NH 772737: OS21

Sometimes mistaken for remains of Milton Castle.

10 Chapelton Point, Newhall NH 707671: OS21

A large ice house on private ground.

FISHING STATIONS

11 Balconie Point NH 624523: OS21

On the north side of the Cromarty Firth. A nineteenth-century salmon fishing station, built on the Inchcoulter estate, with arched windows in imitation of a chapel. It may incorporate stones from the medieval church of Kiltearn. Also at the tip of the point, and elsewhere in the firth, are mounds of stones in the water. Some are still used for salmon fishing by cobles (small boats) and sweep nets – the only form of net fishing *within* the firths to be permitted after the 1860s. Skilled coble fishers are able to detect the movement of the salmon in the shallow waters of the firth.

Later coastal netting stations used fixed bag nets. The catches from the four below were brought to the yard at the east end of the links at Cromarty, where the buildings still stand.

12 Eathie   NH 778635: OS21

The bothy which accommodated the salmon fishers survives.

13 Navity   NH 789645: OS21

14 MacFarquhar's Bed   NH 800653: OS21

With a surviving bothy.

15 Old Shandwick   NH 856741: OS21

On the path to the Well of Health.

WEST COAST STATIONS

16 Big Sand   NG 746792: OS19

North of Gairloch.

17 Charleston   NG 810751: OS19

South of Gairloch, with an ice house built into the slope beside the road.

18 Eilean Tioram   NG 740672: OS19 or 24

South of Redpoint, on the shore opposite the island.

19 Badentarbat   NC 008095: OS15

North of Achiltibuie. The Badentarbat station includes a house with a store, which was probably used for salt, and later, ice.

GAZETTEER 19:
FISHING COMMUNITIES AND
HERRING FISHING

EARLY FISHER COMMUNITIES

1 Cromarty   OS21

The fishertown may once have been on the edge of the burgh, but as the town grew, it was incorporated into the central part of Cromarty (present day Shore Street and behind). Unlike many places, fishers held a clear title to their property. Cromarty expanded with the boom in fishing in the early eighteenth century, and at that time, the Braehead, above the links, was known as 'Pickletown' after its curing yards. See also Gazetteer 23:1.

2 Avoch   OS27

The fishertown of Avoch lies along the shore to the west of the village, according to tradition built on land below the then high-water mark. The present single-storey fisher cottages are nineteenth century. The adaptability of the Avoch fishermen, noted 200 years ago, has enabled this to survive as a fishing settlement, albeit that the boats now fish from the west coast. The siting of the harbour, built in 1815, was the subject of a dispute between the landowner and the fisher community.

3 Balintore   OS21

The fisher town of the abbey of Fearn is recorded in the sixteenth century, when there were fisher crofts, but the link with the land was later lost. Balintore grew from the early nineteenth century, including buildings for curing red herring. A harbour was finally built in 1896.

Although beyond the period covered by this guide, it is worth mentioning the skeletal remains of two boats easily seen from the main road at **Ardullie** (NH 589624: OS21) on the north side of the Cromarty Firth. These are not wrecks, but the remains of the herring boats which were anchored here for the winter by the fishermen of Balintore. Many of them did not return from the First World War, and their boats were left to decay.

LATER EAST COAST FISHER COMMUNITIES

4 Balintraid   NH 73 70: OS21

Balnagowan estate. There were four fishing boats here in the early eighteenth century. A new pier was built by Thomas Telford in 1817, with fisher cottages.

5 Portleich   NH 74 72: OS21

Now Barbaraville, on the New Tarbat estate. A fisher community was established by 1691, and fishers also held land in runrig. There were unsuccessful attempts to expand it in the 1760s by settling former soldiers. A pier was designed by James Smeaton in 1771, but never built. In 1808 there were sixteen fishers, but many had turned to making lime from shell deposits on the Nigg sands.

6 Balnabruach   NH 79 69: OS21

Pitcalzean estate.

7 Balnapaling   NH 79 69: OS21

Dunskaith estate. Both Balnabruach and Balnapaling were established by 1691 and fishers also held crofts of land. The settlements have now almost vanished in the industrial complex at Nigg.

8 Shandwick   NH 85 75: OS21

Ankerville estate. Originally a small fisher settlement like those above, Shandwick grew with the herring boom of the early nineteenth century to become a much larger fishing community, with over sixty fishermen in the 1880s.

9 Hilton   NH 87 76: OS21

Cadboll estate. Developed as a fisher settlement in the early eighteenth century and expanded considerably in the early nineteenth, with its own harbour, admittedly very insubstantial. There were some seventy fishermen at one time.

10 Rockfield   NH 92 82: OS21

Little Tarrel estate. Appears to have been largely a creation of the nineteenth century, with the pier constructed in 1829 and fisher cottages built before 1830.

11 Balnabruach   NH 90 84: OS21

Seafield estate. The original fishertown of Balnabruach is now part of Portmahomack

12 Portmahomack   NH 91 84: OS21

Tarbat estate. Fishermen held crofts near the church and to the east of Balnabruach. Portmahomack's fisher community is first mentioned in 1679. The first pier was built in 1697, and was extended by Thomas Telford in 1813. Like Cromarty, Portmahomack was a centre for the export of salt fish in the early eighteenth century. It was also, from the 1780s, noted for the shipping of live lobsters to London in 'well smacks', with over 50,000 exported in a single year. A nineteenth-century warehouse still stands beside the earlier girnal. There may once have been a fishing settlement at Wilkhaven.

13 Inver   NH 86 82: OS21

Tarbat estate. Inver is the only one of the Easter Ross fishing communities where there is a relic of 'fisher land'. Now in the ownership of two families of fisher descent, it is said to have been once the common property of the fisher community.

14 Skinnerton   NH 86 82: OS21

Arboll estate. Inver and Skinerton, now two parts of the same modern village, lie in different parishes.

15 Saltburn   NH 72 69: OS21

Inverbreakie, later Invergordon, estate. Established by 1691, but with only one boat.

16 Obsdale   NH 67 68: OS21

Fishers are mentioned in the 1720s.

17 Kilmuir   NH 67 49: OS26

Drynie estate, with a ready market in Inverness.

For Kessock and Charleston, both created as estate villages in the early nineteenth century, *see* Gazetteer 24.

WEST COAST FISHING SETTLEMENTS

18 Gairloch
NG 80 75: OS19

Gairloch had emerged a base for cod fishery by the eighteenth century. There were attempts to develop cod and herring fishing at Lochbroom at the same time.

19 Port Henderson
NG 75 73: OS19

Established as a fishing village on the Gairloch estate in 1815, with twenty-two tenants, but later became a crofting settlement.

20 Eilean Horrisdale
NG 78 74: OS19

Opposite Badachro. A well-preserved fishing station, with jetties on the Badachro shore beside Aird House.

21 Isle Martin
NH 09 99: OS19

In 1776 merchants from the south began to build smoke houses to produce red herring, that is herring salted and smoked, a method of preservation which allowed them to be shipped to hot climates such as the West Indies.

22 Tanera Mor
NB 99 07: OS15

A herring curing station was established in 1784 and remains include a two-storey range of buildings with adjoining yards, which included a house for the manager. The pier was rebuilt in 1938 by the ecologist Frank Fraser-Darling.

23 Ullapool

Established by the British Fisheries Society. Ullapool is described in the section on new settlements below.

OTHER SITES

Mussels were an important and jealously guarded source of bait for fisher communities. A century ago there were twenty-one acres of scalp in the Cromarty Firth alone. These have almost all gone, though it is possible to see many remains of the beds at low tides. Of particular interest are the mussel beds in the Dornoch Firth. These form part of the 'common good' of the royal burgh of Tain. The recent revival and expansion of mussel farming provides an important source of finance for a variety of projects benefiting the inhabitants of the town.

24 West of Ardjachie Point   NH 74 85: OS21
Mussel bed.

25 Beside Tain   NH 78 83: OS21
Mussel bed.

26 Ness of Portnaculter   NH 732859: OS21
Mussels are harvested from the station on the point.

GAZETTEER 20: INDUSTRIAL SITES

IRON SMELTING WITH CHARCOAL

1 The Red Smiddy   NG 861798: OS19

2 Furnace   NG 960704: OS19

3 Fasgadh   NH 012655: OS19

Near here is Claod nan Sasganach (NH 006569), 'the burial ground of the southerners', where it is said that ironworkers buried their dead.

MINES AND QUARRIES

4 Munlochy Bay   NH 678532: OS26
The quarry on the north side of the bay was the source of much of the stone for the great fortress of Fort George. It was ferried across the firth in fleets of small boats, providing substantial employment for over twenty years.

5 Findon   NH 596603: OS21
The quarry site is now occupied by a sewage plant, but on the shore to the west of the Cromarty Bridge are remains of what may have been some kind of ship dock.

6 Tarradale
NH 553498: OS26

The now abandoned quarry was the source of stone used throughout the Black Isle and the Inverness area in the nineteenth century.

7 Millstone quarry, Sittenham
NH 654742: OS21

An abandoned quarry with two unfinished millstones.

8 Coalheugh Well, Cromarty
NH 795672: OS21

Below the chapel of St Regulus. Best approached along the side of the field below, by the entrance beyond the bowling green. A well created as the result of a test bore for coal in the 1690s.

9 Lochcarron
NG 849432: OS24

Remains of a copper mine.

OTHER

10 Phippsfield
NH 786764: OS21

Tile works established in 1840s but no visible remains.

GAZETTEER 21:
TEXTILE WORKING

FLAX AND HEMP

1 Inverlael
NH 182860: OS20

At the head of Lochbroom. See below

2 New Kelso
NG 939428: OS25

At the head of Lochcarron. Government bodies promoted flax spinning in the Highlands between 1749 and the 1770s, and funded the building of these two spinning schools in Wester Ross. The schools were abandoned in 1789 and converted to substantial farmhouses, still inhabited.

3 Tarbat House   NH 769736: OS21

Tarbat House stood on the site of the present ruin. Much flax yarn was spun in the east and there was for a short time a linen factory here, with hand spinning and hand looms. Most yarn was shipped to Edinburgh but a limited quantity was woven into linen cloth locally, a process which involved bleaching the finished cloth. Small bleachfields were established on the Cromarty links by the local merchant, William Forsyth, and by Munro of Culcairn, somewhere on his estate.

4 The Cromarty Manufactory   NH 786675: OS21

This hand loom factory was built c.1772 and originally had five ranges. One on the shore side has been demolished to open up the square and a fifth range stood farther inland. There were also central buildings. The factory worked imported Russian hemp. Some of it was spun in the factory in long spinning walks, hence the long ranges of buildings which were later used for rope making. Much of the hemp was, however, distributed for home working. The yarn was then woven into a coarse cloth for sacking and bagging and sold in London, for use in the West Indies trade. The factory employed up to 250 people in the building and over 600 outworkers. It ceased production in the 1850s.

5 Invergordon   NH 70 68: OS21

A branch factory was opened at Invergordon before 1808, but had closed by 1820.

WOOL

6 Gordonsmills   NH 706655: OS21

On the shore of Udale Bay. The spinning mill, four-storeys high, was in operation from January 1797, under a manager and others brought in who had a knowledge of 'sorting, scribbling, carding and spinning'. The owner expressed the hope that the mill would provide employment and 'meliorate the condition of the people, many of whom are yearly emigrating to other countries'. A number of plots were laid out beside the mills to form the nucleus of a new village. There was also a waulk (fulling) mill nearby. The venture failed *c.*1815, and the mill was converted to grind grain.

7 High Mills, Tain NH 772797: OS21

Also known as Moulinard. A pair of early nineteenth-century woollen mills used a single water lade to drive two wheels, one above the other.

GAZETTEER 22:
DISTILLERIES AND BREWERIES

DISTILLERIES

There may be remains of the Ferintosh distillery, built in 1782, near Mulchaich. Smaller stills on the Ferintosh estate, in operation after the rescinding of the Ferintosh privilege, are documented in 1798.

1 Ferintosh NH 578566: OS26

The substantial pier below at **Alcaig** (NH 564576: OS26) may be associated with exports from the distillery.

2 Balblair, original site NH 707847: OS21

Near Edderton. The distillery is said to have been established in 1790 and is documented from 1798. It was moved to its present site (NH 706855: OS21) in 1872, and remains in production in an attractive and unassuming group of buildings on the Ardmore peninsula.

3 Teaninich NH 653692: OS21

Recorded in 1818. Teaninich was established by Captain Hugh Munro with a 200-gallon still and remains in production, though in later buildings.

4 Ord Distillery NH 516507: OS26

Outside Muir of Ord. Established in 1838 and still in production, with an attractive visitor centre. The site also includes maltings, so the whole process of whisky production can be seen.

5 Dalmore NH 666687: OS21

Established in 1839 on a site which also included mills. Still in production.

6 Glenmorangie NH 768838: OS21

Near Tain. Established in 1843 and still in production, with an attractive visitor centre.

7 Balvaird NG 849170: OS33

There are remains here of a small west-coast still, probably from the mid-nineteenth century.

Other recorded stills, but with no remains, are at **Ryefield** (NH 568565: OS26), possibly the site of the Ferintosh distillery destroyed in 1689; **Tighnahinch** (NH 566585: OS26); Findon (NH 60 60: OS21); **Drumcudden** (NH 64 63: OS21); **Dunvournie** (NH 59 57: OS26); **Braes of Dunvournie** (NH 60 57: OS26); **Portleich** (NH 748721- OS21); **Delny** (NH 735723: OS21); **Hartfield** (NH 776811: OS21), outside Tain where there may have been a further distillery; **Ardoch** (NH 716646: OS21), which operated until the distiller became bankrupt in the 1820s; **Fortrose**; **Dingwall** (possibly NH 552585: OS26); Pollo (NH 744718: OS21); **Braelangwell** (NH 69 64: OS21).

BREWERIES

8 Cromarty Brewery NH 792673: OS21

Brewing was common throughout the area, with most estates having their own brewhouse. The only enterprise of any scale for which the original buildings survive is that at Cromarty. It was erected *c.*1770 and operated intermittently until the 1860s. Two ranges still stand, attractively converted to a study centre, but it was originally larger. The building probably incorporates an earlier kiln – the different stonework of the earlier part of the building can be seen on the outside wall nearest to the church.

GAZETTEER 23:
ESTABLISHED TOWNS, BURGHS OF BARONY, PLANNED VILLAGES AND SETTLEMENTS

Essential Viewing
1 Cromarty   OS21

This is an outstanding example of a Scottish coastal town of the late eighteenth and early nineteenth century and can be explored in a number of ways, including a guided tape-tour available from the museum in the courthouse and through the writings of Hugh Miller (1802–56). This description begins at the east end and follows the development of the town over time.

The oldest part of the Cromarty was the Causeway (originally Castle Street), running from below the site of the castle (now replaced by Cromarty House) to the shore, where part of it has been lost to coastal erosion. It was once a busy thoroughfare with the houses of the burgesses on either side. Thief's Row, now gone, ran across the field to the west. Above is the site of St Regulus' Chapel, with many fine gravestones of the seventeenth and eighteenth centuries. Only three houses on the Causeway remain, the earliest being The Old Manse of c.1690 – not, in fact, the old parish manse, but a merchant's house later occupied by the estate gardener and, briefly, by the minister. Clunes House, nearest the shore, has a skewputt (the stone at the bottom of the gable) carved with the date 1724 and the names of the couple who owned or built it; and the gable of The Kennels incorporates a triangular yellow stone which was once a window pediment. All three are on the sites of earlier buildings, and the market cross and tolbooth stood in what is now the garden of Clunes House. The enclosed orchard and garden was created in the seventeenth century and walled in the 1770s with stone from the demolished castle. It occupies a substantial part of the site of the medieval burgh.

To the west, the East Church contains a fourteenth-century carved grave slab and is probably the original parish church. By the seventeenth century, Cromarty had grown to reach the Paye (now a cobbled lane) and Big Vennel, around which was the Fishertown, originally on the outskirts of the burgh but by then incorporated in the town. The burgh's Courthill was on what remains open ground on Gordon's Lane. Church Street was the principal road in this part of the town, with narrow house plots running off on either side. Also from this period is the mid-seventeenth-century Townlands Barn, once the mansion house of the small estate of Sandilands which lay on the edge of the burgh. Although dilapidated, it is an important building.

Cromarty lost its status as a royal burgh c.1680, but trade in salt fish brought renewed prosperity between 1690 and 1720. The Old Manse (see above) and The Retreat, Albion House and Hugh Miller's Cottage, all in Church Street, date from this period. The town also expanded to the west, with the creation of an area known as Pickletown (from the pickling or salting of fish) on the Braehead above the links. Well before this time the harbour had been established at its present site and a large meal girnal was added in the 1690s, only traces of which remain.

The town's principal period of prosperity was between 1770 and 1830. George Ross, who acquired the estate in 1767, built the hemp factory, of which three long ranges survive. It was later used as a rope works, but its principal product was always sacks and bags, produced on hand looms. It is a remarkable survival of early manufacturing in the north of Scotland. Ross was also responsible for the Courthouse (1772), the harbour (designed by Smeaton and built between 1782 and 1786), the brewery (c.1770), the Gaelic Chapel (1784) and Cromarty House. Ross worked along with the principal local merchant, William Forsyth, who built himself the first of the town's Georgian houses, Forsyth House, in

1774. Below ground in front of the house are vaulted brick cellars for storage, and from the back of one a low, slab-roofed tunnel runs towards the street. It is not, as some have it, a smugglers' tunnel, but ran to a well in the garden, now filled in.

During the next sixty years, almost all the houses in the older part of the town were rebuilt and new houses were constructed to the west in a grid of regular streets – the principal ones being Bank Street, George Street, Duke Street and Barkly Street. The rebuilt houses of the old town range from Bellevue and St Ann's to smaller buildings in the fishertown, but all were noted for their 'neatness and cleanness' at the end of the eighteenth century. It is still possible to see the difference between houses rebuilt gable-end to the street, on narrow early sites, and grander houses facing the road, which occupy two or three original plots. Examples of the latter are Miller House, built in the 1790s by Hugh Miller's sea-faring father, and Wellington House, built in the 1820s by a retired sea captain, Alexander Clark. The Cromarty Arms in Church Street, with its large first floor windows, was built as the lodge of the Free Gardeners, a friendly society which flourished in Cromarty in the 1820s.

The failure of herring fishing, the decline of the hemp factory and the development of Invergordon as the port of the Cromarty Firth all contributed to Cromarty's decline. There are few buildings from the rest of the nineteenth century, with the exception of the lighthouse (1847), the school (1872) and the bank. Both world wars, however, brought much activity to Cromarty. There are substantial remains of fortifications on the headlands and the harbour was extended. Beside the harbour is the concrete control tower used in rehearsals for the D-Day landings. Cromarty's most modern housing, at the west of the town, was built in response to the developing North Sea oil industries of the 1970s.

2 Dingwall   OS26

Like Cromarty, Dingwall was a royal burgh from the thirteenth century, though there was an earlier Norse settlement there. The museum, open in the summer months, provides information on Dingwall's history. The site of the Norse *thing* or

assembly was probably at Greenhill, on the side of the hill on
the south of the town. The medieval royal castle was at the
end of Castle Street, on the shore of the firth.

The Tolbooth or Town House is a 1730 tower enlarged in
1774, with two-storey wings added in 1905. The burgh's arms
and a date stone of 1730 can be seen on the east gable. The
tall wooden bell tower is an Edwardian replacement of an
earlier structure. The Tolbooth houses the town's museum,
and in front is the re-erected market cross of *c.*1600. In the
car park between Church Street and Tulloch Street is a further

FIGURE 40. *Dingwall Tolbooth before additions*

early site – the obelisk which marked the burial place of George Mackenzie, 1st Earl of Cromartie, who died in 1714. This was re-sited and re-built in 1923.

Dingwall had shrunk to a town of little importance by 1690, and revival came only at the end of the eighteenth century. The High Street was the principal thoroughfare, and it is still possible to detect something of the earlier and typical burgh arrangement of the long narrow house plots, which created a pattern of lanes and closes running off on either side. A number of these have been re-opened in recent years. Church Street is an early thoroughfare and Tulloch Street was created in the eighteenth century. Much of Dingwall's twentieth-century building has not been sympathetic to the historic nature of the town, but it is possible to see a few remaining early houses. No. 64 High Street at McGregor's Close, just east of its junction with Tulloch Street, is a substantial town house dated 1786, and was once used as the Council Chamber. The Retreat, off the High Street in Lochiel Place, was the parish manse, built between 1789–91. Farther along is an early eighteenth-century gable end, the lower half filled by plate glass. Opposite the National Hotel, and hidden in a close, is the front of the late eighteenth-century Park House.

Dingwall was a market centre serving a large hinterland, though its harbour was poor. To rectify this, an Act of Parliament was passed in the early 1800s providing for the construction of a canal to allow small boats access from the firth to Peter's Bridge, close to the centre of the town. Work began in 1815 and was completed in 1817. The canal, however, suffered badly from silting, and although it was deepened in 1868, it was never a success. It is still possible to detect the route of the canal from the mouth of the Peffery to the centre of the town.

It was improved road communications and the coming of the railway which led to the growth of Dingwall in the nineteenth century. In 1843, after decades of dispute with Tain, it became the administrative centre for Ross-shire and, later, for the amalgamated county of Ross and Cromarty. A number of early nineteenth century houses reflect this growth in prosperity, including The Castle (1821) at the end of Castle Street, built for Captain John Maclennan, with a memorial on which is carved an image of his ship the *Dart*; and Park Cottage (*c.*1830), a villa on Greenhill Street now incorporating a petrol station. A substantial prison completed in 1843 still stands, converted to housing, at the back of the later sheriff court buildings in Ferry Road. This had an exercise yard guarded by towers which can still be seen among the surrounding buildings.

3 Fortrose   OS27

Fortrose was a bishop's burgh, and its cathedral, chanonry and castle, originally built by the bishop, have been described in earlier sections. The present High Street, with its market cross of *c.*1590, is flanked by many simple eighteenth- and nineteenth-century houses. Notable among eighteenth-century houses in the town are Rose Court and Angel Court, both in Rose Street and both largely from early in the century (but with some sections which may be pre-Reformation). The Deanery, on the corner of the street, is mid-eighteenth century, with a garden pavilion of the same period. The 1740 date on Woodside in the High Street refers to the rear section of the house. From later in the century are Seaforth Place (1783 date stone) in Academy Street and Meadowbank (*c.*1800). The Bank of Scotland on High Street incorporates a marriage stone of 1719.

The pier and Ferry House at Chanonry Point are mid-eighteenth century, a reminder of the importance of the Chanonry–Ardersier ferry crossing. Nearby is the early nineteenth-century ice house and the lighthouse (1846). A new harbour was built in Fortrose itself in 1813–17 to a design by Thomas Telford, with a granary (1813). The Royal Hotel was built *c.*1835, and Flowerburn Cottage, at the junction of Academy Street and High Street, was built *c.*1838 The house beyond the Royal Hotel has skewputts (stones at the bottom of the gables) from the early nineteenth century carved with human heads.

4 Tain   OS21

A tape-tour of part of the town, also available in Gaelic, is supplied by Tain Museum. The collegiate church and related sites, including the bounds of the sanctuary of the girth of

FIGURE 41. *Tain Tolbooth – view from the north-west* c. *1880*

Tain, have been described above in the section on the medieval church. The description below concentrates on the town's later history.

Tain's origins are intriguingly obscure. It probably began as a religious centre and may, in some form, be earlier than the eleventh-century date attributed to it. In 1439, the town claimed that it also had trading rights granted as early as the second half of the eleventh century. Even if this is not correct, Tain developed with a status similar to that of a royal burgh by the early sixteenth century, dealing principally in skins, hides and salted fish from the lands around the Oykell. The importance of the shrine of St Duthac as a place of pilgrimage increased under James IV (1488–1513). Although this ceased to be significant after the Reformation (1560), Tain was well established and was granted a charter as a royal burgh in 1588.

Tain is centred on the complex of buildings around the medieval collegiate church, the most prominent of the secular structures being the tolbooth, erected in 1706–08 to replace an earlier building, destroyed by a storm in 1703. The sheriff court, which adjoins the tolbooth, was added in 1848. The bell of the earlier tolbooth, cast by the Flemish bell-founder Michael Burgerhuys, survives. The market cross of Tain, restored in 1895, stands at the base of the Tolbooth. The 'castle' of Castle Brae, which runs down on the other side of the Tolbooth, was probably a substantial and perhaps fortified town house, similar to Seaforth Castle in Fortrose. Like Seaforth Castle, nothing remains.

The buildings now standing in Tain reflect prosperity which came with the improvement of agriculture in the late eighteenth century and its subsequent growth as a market town in the fertile lands of Easter Ross. For many years Tain was regarded as the head burgh of Ross-shire. While it lost this position to Dingwall in 1843, a role as an administrative centre also enhanced its status in the early nineteenth century. From 1827, the town expanded with the laying out of new streets (Knockbreck, Geanies, Shandwick and Ankerville) to the east, on land feued by Macleod of Geanies as principal landowner. The level of the High Street was also raised during the nineteenth century by bridging a number of small streams.

Nos 1–25 High Street, opposite the Tolbooth, are all well-constructed early nineteenth-century buildings, some with original shop fronts. Many windows on the first floor have, in addition to the large central section, two narrow side lights. These were popular in Easter Ross in the early nineteenth century, providing extra light for dining and drawing rooms. On the other side of the street, the council offices were built as the Commercial Bank in 1828. At the other end of High Street are The Grove (c. 1800), on the north side, and opposite, Nos 33–43 (1830s). On Stafford Street, at the eastern approach to the town, is the Duthac Centre, built in 1811–14 as a new parish church to replace the decaying collegiate church building. It is elegant and very unlike other churches in the area. At the opposite end of Tain, in Academy Street, is Duthac House built in 1803–13 as Tain Academy and considered at the time to be one of 'the handsomest and chastest erections in the north of Scotland'.

Many of Tain's streets are lined with simple two-storey nineteenth-century houses, but some, such as No. 10 Knockbreck Street (c. 1830–40), are decidedly elegant. Around the town are more impressive houses, set in their own grounds, such as Knockbreck House (c. 1820), Mayfield (c. 1830) in Morangie Road, and Hartfield (c. 1830). There is a considerable amount of building from later in the nineteenth century, which is beyond the scope of this guide.

BURGHS OF BARONY

5 Portmahomack   NH 91 84: OS21

Portmahomack was created a burgh of barony in the 1690s by George Mackenzie, later 1st Earl of Cromartie, who renamed it Castlehaven, but the new name did not stick. A pier was built in 1699 and is probably incorporated in the later harbour of the early nineteenth century. The girnal and storehouse beside the harbour are detailed in the section on girnals. There are a number of eighteenth- and early nineteenth-century houses in the main street which follows the curve of the bay.

6 Milton of New Tarbat   NH 76 74: OS21

Milton was also established by the 1st Earl of Cromartie, close to his principal residence of New Tarbat House. Milton is clearly a planned settlement, built around a green on which is the mercat cross, dated 1779. The houses around the green are mostly of the late eighteenth and early nineteenth centuries, and include the mid-eighteenth-century Old Drovers Inn with a circular rear stairwell.

7 Invergordon   NH 70 68: OS21

The Inverbreakie estate had been bought before 1700 by Sir Adam Gordon and renamed Invergordon. In 1755 his grandson, Sir John Gordon, drew up plans for a village which was to have not only 'Ferries and Fisher Houses', but a public house, a pier with a crane, a smithy, a lumber yard, a bleach field, a waulk (fulling) mill, a grain store with a weather vane and clock, and pleasure boats and bathing machines. Had he succeeded, this would have been the first planned village in Easter Ross. However, it was only when the MacLeods of Cadboll took over the estate in the 1780s that Invergordon developed with the laying out of ninety-eight plots along the present High Street, forming the pattern of streets which survives today. The Ness of Invergordon had a further twenty-nine plots, including a number later taken up by the hemp factory, and Saltburn had thirty. In 1818 the ferry pier was built and the harbour pier followed in 1828. As early as 1803, a report to Parliament proposed that a naval base be created in the Cromarty Firth, with a small pier at Invergordon to enable ships to take on water barrels, with water piped from a nearby well. The report was ignored and no base was created but individual naval vessels continued to call. 1863 was a vitally important year for Invergordon for two reasons. First, a full Naval Fleet – the Channel Squadron, consisting of nine ships and nearly 5,000 men – visited the firth for the first time; and second, the railway reached the town, linking it with the south and providing a means of supplying vessels.

8 Drummond   NH 60 65: OS21

Drummond, on the west side of the Sgitheach river was later supplanted by the planned village of Evanton on the east side.

ESTATE VILLAGES
Planned villages began to appear in the mid-eighteenth century and can all be associated with particular estates. They were intended as centres for established trades which had previously

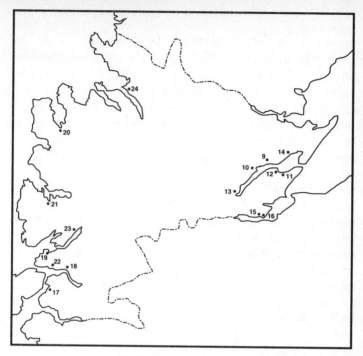

PLANNED VILLAGES

been carried out in the fermtouns, and as new centres for industry and manufactures.

West coast villages were created at the time of clearances in the early nineteenth century. They represent a phase during which many landowners believed it possible to introduce manufactures, particularly using wool from the sheep farms. There was also a heavy dependence on fishing, but these planned villages should be distinguished from the linear crofting settlements created when tenants were cleared to the shore.

EAST COAST

9 Alness and Bridgend of Alness NH 65 69: OS21

Modern Alness is in fact two villages on either side of the River Alness or Averon. In Bridgend, created by Munro of Teaninich on the west bank, there were fifteen tenants in 1819: a carpenter, a merchant, seven masons, a wright, a smith, a tailor and three labourers. The village on the east side was the larger, laid out on either side of an impressively wide main street.

10 Evanton   NH 60 62: OS21

Created in 1807 by Fraser of Inchcoulter (later known as Balcony). In 1819 there were twenty-seven tenants, including a postmaster.

11 Jemimaville   NH 71 65: OS21

Created before 1820 by Munro of Poyntzfield and named after his wife, Jemima Graham. The village inn is set back from the main line of houses. The two village pumps can still be seen on the side of the road opposite the houses.

12 Gordonsmills   NH 70 65: OS21

A failed attempt to create a village based around the woollen mill established by Gordon of Newhall in 1796.

13 Maryburgh   NH 54 56: OS26

Laid out by Mackenzie of Seaforth in the early nineteenth century as the village of the Brahan estate.

14 Barbaraville   NH 74 72: OS21

An extension of the earlier settlement of Portleich.

15 Charleston   NH 64 48: OS26

Created on the estate of Kilcoy in 1812 and named after Charles Mackenzie of Kilcoy, who died the following year. One of the houses has an inscription on its porch: 'Erected by Kenneth Stewart (Founder of this Village) in 1812 and Rebuilt 1852.' The village consisted largely of fisher cottages but once had a smithy and a mill.

16 North Kessock   NH 65 48: OS26

Established in 1828 by William Fettes, the then owner of Redcastle, who also built the pier and the inn.

WEST COAST

17 Glenelg
NG 81 92: OS33

A survey was made in 1787 and buildings were erected in the following year. The population soon rose to 100.

18 Dornie
NG 88 26: OS33

Plans for the village were drawn up in 1794 for Mackenzie of Seaforth, but settlers had difficulty finding wood for building. A new survey was undertaken in 1801, and by 1812 it had over 400 inhabitants. Nearby **Bundalloch** (NG 89 27) was included in the 1801 survey and laid out in plots, but later cleared.

19 Plockton
NG 80 33: OS19

The village was planned for Mackenzie of Seaforth in 1794, but only seems to have been laid out in 1801 when it had been acquired by Sir Hugh Innes. It was made a burgh of barony in 1808 and plots were being advertised between 1811 and 1813.

20 Poolewe
NG 85 80: OS19

Created in 1808 for Mackenzie of Gairloch, who was hopeful of establishing a 'manufactory for woollen cloth'.

21 Shieldaig
NG 81 53: OS24

Erected *c.*1810 but very much depleted by 1859.

22 Innestown
NG 84 27: OS33

Built in the bay of Auchtertyre by Hugh Innes of the Balmacara estate *c.*1813.

23 Jeantown, now named Lochcarron
NG 90 40: OS24 & 25

Created by Mackenzie of Applecross before 1813 on the site of a farm.

OTHER PLANNED SETTLEMENTS

Essential Viewing

24 *Ullapool* OS19

Ullapool was a creation of the British Fisheries Society, one of three fishing villages established by them – the others being Tobermory on Mull and Lochbay on Skye. It is an important example of attempts to develop the economy of the Highlands. Like Cromarty and Tain, Ullapool can be explored with a tape-tour available from the local museum. Work began in 1788 when the society laid out building plots on a spacious grid of streets. The plots were gradually taken up by settlers and the society financed various buildings including the pier. The three-storey building now known as the Captain's Cabin, with a fore stair, is a late eighteenth-century warehouse, and the Caledonian MacBrayne office on West Street is another of c.1800, possibly to a design by Thomas Telford.

Ullapool fared badly in its early days and it was described by Sir George Steuart Mackenzie in 1808 as a 'nest of wickedness', where enforced idleness had led to vice – presumably heavy drinking. He argued that it had been a mistake to promote only fishing and that manufactures ought to have been promoted, perhaps involving locally grown hemp. Nevertheless, in 1814 there were seventy-two houses, over half of which had slate roofs. A new church, now Ullapool Museum, was built in 1829. Ornsay House on Shore Street is the former manse. Ullapool's fortunes have followed those of the fishing industry and there was a decline in the late nineteenth century.

Essential Viewing

25 *Strathpeffer Spa* OS26

The qualities of the mineral springs at Strathpeffer were brought to the attention of the Royal Society in 1772. Subsequently, the reputation of its curative powers increased. An inn was built in 1778 and plots for a village were laid out. In 1819, a pump room was opened, but this did not greatly increase the numbers of visitors, and it was not until the 1860s, with the coming of the railway, that it became more widely popular. A branch line from Dingwall was opened in 1885. Most buildings are Victorian – and Strathpeffer is a wonderful example of a spa town of this period – but Spa Cottage, in the southwest corner of the square, is earlier.

GAZETTEER 24:
ROADS, BRIDGES, FERRIES AND HARBOURS

The road from Evanton to Ardgay over the Struie was built between 1810 and 1815 and created a more direct route to the north. One of the last of the roads to be built under the Highland Roads and Bridges scheme was in the west, over the **Bealach nam Bo** ('pass of the cattle') to Applecross in 1822. This remains a spectacular journey, though it is no longer necessary, as it was with cars of the 1930s, to reverse up the hairpin bends.

A turnpike road from Beauly to Dornoch, with toll-houses every six miles, was begun in 1807. A further toll road to Fortrose followed.

TOLL HOUSES

1 Artfallie   NH 630495: OS26

Dating from *c.*1830, but much altered by recent additions.

2 Conon Bridge   NH 541559: OS26

1828.

3 Tain   NH 788806: OS21

On the north side of the A9 before Tain.

BRIDGES

4 Aultgraad   NH 608662: OS21

This bridge in Evanton was designed by James Smeaton and built in 1777. The original structure can still be seen from underneath the bridge.

5 Conon   NH 542559: OS26

This elegant five-span bridge, by Telford, was built between
1806 and 1809 and was of great importance in improving
communications.

6 Alness   NH 665695: OS21

1810 by Telford.

7 Contin   NH 454566: OS26

1812–13, a three-arched bridge over the Blackwater by Telford,
now by-passed.

8 Dalneich   NH 637723: OS21

A wide single-span bridge over the fast-flowing Alness or
Averon river. Telford 1810–15.

9 Strath Rory   NH 660776: OS21

A low bridge with a double span. Telford 1810–15.

10 Easter Fearn   NH 645867: OS21

A high single-span bridge by Telford, c.1812, with a long stone
causeway on the approach from the east.

11 Inverlael   NH 182855: OS20

An estate bridge of the 1790s.

12 Dundonnel   NH 103880: OS19

A high single-arched estate bridge of the 1790s.

13 Ledgowan   NH 158583: OS25

Built c.1815.

14 Aultbea   NG 873890: OS19

A seven-span 'clapper bridge', possibly eighteenth century.

FERRIES

A number of ferry piers were improved in the early nineteenth
century.

14 Kessock north pier   NH 655478: OS26
1821.

15 Invergordon ferry pier   NH 706683: OS21
Built by Telford in 1817.

16 Strome Ferry piers   NG 86 34 and 86 35: OS24
1814.

Chanonry Ferry pier is earlier, probably mid-eighteenth
century.

INNS

With better communications came the need for inns to accommodate travellers.

17 Chanonry Point   NH 750558: OS27
The ferry house is probably a mid-eighteenth century inn.

18 Sittenham   NH 651744: OS21
Built in 1835 by the Sutherland estate as the last staging post
on the road to Dunrobin and much altered by Matheson of
Ardross in 1847. It also served the nearby droving stance.

19 Drover's Inn   NH 767742: OS21
This inn in Milton of New Tarbat is late eighteenth century,
now converted to housing.

20 Balblair Inn   NH 704667: OS21
Built *c.*1820 replacing an earlier building, the inn served the
south side of the Invergordon ferry and is still a public
house.

HARBOURS AND PIERS

21 Portmahomack   NH 915846: OS21
The pier was built in 1697 and enlarged by Telford in 1813.

22 Cromarty   NH 785678: OS21

The harbour was built to a design by James Smeaton (1782–86) with two piers and an outer landing stage. In 1835–37, the west pier was widened, Smeaton's work was repaired and a sloping access to the harbour basin was added. The curved and bull-nosed eastern pier is still attractive, but the outer landing stage is less easy to see under later concrete work. Note the blocked arch in the harbour basin, which was built in an attempt to use the tide to scour the harbour.

23 Ullapool   NH 128938: OS19

The harbour was built in the 1790s to a design by Telford.

24 Fortrose   NH 725563: OS27

The harbour was built *c*.1810.

25 Avoch   NH 705550: OS27

The harbour was built by Telford in 1815 beside a warehouse of slightly earlier date.

26 Balintraid pier   NH 741711: OS21

Built, with adjoining workers cottages, by Telford in 1817.

27 Invergordon   NH 708683: OS21

Two piers, one L-shaped the other straight, were completed in 1828

28 Rockfield pier   NH 925828: OS21

Built in 1829.

29 Alcaig pier   NH 564576: OS26

Built in the late 1780s, probably in connection with shipping of whisky from Ferintosh.

The development of both Cromarty and Invergordon piers in the 1830s allowed the introduction of steamships, providing regular and reliable sailings. Navigation was made safer by the construction of lighthouses designed, as were most Scottish lighthouses, by Robert Stevenson and his sons. The author Robert Louis Stevenson was a grandson of his.

30 Tarbatness   NH 946875: OS21

1830 heightened in 1892 to make it second tallest lighthouse in Britain.

31 Chanonry   NH 749557: OS27

1846.

32 Cromarty   NH 786677: OS21

1846.

Details of the Dingwall Canal have been given in the description of the town and is the subject of a booklet published by Dingwall Museum.